Backgrounds to Victorian Literature

RICHARD A. LEVINE
University of California, Riverside

CHANDLER PUBLISHING COMPANY
124 Spear Street, San Francisco, California 94105

Previously published and copyrighted materials are reprinted with the permission of authors, publishers, or copyright owners as listed below:

Walter E. Houghton, "Character of the Age." Reprinted by permission of Yale University Press from Walter E. Houghton, *The Victorian Frame of Mind, 1830–1870.*

Jerome Hamilton Buckley, "Victorianism." Reprinted by permission of the publishers from Jerome H. Buckley, *The Victorian Temper,* Cambridge, Mass.: Harvard University Press, Copyright, 1951, by the President and Fellows of Harvard College.

Mario Praz, "The Victorian Mood: A Reappraisal." From *The Nineteenth Century World: Readings in the History of Mankind,* edited by Guy S. Métraux and François Crouzet. Published by arrangement with The New American Library, Inc., New York. Copyright © 1963 by UNESCO.

Asa Briggs, "Religion and Science." From *The Age of Improvement* by Asa Briggs. New York, 1959. Used by permission of David McKay Company, Inc., and Longmans, Green & Co. Limited.

Noel Annan, "Science, Religion, and the Critical Mind." Reprinted by permission of Indiana University Press from Philip Appleman, William A. Madden, and Michael Wolff, eds., *1859: Entering an Age of Crisis.*

Northrop Frye, "The Problem of Spiritual Authority in the Nineteenth Century." Reprinted from *Literary Views: Critical and Historical Essays,* edited by Carroll Camden, by permission of The University of Chicago Press. Copyright © 1964 by William Marsh Rice University.

William S. Knickerbocker, "Victorian Education and the Idea of Culture." Reprinted from *The Reinterpretation of Victorian Literature,* edited by Joseph E. Baker, by permission of Princeton University Press. Copyright 1950 by Princeton University Press. This selection includes matter from Beatrice Webb, *Our Partnership,* 1948; reprinted by permission of The Passfield Trust, Drake, Sturton & Co., London.

E. D. H. Johnson, "The Role of the Artist." Reprinted with the permission of Charles Scribner's Sons from *The World of the Victorians,* pages 253–262, by E. D. H. Johnson. Copyright © 1964 Charles Scribner's Sons.

Richard A. E. Brooks, "The Development of the Historical Mind." Reprinted from *The Reinterpretation of Victorian Literature,* edited by Joseph E. Baker, by permission of Princeton University Press. Copyright 1950 by Princeton University Press.

Richard D. Altick, "The Social Background [to the Growth of a Mass Reading Public]." Reprinted from *The English Common Reader* by

[The following facing page is a continuation of this page.]

for Fredric and Jessica

Contents

Backgrounds to Victorian Literature

Introduction

As our age pays increasing attention to the Victorian years, we are becoming ever more aware of the complexity of nineteenth-century England. Neither the rather easy and urbane dismissal of all things Victorian which marked so many sophisticated literary discussions of Edwardian England nor the scoffing, derisive laughter of the post-Edwardians remains meaningful to students of the nineteenth century—except as indicators of aspects of the post-Victorian sensibility. Not only have we come to perceive the validity of Chesterton's comment that many of the most memorable Victorian writers rode contrary to the dominant ethics of their age, but our examination of the Victorians has also reached a degree of maturity which has given a new dimension to Victorian studies in general and produced an atmosphere in which the primary burden of the scholar is not to defend or judge the Victorians, but to understand them. This happy situation at once denies all simplistic readings of the age and lays new stress on interdisciplinary cooperation as the most effective means for achieving the fullest and richest reading of Victoria's England. One might venture the suggestion that the single most significant breadth approach to literature in the last twenty years has been in the area of Victorian scholarship, and it has been an approach which has managed to combine historical scholarship and critical analysis in a way at once exciting to the individual student and meaningful to the entire discipline of letters. No longer can it be fashionable to talk of Dickens, for example, as a "great writer . . . *although* a Victorian." To be sure, we now approach the Victorians with sensibilities to a large degree shaped by Proust and Joyce, by Pound and Eliot—in a word, by the artists, critics, and theoreticians of our own century —and because of this we often read the nineteenth-century writer in a twentieth-century critical frame of reference. More important, however, coupled with our modern literary sense is our realization that Dickens is a great writer *and* a Victorian,

that it was the world of the nineteenth century which surrounded him and to which he responded, that to understand
the Victorian writer best the reader must understand that
writer's age. And the task is not an easy one.

Victorian England was not the complacent monolith that the
debunkers of the age would lead us to believe. England in the
nineteenth century produced an exceptionally large number of
fascinatingly complex personalities. It was not at all uncommon
for Victorian Englishmen to work simultaneously in several
fields. There were clergymen who were also creative writers;
both Kingsley and Newman, for example, wrote novels. John
Ruskin, scholar, critic, essayist, founded a corporate social movement, the St. George Guild. William Ewart Gladstone wrote
religious tracts and Homer criticism. Ebenezer Elliott, a middle-
class iron manufacturer, composed and published poetry. And so
the list goes on. The Victorian Age witnessed a keen interest on
the part of many of its members in various and often apparently
uncongenial areas of life. Perhaps not since the Renaissance had
England produced so many versatile and far-ranging men—men
whose breadth of interests moved far beyond their peculiarly
personal concerns and activities.

One of the major factors which helped shape such a situation
was the "condition of England" question and its many ramifications. Nineteenth-century England was an age of anxiety, an
age of flux. Traditional institutions—religious, social, political—
were challenged from every corner. Individual man's relationships to his church, class, and government were coming under a
new scrutiny. No longer sure of these relationships, Victorian man
had to examine their very basis or, at least, have them examined
for him. Wesleyanism, the Oxford Movement, parliamentary Reform Bills, Chartism, Utilitarianism, a new Traditionalism, the
impact of science, and, above all, the Industrial Revolution made
new intellectual and emotional demands upon the Victorian
man. The traditional relationships between men and their fellow
men, and between men and their institutions were crumbling.
Often the newly created or suggested relationships were unsatis-
factory. For example, in theory, the Industrial Revolution was a
magnificent success, a giant step into the future, supplying the

mechanized means for achieving undreamed-of progress. In practice, however, this same Industrial Revolution led to social problems of such magnitude that many thoughtful Englishmen could not help viewing it as, at best, a dubious blessing. Never before in modern times had an age been forced to re-evaluate so thoroughly the very roots of its existence. Never before had a people been faced with so many disruptive shocks—shocks brought on by the upheaval of values which their grandparents in the eighteenth century had considered permanent and true. In fact, by the middle of the nineteenth century, the average Victorians (those, at least, above the great class of paupers in the new industrial centers) found it best to ignore such questions and settle down to enjoy complacently their greater salary, the nation's peace, and the "great exhibitions." But others refused to be engulfed by mid-century complacency as they saw great problems and responded to them.

It was the complex social, moral, and political problems of Victorian England which produced the unusually large number of many-sided intellects. In an age shaken by the onslaughts of science and an emerging technology, poverty and squalor, Rome and Evangelicalism, Utilitarianism and radicalism, thinking men had to take sides. And to consider the issues, they had to become aware of them—a difficult task in any age but a greater task for men in an age of such great change. Such, then—in broad terms—was the milieu out of which came the Victorian man of letters.

The concept of the man of letters is peculiarly meaningful within the Victorian context, for out of the welter of interrelationships between literary artists and their environment emerged the artist as man of letters. Certainly one reason for the richness of the nineteenth-century literary and historical texture is the interweaving of life and art. If the Victorian writer did not respond more immediately and vigorously to his world than does our contemporary writer, he nevertheless found himself playing a more meaningful and responsible social and cultural role than does the writer of our own day. E. D. H. Johnson, in writing of the role of the Victorian artist, invokes Archibald MacLeish's conception of the nineteenth-century man of letters:

A century ago the professions of the writer and the scholar were united in the single profession of the man of letters and the man of letters was responsible in everything that touched the mind. He was a man of wholeness of purpose, of singleness of intention—a single intellectual champion, admittedly responsible for the defense of the inherited tradition, avowedly partisan of its practice . . . Whatever threatened learning or the ends of learning challenged the man of letters. Whatever struck at truth or closed off question or defiled an art or violated decency of thinking struck at him. And he struck back with every weapon masters of the word could find to strike with.*

It should be clear that the very nature of such a role involved the artist in the broad world surrounding his art, in the world of ideas and opinions above or below his art. Here is one major reason for the critical-historical synthesis which has become so apparent in Victorian studies and which—when in proper balance—should afford the reader the most fruitful response to any literary work, Victorian or not. This collection of essays is predicated upon that premise. The student's response to nineteenth-century literature should be more meaningful if it is broadened by an examination of the background to the age, an overview of which is presented in this volume. Although the book is divided into five topical areas, the distinctions are arbitrary and convenient. The fact of the matter is that a wide variety of subjects is treated in the volume and most significant areas of the Victorian environment are alluded to if not discussed at length.

Walter Houghton begins his discussion of the character of the Victorian era by underscoring the pervasive use among Victorians themselves of *age of transition* as an epithet for the times. When Houghton quotes John Stuart Mill's "mankind have outgrown old institutions and old doctrines, and have not yet acquired new ones," he casts the reader into the midst of the Victorian vortex. England was in the process of enormous change, embracing the obviously visible and consequential

---

* Except where otherwise noted, all quotations are from the essays in this collection.

movement from an agrarian, rural society to an urban, industrialized one and also the subtle and less visible though equally consequential movements in thought and ideological commitment. In the background of the intellectual turmoil was the change brought about by the Industrial Revolution. Just a few facts can illustrate vividly the enormity of that change. In 1833, a girl working a steam loom could produce 9 times as much cloth as an experienced handloom weaver; in 1835, one man could spin as much yarn as 250 men in 1760. The new industrialized situation obviously led to a relocation of great numbers of people. In addition to mechanization applied to industry and commerce, roads improved, and the great locomotive and steamship boom began in the thirties. Perhaps we can see the nature of the change from another statistical vantage point: in 1648, three-quarters of the population was engaged in agriculture; in the 1840's, only one-quarter. These figures represent a net shift of one-half of the country's population from agriculture to industry! Houghton couples with this shattering social and economic change the problems produced by the transfer of power in society, the emerging middle class and its ultimate influence in the age, the spread of knowledge and education, and the increasing prominence of scientific and rationalistic thought accompanied by a disintegrating religious certitude.

Even though W. R. Greg could say that life was being lived "without leisure and without pause—a life of *haste*—above all a life of excitement, such as haste inevitably involves—a life filled so full . . . that we have no time to reflect where we have been and whither we intend to go . . . still less what is the value, and the purpose, and *the price* of what we have seen, and done, and visited," Houghton correctly suggests that one of the age's intellectual certitudes (at least until about 1870) was a "faith in the existence of ultimate truths in religion and ethics, in politics, economics, and aesthetics (as well as in the natural sciences), and in the capacity of the human mind to discover them, by some form of reason or of intuition . . ." But counterpointed against this optimistic melody are the strains of great doubt—even in the mid-Victorian period, which one writer wryly has called the period of "peace, plenty, and doubt." Thus the

Victorian optimism is shaky; the Victorian doubt rarely total.

After 1870 discords became more audible as the age moved to its dissonant coda. Houghton contrasts Arnold and Pater as representatives of views prior to and after 1870:

The contrast of Pater and Arnold is pointed by their respective conceptions of the "modern spirit." To Pater, of course, it is the relative spirit, which considers that "truth itself is but a possibility, realisable not as a general conclusion, but rather as the elusive effect of a particular personal experience"; and which "must needs content itself with suspension of judgment, at the end of the intellectual journey, to the very last asking: *Que sais-je?* Who knows?" For Arnold the modern spirit is the awareness that traditional beliefs and institutions are no longer adequate to embody contemporary life; and the representatives of the modern spirit, "the would-be remodellers of the old traditional European order," are "the invokers of reason against custom." For them the end of the intellectual journey is not doubt but reconstruction.

Throughout his essay Houghton plays on the double themes of the modernity of Victorian England (that is, the continuity rather than the contrast between our world and the Victorian) and the complexity of the age. It is with the latter theme in particular that Jerome Hamilton Buckley deals in the opening chapter of his *The Victorian Temper.* For Buckley, the hallmarks of Victorian England are diversity and complexity, and he demonstrates those features of the age by initially and energetically surveying a series of contradictory charges: the Victorians were complacent yet troubled, materialists yet idealists, conformists yet individualists, sentimental yet hard-boiled; they were "iconoclasts who worshiped the idols of authority"; their literature was didactic yet escapist. The conclusion is obvious: the very term *Victorianism* cannot be defined, let alone be considered pejorative. With this realization of the age's complexity, Buckley believes we are ready for a careful re-examination of Victorian England, the broad strokes of which he outlines in his essay.

Where Houghton and Buckley deal with dominant ideas and movements, Mario Praz considers the externals of the age as another way of getting at the Victorian temper. Contrary to

Buckley's position, Praz argues that there is a dominant Victorian mood which is—put briefly—middle-class, didactic, and vulgar. Even though many nineteenth-century writers become even more striking against the backdrop of Praz' comments, we must realize that Praz has no monopoly on correct judgments of either the age or of individual figures. Like a new-wave French novelist and, perhaps, suffering from some of the same faults, Praz has decided to study the period only from its externals: "Let the monuments of the past speak for themselves— and by monuments I do not only mean a triumphal arch or a cathedral, but also a humble utensil or a fashionable knickknack." Thus he examines areas such as taste and painting, interiors of houses, clothing fashions and colors, and education. Inevitably such an approach rigidly adhered to must lead to incomplete if not untenable positions: "It is easier to form a general impression [of an age] from a gallery of paintings or a collection of photographs of them than from reading the contents of an entire library." Although it is clear that the results of such a procedure can be only an imperfect view, we learn a good deal about the externals Praz talks about and encounter a number of exciting insights. Praz himself underscores the essential thrust of his approach when he discusses the "apoplexy of art" in Victorian England: the approach is more that of the literary sociologist than either the literary critic or historian. And within that frame of critical reference, Praz can be very good indeed. Thus even though he fails to qualify his conception of Victorian fiction, "with its increasing interest in the lower classes and everyday life, in the tragedies of humble folk and scenes of crowds, almost invariably with a moral or social lesson to impart," he is most acute in suggesting the broad relevance of the darkening colors of men's fashions: "Up to the beginning of the century masculine dress had been that of the gallant, of the man whose chief occupation was to court the ladies; by midcentury it became that of the financier, of the man managing public money. His sober attire can be traced back to the severe style of the Puritans; this link in fashion may confirm the opinion of those who have seen the origins of modern capitalism in the Puritan conception of life." While he fails to notice the symbolic significance of

Carker's death by a train in *Dombey and Son,* he has a great deal to say about the new mechanized age. If he does not assess judiciously the nature of the rebellion practiced by so many Victorian writers, he nevertheless cogently discusses the influence of romanticism and the French Revolution throughout nineteenth-century English thought.

From another vantage point, however, any criticism of Praz' approach must be tempered by an awareness of his method. Since he is playing the role of literary or cultural sociologist in the attempt to reappraise the Victorian age, his conclusions must deal with large segments of people and their ideas rather than with individual points of view, with the mainstream rather than with the counter-currents. Certainly from this perspective Praz has given us a good deal to consider, but one must combine his approach with those represented in the Houghton and Buckley essays in order to arrive at a fuller conception of the Victorian environment. Praz himself, before the essay concludes, comes close to the now orthodox conception of Victorian England as a time of complexity, diversity, and transition. He sees the charge of the Light Brigade as symptomatic of a confused age groping for order:

Six hundred horsemen, in consequence of a confused and misunderstood order, charged in the valley of death in perfect parade style, with no other prospect than being mowed down by the Russian cannons; Lord Cardigan, galloping in front of all, offered himself alone to the astonished Russians, dressed in his splendid uniform glittering with gold braid, heroic and grotesque like somebody facing a public meeting naked: these are the symptomatic signs of a period and a society that, under the veneer of a debased enlightenment, were harboring a confusion of principles and purposes that eventually had to come to a head.

Finally, as his own comment on the method he employed, Praz says, "I take the nineteenth century to be such a period of *âge ingrat,* of laborious transition. This manifestly implies an adverse judgment on many of the manifestations that passed for art in the nineteenth century . . ."

So it is that the opening section of this book offers an overview of the Victorian years and readies the reader for the more specialized studies which follow. And it is through those studies that the student will come to grips with the very problems which surrounded the Victorian writer and compelled his attention: religion, science, education, the spread of knowledge, economics, politics, and their myriad and sometimes subtle ramifications.

The critical-historical synthesis to which I have alluded already and to which approach this volume is directed occupied a valuable moment during a recent Dickens symposium:*

Professor George H. Ford:

But to think back to the papers, rather than to the discussion that has followed them, I have the impression that there was one area where perhaps at least some element of disagreement might exist. It is in Mr. Miller's emphasis on the importance of the pure critic and my own suggestion that the pure critic is not necessarily threatened by some historical resurrection of the Victorian background in which Dickens' books were presented.

I can say, like Professor Monod, myself, that I have fluctuated in this respect, not just tonight, but at other times. As far as the Indiana Conference is concerned I can recall, four or five years ago, talking to the young men at Indiana who founded the magazine *Victorian Studies,* young men who have a strongly developed preference for an historical approach to literature. And I recall recommending to them that what Dickens needed was pure criticism and advising them to stay away from history. And here I am tonight saying, it seems, just the opposite.

But I say this with the experience of a recent re-reading in mind, during which I became aware of the gaps in our own knowledge of Dickens' age. And I think the only place where I might disagree with Professor Miller would be in this area, when he speaks about transcending a context.

---

* *Dickens Criticism: Past, Present, and Future Directions.* A Symposium with George H. Ford, Edgar Johnson, J. Hillis Miller, Sylvère Monod. Noel C. Peyrouton, moderator. The Charles Dickens Reference Center, 1962.

Is the knowledge of historical context really detrimental to his significant work of literature? Isn't it something that reduces to the level of mere historical fact the secondary work but not the great work? . . .

Professor J. Hillis Miller:

. . . we do agree—that is, I think there is a distinction to be made and, once that distinction is made, I think there is no real difference in our positions. I certainly feel that all the footnotes we can get are necessary. We need to know who the Red-Faced Nixon [alluded to in *Pickwick Papers*] was and everything else of that sort, from minor details to the most elaborate background for a big novel like *Bleak House*.

I think the real question then comes as to what you do with this information when you've got it, and this is where people divide. I am not saying that one way of using literature is better or worse than the other, but that they are essentially different. In one case you use *Bleak House* as an example of attitudes which were shared by a whole lot of people; on the other hand you can put this knowledge, the identification of all the allusions, back into the novel and try and see what the novel means in itself.

There are really two issues here: (1) the question of the value of identifying the facts; (2) the question of ways of using them.

Professor Edgar Johnson:

I am sorry to make this gathering into a chorus of "I agree and you agree," but I cannot really see that we can do otherwise.

In a very striking volume of literary criticism issued within the last year or so, Mr. Leslie Fiedler takes it as his point of view that the critic and the artist must constantly be attacking whatever they find to be the predominant scheme of values of their time. This they must attack very emphatically and violently. The title of Mr. Fiedler's book is *No, In Thunder,* and a critic must say, "No! In Thunder," according to him, all the time.

Now, I agree that it is perfectly legitimate and right for the critic to say "No" thunderously or in a whisper, whenever he feels like saying "No." But to my mind the most fruitful of approaches is to say, "Not only, but also," and to be finding all that is valuably and truly, to the best of your own insights, present in a work of art that you can discover there. The more that can be found, whether affirmation or negation, that is actually there, the richer the total work becomes.

Consequently, I welcome every kind of insight, both that of rejection and that of the affirmation of the previously unobserved.

It is toward the kind of critical understanding of literature suggested by Professors Ford, Miller, and Johnson that this backgrounds book is offered.

I

The Victorian Years: An Overview

WALTER E. HOUGHTON
Character of the Age

JEROME HAMILTON BUCKLEY
"Victorianism"

MARIO PRAZ
The Victorian Mood: A Reappraisal

Character of the cAge

WALTER E. HOUGHTON

In 1858 a Victorian critic, searching for an epithet to describe "the remarkable period in which our own lot is cast," did not call it the age of democracy or industry or science, nor of earnestness or optimism. The one distinguishing fact about the time was "that we are living in *an age of transition.*" [1] This is the basic and almost universal conception of the period.[2] And it is peculiarly Victorian. For although all ages are ages of transition, never before had men thought of their own time as an era of change *from* the past *to* the future. Indeed, in England that idea and the Victorian period began together. When John Stuart Mill in 1831 found transition to be the leading characteristic of the time—"mankind have outgrown old institutions and old doctrines, and have not yet acquired new ones"—he noted that this

---

[1] "The Progress and Spirit of Physical Science," *Edinburgh Review,* 108 (1858), 71. The writer (who was kindly identified for me by Professor R. D. Altick) was Sir Henry Holland. The article was reprinted in his *Essays on Scientific and Other Subjects Contributed to the Edinburgh and Quarterly Reviews,* London, 1862.

[2] The specific words "transition" or "transitional" are used by Prince Albert, Matthew Arnold, Baldwin Brown, Carlyle, Disraeli, Frederic Harrison, Bulwer Lytton, W. H. Mallock, Harriet Martineau, John Mill, John Morley, William Morris, Herbert Spencer, Hugh Stowell, J. A. Symonds, Tennyson, and no doubt many others.

From Walter E. Houghton, *The Victorian Frame of Mind, 1830–1870* (New Haven: Yale University Press, 1957), pp. 1–23.

had become obvious to the more discerning only "a few years ago," and that now "it forces itself upon the most inobservant." [3]

To Mill and the Victorians the past which they had outgrown was not the Romantic period and not even the eighteenth century. It was the Middle Ages. They recognized, of course, that there were differences between themselves and their immediate predecessors, but from their perspective it was the medieval tradition from which they had irrevocably broken—Christian orthodoxy under the rule of the church and civil government under the rule of king and nobility; the social structure of fixed classes, each with its recognized rights and duties; and the economic organization of village agriculture and town guilds. That was "the old European system of dominant ideas and facts" which Arnold saw dissolving in the nineteenth century.[4] But the process had begun much earlier, starting with the Renaissance and the Reformation, gaining momentum, quietly but steadily, through the next two centuries of philosophic rationalism and expanding business, until it finally broke into the open when the French Revolution of 1789 proclaimed the democratic Rights of Man and the atheistical worship of the Goddess of Reason. That was the first overt manifestation, in Mill's opinion, that Europe was in a state of transition.[5] But it was not realized at the time, not in England. There it was not until the rising agitation for a reform bill (finally successful in 1832), the passage of Catholic Emancipation, the attack on the Church by Whig Liberals and Benthamite agnostics, together with the outbreak of the 1830 revolutions abroad, that men suddenly realized they were living in an age of radical change.[6] Then they began to say that "old opinions, feelings—ancestral customs and institutions are crumbling away, and both the spiritual and temporal worlds are darkened by the shadow of change." [7]

For "old" and "ancestral" we may read "medieval" or "feudal."

---

[3] *The Spirit of the Age*, p. 6, and cf. p. 1 . . .

[4] "Heine," *Essays in Criticism, First Series*, pp. 186–7.

[5] *The Spirit of the Age*, p. 67. Cf. Carlyle, "Signs of the Times," *Essays*, 2, 82.

[6] See Mill, "The Claims of Labour," *Dissertations and Discussions*, 2, 188; and George Eliot, *Felix Holt*, 1, chap. 3, pp. 66–7.

[7] Edward Bulwer Lytton, *England and the English*, p. 281. But this

When Arnold observed that many people thought it possible to keep a good deal of "the past," his next sentence defined the term: the extremists, indeed, hoped "to retain or restore the whole system of the Middle Ages." [8] "Until quite recently," wrote Baldwin Brown in his important lectures of 1869–70, *The Revolution of the Last Quarter of a Century*, ". . . our modes of thought and speech, our habits of action, our forms of procedure in things social and political, were still feudal." [9] To Carlyle and Ruskin and Thomas Arnold, the period is one of decaying or dying feudalism.[10] This was not an abstract idea. Victorians like Thackeray who had grown up in the 1820's felt they had lived in two distinct worlds:

It was only yesterday; but what a gulf between now and then! *Then* was the old world. Stage-coaches, more or less swift, riding-horses, pack-horses, highway-men, knights in armour, Norman invaders, Roman legions, Druids, Ancient Britons painted blue, and so forth—all these belong to the old period. I will concede a halt in the midst of it, and allow that gunpowder and printing tended to modernise the world. But your railroad starts the new era, and we of a certain age belong to the new time and the old one. We are of the time of chivalry as well as the Black Prince of Sir Walter Manny. We are of the age of steam.[11]

From a mere glance at the title page of Carlyle's *Past and Pres-*

---

passage may have been written by Mill: see his *Autobiography*, chap. 6, p. 168.

[8] "Democracy" (1861), *Mixed Essays*, p. 22. Robert Vaughan began *The Age of Great Cities* (1843) with a section "On the Conflict between Feudalism and Civilization in Modern Society" in which he noticed (pp. 5–6) a reactionary movement that would "diminish everything commercial and civic, so as to place the military and the feudal in its old undisturbed ascendancy" and would "restore the power of the Christian priesthood in much of the form and greatness which distinguished it during the middle age."

[9] *First Principles of Ecclesiastical Truth*, p. 273. The lectures are on pp. 209–364. For their date see p. vii.

[10] Thomas Arnold and Carlyle are quoted below . . . for Ruskin, see *The Crown of Wild Olive, Works, 18*, Lecture 4, p. 494. Cf. Dowden, quoted below, note 14.

[11] "De Juventute" (1860), published in the *Roundabout Papers, Works, 12*, 232. For the tendency to idealize the prerailroad world of the early century, see Kathleen Tillotson, *Novels of the Eighteen-Forties*, pp. 102–9, where Thackeray's essay is quoted.

ent, any Victorian might have guessed that the book was a comparison of the Middle Ages with the nineteenth century.

By definition an age of transition in which change is revolutionary has a dual aspect: destruction and reconstruction. As the old order of doctrines and institutions is being attacked or modified or discarded, at one point and then another, a new order is being proposed or inaugurated. Both tendencies were apparent by 1830. After his description of the breakup of timeworn landmarks, Bulwer Lytton continued: "The age then is one of *destruction!* . . . Miserable would be our lot were it not also an age of preparation for reconstructing." [12] Twenty years later at the center of the Victorian period, what new construction had emerged? Or rather—for this is the important question for getting at the temper of the age—what did men think distinguished their time most significantly from the past? What did they think was peculiarly Victorian about "the state of society and of the human mind?" [13]

1. The State of Society

By the late nineteenth century it was clear that the feudal and agrarian order of the past had been replaced by a democratic and industrial society.[14] The emergence of democracy meant not only the transference of political power from the aristocracy to the people, mainly by the successive Reform Bills of 1832, 1867, and 1884, but also the arrival of what is often called a democratic society. The latter, indeed, was so striking that Mill once called the distinguishing feature of modern institutions and of modern life itself the fact "that human beings are no longer born to their place in life . . . but are free to employ their faculties, and such favourable chances as offer, to achieve the lot

---

[12] *England and the English,* p. 281; but see note 7. Cf. Carlyle, *Sartor Resartus,* Bk. III, chap. 7, p. 244.

[13] These are Mill's categories in *The Spirit of the Age,* pp. 2, 6.

[14] Cf. Dowden, "Victorian Literature" (1887), *Transcripts and Studies* (London, 1896), p. 159: "Society, founded on the old feudal doctrines, has gone to wreck in the storms that have blown over Europe during the last hundred years. A new industrial and democratic period has been inaugurated."

which may appear to them most desirable." [15] This breakdown of the old conception of status owed something to democratic ideas about the rights of man, but its primary cause was economic. The development of commerce, drawing men off from the land and opening new and independent careers to talent, had been the main instrument in dissolving the feudal nexus of society.[16] In politics, too, the Industrial Revolution underlay the democratic revolution. What Thomas Arnold had in mind when he remarked, on seeing the first train pass through the Rugby countryside, that "feudality is gone for ever," [17] is made explicit by a passage in *Sartor Resartus*, written on the eve of the Reform Bill of 1832: "Cannot the dullest hear Steam-Engines clanking around him? Has he not seen the Scottish Brassmith's IDEA (and this but a mechanical one) travelling on fire-wings round the Cape, and across two Oceans; and stronger than any other Enchanter's Familiar, on all hands unweariedly fetching and carrying: at home, not only weaving Cloth; but rapidly enough overturning the whole old system of Society; and, for Feudalism and Preservation of the Game, preparing us, by indirect but sure methods, Industrialism and the Government of the Wisest?" [18]

Whether wisest or not, the bankers and manufacturers who rose to political power through the revolutionary legislation of 1828–1835—the repeal of the Test and Corporation Acts, the Municipal Reform Act, and above all, the Reform Bill—owed their victory to the financial and psychological power they acquired from the Industrial Revolution. Both factors are seen in Disraeli's analysis of the capitalist mind in *Coningsby*. Mr. Millbank is discussing the English peerage: "I have yet to learn they are richer than we are, better informed, wiser, or more distinguished for public or private virtue. Is it not monstrous, then, that a small number of men, several of whom take the titles of

---

[15] *The Subjection of Women,* chap. 1, p. 445. Cf. Brown, *First Principles,* pp. 274–9.

[16] Brown, pp. 280–1, and cf. Mill, "Democracy in America," *Dissertations,* 2, 62–71.

[17] A. P. Stanley, *Life of Thomas Arnold,* appendix D, p. 723 n., with the journal entry for August 4, 1839.

[18] Bk. II, chap. 4, p. 118. The Scottish Brassmith is James Watt.

Duke and Earl from towns in this very neighbourhood, towns which they never saw, which never heard of them, which they did not form, or build, or establish,—I say, is it not monstrous that individuals so circumstanced should be invested with the highest of conceivable privileges, the privilege of making laws?" [19] Those are the social forces, wealth and outraged pride, which demanded the Reform Bill. And once the middle class attained political as well as financial eminence, their social influence became decisive. The Victorian frame of mind is largely composed of their characteristic modes of thought and feeling.

But far more striking at the time than democracy was the tremendous industrial development that came with the use of new machines for manufacturing and communication.[20] The great inventions date from the later eighteenth century; and in the early decades of the nineteenth the introduction of more canals, macadam roads, railways, and steamboats hastened the growth of large-scale production by making possible a vast expansion of commerce. This development revolutionized the economic life of England. The old system of fixed regulations, which paralleled that in fixed social relations, was abandoned for the new principle of laissez-faire, on which the manufacturer bought his materials in the cheapest market and sold them in the highest, and hired his labor wherever he liked, for as long as he pleased, at the lowest wages he could pay. In Southey's *Colloquies on the Progress and Prospects of Society* (1829) and Macaulay's fighting review of it (1830), the world of big business and unlimited competition was debated by the old conservatism and the new liberalism.

To live in this dynamic, free-wheeling society was to feel the

---

[19] *Works, 12*, chap. 26, p. 225. Cf. Brougham's speech in the House of Lords advocating the Reform Bill, quoted in A. V. Dicey, *Lectures on the Relation of Law and Public Opinion in England*, pp. 184–5.

[20] Cf. T. H. Huxley, "The Progress of Science, 1837–1887," *Method and Results*, p. 42: "The most obvious and the most distinctive feature of the History of Civilisation, during the last fifty years, is the wonderful increase of industrial production by the application of machinery, the improvement of old technical processes and the invention of new ones, accompanied by an even more remarkable development of old and new means of locomotion and intercommunication."

enormous pressure of work, far beyond anything known before. When new and more distant sources of supply and demand were constantly being opened up by the railroad and the steamship, the battle for new markets became intense. To neglect them could mean ruin. So could failure to take advantage of the latest invention or adapt one's business methods to the most recent developments. Disraeli's Coningsby is startled to learn from Mr. Head, who is building a new mill at Staleybridge, that Manchester is already gone by. "If you want to see life," he says, "go to Staley-bridge or Bolton. There's high-pressure." Only the Manchester Bank has kept up with the times: "That's a noble institution, full of commercial enterprise; understands the age, sir; high-pressure to the backbone." [21] The masters had to work almost as long hours as their hands—the Messrs. Carson, for example, who did not become acquainted with their agreeable daughters until their mill was burned down: "There were happy family evenings now that the men of business had time for domestic enjoyments." [22] The same pressure was felt in the professions. "The eminent lawyer, the physician in full practice, the minister, and the politician who aspires to be a minister—even the literary workman, or the eager man of science—are one and all condemned to an amount and continued severity of exertion of which our grandfathers knew little." [23] That was due as much to the social system as to business conditions. When class lines broke down and it became possible as never before to rise in the world by one's own strenuous efforts, the struggle for success was complemented by the struggle for rank.[24] Even apart from personal ambitions, the very existence of hundreds of objects, once unknown or within the reach of few, now made widely available and therefore desirable, increased the size of one's expenses and the load of his work.[25] Moreover, the growing

---

[21] *Works, 12,* chap. 24, p. 210. The date is 1844.

[22] Mrs. Gaskell, *Mary Barton* (first ed., 1848; London, 1911), chap. 6, p. 67.

[23] W. R. Greg, "Life at High Pressure" (1875), *Literary and Social Judgments, 2,* 272.

[24] This is discussed below, Chap. 8 ["The Commercial Spirit"].

[25] Cf. Mark Pattison, "The Age of Reason," *Fortnightly Review, 27* (1877), 357: "To live at all is a struggle; to keep within reach of the

wealth of the wealthy advanced the style of living in the middle and upper classes to a point where the Victorian had to struggle for things his father had been able to ignore. George Eliot remarked that £3,000 a year had seemed wealth to provincial families in 1830, "innocent of future gold-fields, and of that gorgeous plutocracy which has so nobly exalted the necessities of genteel life." [26]

Not only the tempo of work but the tempo of living had increased with striking impact, so much so that one observer thought that "the most salient characteristic of life in this latter portion of the 19th century is its SPEED." [27] Until the Victorian period the rate of locomotion and communication had remained almost what it had been for centuries. The horse and the sailing vessel were still the fastest things on earth. But within a few years the speed of travel by land increased from twelve to fifty miles an hour on the new railroads (over 400 per cent) and the new steamships were doing fifteen knots "with wonderful regularity, in spite of wind and tide." [28] But it was less the mechanical speed of the new inventions than the speed of living they produced which impressed the Victorians. Faster locomotion, of goods and letters and people, simply increased the number of things one crowded into a day, and the rush from one to another. Once upon a time "people did not run about the town or the land as we do." They traveled less often, did not hurry to catch trains, wrote one letter a morning instead of ten. Now "we are whirled about, and hooted around and rung up as if we were all parcels, booking clerks, or office boys." [29] It seems far more modern than Victorian. But if the speed of life has increased in the twentieth century, the sense of speed has declined, for what

---

material advantages which it is the boast of our century to have provided is a competition in which only the strong can succeed—the many fail."

[26] *Middlemarch, 1,* Bk. I, chap. 1, p. 6; and cf. Greg, p. 278.

[27] Greg, p. 263.

[28] Ibid., p. 264, quoted from Greg's earlier *Enigmas of Life,* pp. 38–9. Cf. Frederic Harrison, "A Few Words about the Nineteenth Century," *The Choice of Books,* pp. 421–2.

[29] Frederic Harrison, *Autobiographic Memoirs, 1,* 12, 18–19. Though he was writing in the 1880's, he was comparing conditions in his later life with those of his youth (he was born in 1831).

has become commonplace today was then a startling novelty. Our great-grandfathers may have had more leisure than we do but it seemed less. Even more than ourselves they felt they were living "without leisure and without pause—a life of *haste*—above all a life of excitement, such as haste inevitably involves—a life filled so full . . . that we have no time to reflect where we have been and whither we intend to go . . . still less what is the value, and the purpose, and *the price* of what we have seen, and done, and visited." [30]

This sense of faster and more crowded living had its intellectual as well as its mechanical basis. The spread of education coupled with the enormous expansion of knowledge and the corresponding increase of publication, books and periodicals and newspapers, gave "every man . . . a hundred means of rational occupation and amusement which were closed to his grandfather," [31] and led George Eliot, in a threnody on the death of leisure ("gone where the spinning-wheels are gone, and the pack-horses, and the slow wagons, and the pedlers, who brought bargains to the door on sunny afternoons") to say that "even idleness is eager now,—eager for amusement; prone to excursion-trains, art-museums, periodical literature, and exciting novels; prone even to scientific theorizing, and cursory peeps through microscopes." [32] By the sixties Frances Cobbe was comparing her own generation with that of 1800–30 in words which sound exactly like someone today comparing the generation of 1950 with that of 1850: "That constant sense of being driven—not precisely like 'dumb' cattle, but cattle who must read, write, and talk more in twenty-four hours than twenty-four hours will permit, can never have been known to them." [33]

---

[30] Greg, p. 268.

[31] Kingsley, "Great Cities and Their Influence for Good and Evil" (1857), *Sanitary and Social Essays*, p. 203.

[32] *Adam Bede*, 2, chap. 28, p. 339. In editions where the chapters are numbered consecutively this is chap. 52.

[33] "The Nineteenth Century," *Fraser's Magazine*, 69 (1864), 482 . . . Cf. Brown, *First Principles*, pp. 222–3, inviting his hearers in 1869 to compare "the rate at which you are living, . . . the rate of thought, feeling, and energy—in these as compared with those quiet and comfortable times" in the first decades of the century.

2. The State of the Human Mind

The radical transition in the human mind was less apparent at first than that in society, but sensitive observers were soon aware that the traditional framework of thought was breaking down. By 1838 Thomas Arnold had noticed a new "atmosphere of unrest and paradox hanging around many of our ablest young men of the present day." He was speaking not merely of religious doubts but "of questions as to great points in moral and intellectual matters; where things which have been settled for centuries seem to be again brought into discussion." [34] This is the atmosphere reflected in the early essays of Macaulay and Carlyle, in *Sartor Resartus* and Mill's *Spirit of the Age,* and the novels of Sterling and Maurice. All of them, written between 1825 and 1834, show that the old certitudes are certain no longer and that a reconstruction of thought is now a prime necessity. "The Old has passed away," wrote Carlyle in 1831, "but, alas, the New appears not in its stead; the Time is still in pangs of travail with the New." [35] There was, of course, more destruction to come, for the old was by no means gone (traditional Christianity, indeed, under Wesleyan and presently Tractarian influence was reviving). And there had been earlier efforts to bring forth the new, most notably by Bentham and Coleridge, the respective heirs of the French *philosophes* and the German transcendentalists, "the two great seminal minds of England in their age." [36] But *the New* had not yet appeared by the thirties. All that was then clear to the intellectuals was that their task was precisely what Carlyle found attempted in the two books he had under review in the essay "Characteristics": "Both these Philosophies are of the Dogmatic or Constructive sort: each in its way is . . . an endeavour to bring the Phenomena of man's Universe once more under some theoretic Scheme . . . they strive after a result which shall be positive; their aim is not to question, but to establish." [37]

---

[34] Stanley, *Life of Arnold,* p. 484, from a letter dated October 5, 1838. The next sentence justifies my insertion of "merely."

[35] "Characteristics," *Essays, 3,* 32.

[36] Mill, "Bentham," *Dissertations, 1,* 331.

[37] *Essays, 3,* 33.

That is the starting point. What was the situation a generation later? What corresponds in the intellectual world to the establishment of bourgeois industrial society? The answer is—nothing. In 1850 the age is still one "of fusion and transition. . . . Old formula, old opinions, hoary systems are being thrown into the smelting-pan; they are fusing—they must be cast anew: who can tell under what new shapes . . . they will come forth from the moulds?" In the seventies men are still searching—"amid that break-up of traditional and conventional notions respecting our life, its conduct, and its sanctions, which is undeniably befalling our age,—for some clear light and some sure stay." By the eighties "the disintegration of opinion is so rapid that wise men and foolish are equally ignorant where the close of this waning century will find us." [38] Though the Victorians never ceased to look forward to a new period of firm convictions and established beliefs, they had to live in the meantime between two worlds, one dead or dying, one struggling but powerless to be born, in an age of doubt.[39]

The phrase is ambiguous—and at first glance dubious. When one thinks of Macaulay, Spencer, and Huxley, or of Browning, even of Mill and Ruskin, let alone thousands of pious Evangelicals and Anglicans, one is ready to deny it. Indeed, it was still common until very recently to draw a radical contrast between the Victorians and ourselves. One modern critic thought that "a spirit of certitude, wonderful to us who live in an age which has taken the note of interrogation as its emblem, impregnated the great Victorians." Another has claimed that it was only after 1900 that "the old certainties were certainties no longer," and "everything was held to be open to question"; and that "the Victorians seemed to themselves to be living in a house built on

---

[38] The three quotations are by Hugh Stowell, "The Age We Live In," in *Exeter Hall Lectures*, 6 (London, 1850–51), 45–6; Matthew Arnold, "Bishop Butler and the Zeit-Geist," *Last Essays on Church and Religion,* p. 287; and J. A. Froude, preface to *Short Studies,* 4, v–vi.

[39] See Arnold, "Stanzas from the Grande Chartreuse" (1855), lines 85–8. After Bulwer Lytton in *England and the English* refers (p. 281) to living in an age of transition, he adds in apposition, "an age of disquietude and doubt." Cf. Winwood Reade, *The Martyrdom of Man* (first published in 1872), p. 540: "We are now in the dreary desert that separates two ages of belief." . . .

unshakable foundations and established in perpetuity . . . the Home, the Constitution, the Empire, the Christian religion—each of these . . . was accepted as a final revelation." [40] From such assumptions we could predict the reversal, under the powerful incitement of nostalgia, of the anti-Victorian movement represented by Lytton Strachey:

If, after the first World War, we were all debunking the nineteenth century, after the second we are deferring to it, and even yearning nostalgically after it: *tendentesque manus ripae ulterioris amore*. In our own unpleasant century we are mostly displaced persons, and many feel tempted to take flight into the nineteenth as into a promised land . . . In that distant mountain country, all that we now lack seems present in abundance: not only peace, prosperity, plenty and freedom, but faith, purpose and buoyancy.[41]

Though this contrast of the Victorian period with our own has its element of truth, the tendency to invest the past with the virtues one finds lacking in the present has led to a serious misconception. The fact is, while moral values were firm until about 1870, all intellectual theories, including those of morality, were insecure. What John Morley said of the fifties and sixties applies to the entire period, though with greater intensity and wider repercussions as the years passed: "It was the age of science, new knowledge, searching criticism, followed by multiplied doubts and shaken beliefs." [42] The very effort to resolve the situation made it worse. New solutions raised new controversies, which raised new questions. "Intellectually," wrote J. A. Froude

---

[40] The two critics are D. Willoughby in *The Great Victorians*, ed. H. J. Massingham and Hugh Massingham (Garden City, N.Y., 1932), p. 242, and A. C. Ward, *Twentieth-Century Literature. The Age of Interrogation, 1901–1925* (London, 1930), pp. 2, 4.

[41] Basil Willey, *Nineteenth Century Studies*, p. 52.

[42] *Recollections*, 1, 100. The view of the period I am advocating—not that doubt existed, which has long been recognized, but that it was an "age of doubt" rather than of certitude—emerged, here and there, in *Ideas and Beliefs of the Victorians* (1949): see pp. 19, 23–5, 71–7, 423; and in 1953 Gaylord C. LeRoy published a book on Victorian writers called *Perplexed Prophets*. But as recently as June 19, 1953, a critic in the *Times Literary Supplement* (p. 397) wrote of the era: "We may envy the unquestioning firmness of its faith, whether the object of that faith was religion, or science, or humanity."

—with religion in mind, but his remark has broader relevance— "the controversies to which I had listened had unsettled me. Difficulties had been suggested which I need not have heard of, but out of which some road or other had now to be looked for." [43] But which road? The choice was baffling. "None of the ways in which . . . mental regeneration is sought," Mill recognized in 1842, "Bible Societies, Tract Societies, Puseyism, Socialism, Chartism, Benthamism, etc.—will *do*, though doubtless they have all some elements of truth and good in them"; with the result that he was finding it very hard to make up his mind "as to the course which must be taken by the present great transitional movement of opinion and society." [44]

The range of discussion reflected by Mill's list is significant. It was not only in religion that one faced a series of alternatives: is there a God or is there not, and if so, is he a person or an impersonal force? Is there a heaven and a hell? or a heaven but no hell? or neither? If there *is* a true religion, is it Theism or Christianity? And what is Christianity? Roman Catholicism or Protestantism? Is it Church or Chapel? High Church? Broad Church? Low Church? Similar questions, if not so pressing or so widespread, invaded ethical theory and the conception of man: have we free-will or are we human automatons? and if we have the power of moral choice, what is its basis? a God-given voice of conscience? or rational calculation deciding which of two actions will promote the greatest happiness of the greatest number? Is man a man or simply a higher ape? Even the political-economic order of bourgeois capitalism, if an established fact of the outer environment in 1850, held no unquestioned supremacy in the world of ideas. The sanctity and

---

[43] "The Oxford Counter-Reformation," *Short Studies*, 4, 311–12. On p. 252 Froude notices that the Oxford Tracts, designed to check the advance of liberalism and atheism, "provoked doubts, in those whom they failed to persuade, about Christianity itself." Also cf. "The Age We Live In," *Fraser's Magazine*, 24 (1841), 5: "The very truths which have come forth have produced doubts . . . and the very lights that have shone in one quarter have only dazzled in others, and this dazzle too often has ended in darkness."

[44] From a letter to R. B. Fox printed in Caroline Fox, *Memories of Old Friends,* ed. H. N. Pym (Philadelphia, 1882), pp. 393–4.

blessings of private property, laissez-faire, and unlimited competition were challenged, in one aspect or another, by Owen and Mill, Carlyle and Ruskin, the Chartists and the Christian Socialists. The abortive "communism" of 1848 in France further opened Victorian eyes to the possibility that the old political economy was limited and temporary. And the provisional character of middle-class government, suggested by the Chartist agitation of the forties, was confirmed by the Reform Bill of 1867. By 1870 the uncertain future seemed to belong to the unpredictable populace.

It was not, however, the mere existence of competing philosophies which called all in doubt. It was also the prevailing atmosphere. As one prophet after another stepped forward with his program of reconstruction, the hubbub of contending theories, gaining in number as the century advanced, and spreading out from the intellectuals to the large audience of the periodicals, created a climate of opinion in which, quite apart from any specific doubts, the habit of doubt was unconsciously bred. One had an uneasy feeling, perhaps only half-conscious, that his beliefs were no longer quite secure. Nor should we forget the complementary effect of the vast increase of knowledge, scientific and historical, that almost inundated the Victorians and left them often baffled by the sheer number and complexity of its implications. The yeasty state of mind which Kingsley ascribed to the young men of 1851 was not only one in which "the various stereotyped systems which they have received by tradition [are] breaking up under them like ice in a thaw"; it was also one in which "a thousand facts and notions, which they know not how to classify, [are] pouring in on them like a flood." [45] Three years later Mill's diary for January 13, 1854, contains what is perhaps the best single statement on Victorian doubt:

Scarcely any one, in the more educated classes, seems to have any opinions, or to place any real faith in those which he professes to have. . . . It requires in these times much more intellect to marshal so much greater a stock of ideas and observations. This has not yet

---

[45] "Epilogue" to *Yeast,* p. 312. Cf. Harrison, "A Few Words about the Nineteenth Century," pp. 437, 442; and Matthew Arnold, *Letters of Arnold to Clough,* p. 130: "Yes—*congestion of the brain* is what we suffer from—I always feel it and say it—and cry for air like my own Empedocles."

been done, or has been done only by very few: and hence the multitude of thoughts only breeds increase of uncertainty. Those who should be the guides of the rest, see too many sides to every question. They hear so much said, or find that so much can be said, about everything, that they feel no assurance of the truth of anything.[46]

Without contrary evidence, who would be surprised if the passage were dated 1954?

This evidence—and much more could be given—suggests that continuity rather than contrast is the conclusion to be drawn from comparing the Victorians with ourselves. And yet, if both periods can be called ages of doubt, it is certainly with a difference. Neither the kind of doubt nor the strength of its hold was the same in 1850 as it is today.

In the four decades under inspection, doubt never reached the point of positive or terminal skepticism. It never involved a denial of the mind as a valid instrument of truth. No mid-Victorian ever described his age as Dobrée described the 1930's: "All the previous ages . . . had something they could take for granted. . . . We can be sure of nothing; our civilization is threatened, even the simplest things we live by. . . . In our present confusion our only hope is to be scrupulously honest with ourselves, so honest as to doubt our own minds and the conclusions they arrive at. Most of us have ceased to believe, except provisionally, in truths, and we feel that what is important is not so much truth as the way our minds move towards truths." [47] Though the seeds of that radical doubt were planted by the 1870's, as we shall see in a moment, they did not grow up until the dissolving influences of modern sociology, anthropology, and psychology had done their work, and mined the old confidence with relativism and rationalization.[48] The Victorians might

---

[46] *Letters*, 2, 359.

[47] *Modern Prose Style* (Oxford, 1934), p. 220.

[48] Cf. W. H. Auden, writing of these modern studies in *Poets of the English Language*, ed. W. H. Auden and N. H. Pearson (5 vols. New York, 1950), 5, xxii–xxiii: "Their exhibition of the mind's capacity for self-deception, of the unconscious effect upon its thinking of social status and sex, their demonstration that the customs and beliefs of other peoples could not be dismissed as merely savage, irrational, and quaint but must be

be, and often were, uncertain about what theory to accept or what faculty of the mind to rely on; but it never occurred to them to doubt their capacity to arrive at truth. When Mill thought of his age as one of intellectual anarchy, his reaction to such a condition was quite different from ours. He could see it as a momentary and necessary stage in a process of growth: "So long as this intellectual anarchy shall endure, we may be warranted in believing that we are in a fair way to become wiser than our forefathers; but . . . we have not yet advanced beyond the unsettled state, in which the mind is, when it has recently found itself out in a grievous error, and has not yet satisfied itself of the truth." [49] Not yet but soon! "If your opinions, or mine, are right," he told Sterling, "they will in time be unanimously adopted by the instructed classes." [50] It is this faith in the existence of ultimate truths in religion and ethics, in politics, economics, and aesthetics (as well as in the natural sciences), and in the capacity of the human mind to discover them, by some form of reason or of intuition, which unites the partisans of every school. That, one is tempted to say, is the one intellectual certitude in Victorian England. But it is a great one, for on such a foundation the universe can be held together: it can remain rational. That is why Chesterton could claim that the Victorian period was "orderly compared with what came after." (But not, he added, "compared with the centuries that came before.") [51] On that foundation it was still possible, as it no longer is, to find comfort in the thought

> That, though I perish, Truth is so:
> That, howsoe'er I stray and range,
> Whate'er I do, Thou dost not change.[52]

It was still possible to adopt this or that theory of Church or State with full confidence that it might well be true—though not that it *was*.

But less possible after 1870. For about that time a number of

---

accepted as rival civilizations complete in themselves, cast doubts on the finality of any truth."

[49] *The Spirit of the Age*, pp. 12–13.
[50] *Letters, 1*, 6. Cf. *The Spirit of the Age*, p. 33.
[51] *The Autobiography of G. K. Chesterton* (New York, 1936), p. 20.
[52] Arthur Hugh Clough, "It fortifies my soul to know," *Poems*, p. 75.

things converged to suggest the relativity of knowledge and the subjective character of thought. This radical change, bounding the mid-Victorian temper, is documented in the popular work of Walter Pater.

The historical method, as it was formulated under the influences of Romantic and scientific conceptions of development, meant the study of social phenomena of all kinds, institutions, customs, beliefs, as the natural product of a given time and place; with the result that the type of question one put to the past underwent a crucial change. One no longer asked, What do I think of this? is it good? is it true? For once everything was thought relative, good or true only for a particular society at a particular stage in its cultural evolution, the right questions became: How shall I account for it? Why did men believe that it was good or true? [53]

In the intellectual as in the organic world the given product, its normal or abnormal characteristics, are determined, as people say, by the "environment." The business of the young scholar therefore, in reading Plato, is not to take his side in a controversy, to adopt or refute Plato's opinions . . . still less, to furnish himself with arguments on behalf of some theory or conviction of his own. His duty is rather to follow intelligently, *but with strict indifference,* the mental process there, as he might witness a game of skill. . . . To put Plato into his natural place, as a result from antecedent and contemporary movements of Greek speculation, of Greek life generally: such is the proper aim of the historic, that is to say, of the really critical study of him.[54]

The phrase I have italicized adds the final touch: nothing could be less Victorian. Though recognized earlier, the awareness that the historical attitude could issue in skepticism did not reach general consciousness, I think, until after 1870 when it came to be debated in the periodicals by men like John Morley, Edward Dowden, and Henry Sidgwick.[55]

---

[53] See Morley, *Recollections, 1,* 71–2, and Wilfrid Ward, "The Time-Spirit of the Nineteenth Century," *Edinburgh Review, 194* (1901), 92–131, reprinted in his *Problems and Persons,* London, 1903.

[54] Pater, *Plato and Platonism* (New York, 1901), p. 6. The italics are mine.

[55] Morley, *On Compromise,* pp. 18–21; Dowden, *Studies in Literature,* pp. 106–9; Sidgwick, "The Historical Method," *Mind, 11* (1886), 213–15.

At the same time the scientific view that all things, material and human, were in constant flux, changing under the inevitable influences of many and complex factors, could make all truths seem relative only to a particular moment. In the opening paragraphs of the "Coleridge" (1866) and the "Conclusion" to *The Renaissance* (1873), Pater revived the skepticism of Hume and reduced all knowledge to a series of "impressions unstable, flickering, inconsistent," each of which "is the impression of the individual in his isolation, each mind keeping as a solitary prisoner its own dream of a world." [56] On such assumptions the intellectual life was ridiculous. Only the aesthetic life of delicate perceptions and sensitive response had any importance. Not that philosophy or "speculative culture" was ruled out. It still had value for the human spirit—but only "to rouse, to startle it into sharp and eager observation." By suggesting "points of view" it could "help us to gather up what might otherwise pass unregarded by us." [57]

To turn back from Pater to Arnold is to return to the Victorian world. For Arnold threw his whole weight against relativism. Not, it is true, with reference to historical or scientific theories, but to the liberal dogma of individualism and its assertion of private judgment, which in society as a whole was the major force that undermined the belief in absolute truths. By 1864 Arnold was aware of a "baneful notion that there is no such thing as a high, correct standard in intellectual matters; that every one may as well take his own way." [58] To the contemporary boast that every Englishman could believe what he liked, what was

---

[56] *Appreciations,* pp. 65–7, and *The Renaissance,* pp. 246–9. The quotation is on p. 248. The "Conclusion" was first written in 1868. On Pater's skepticism, see Helen H. Young, *The Writings of Walter Pater. A Reflection of British Philosophical Opinion from 1860 to 1890* (1933), chap. 3, esp. pp. 27–9, and Milton Millhauser, "Walter Pater and the Flux," *Journal of Aesthetics and Art Criticism,* 11 (1952–53), 214–23. Cf. Karl Pearson, *The Grammar of Science* (1892), where the same skeptical conclusions were systematically advanced. That book and its impact are discussed in *The Education of Henry Adams,* chap. 31.

[57] *Renaissance,* pp. 249, 251.

[58] "The Literary Influence of Academies," *Essays in Criticism, First Series,* p. 66.

true for him, Arnold kept asking whether it was not important that what people were free to believe should be worth believing; whether, in short, the anarchy of individualism should not be checked by the authority of Culture, with its inherent power of discovering truth. For Culture, "bent on seeing things as they are," can dissipate delusions like the worship of freedom for its own sake, and fix "standards of perfection that are real!" [59] What is meant here by things as they are or standards that are real is the very absolutes which Plato affirmed and Pater denied. "To see things as they are" is "to draw towards a knowledge of the universal order which seems to be intended and aimed at in the world . . . to learn, in short, the will of God"; and this insight comes from the use of right reason, meaning intuitive judgment, by a man of wide learning and flexible intelligence. Indeed, Arnold cites Plato by name as explicitly denying to the mere man of virtue the Greek instinct for what he (Plato) calls "the true, firm, intelligible law of things." "He reserves it for the lover of pure knowledge, of seeing things as they really are,—the φιλομαθής." [60]

The contrast of Pater with Arnold is pointed by their respective conceptions of the "modern spirit." To Pater, of course, it is the relative spirit, which considers that "truth itself is but a possibility, realisable not as a general conclusion, but rather as the elusive effect of a particular personal experience"; and which "must needs content itself with suspension of judgment, at the end of the intellectual journey, to the very last asking: *Que sais-je?* Who knows?" [61] For Arnold the modern spirit is the

---

[59] *Culture and Anarchy,* chap. 1, p. 51. Cf. Lionel Trilling, *The New Yorker Magazine* (June 18, 1949), p. 74, where—with Arnold plainly in his mind—he spoke of George Orwell's "commitment to intellect" as "fortified by an old-fashioned faith that the truth can be got at, that we can, if we actually want to, see the object as it really is."

[60] *Culture and Anarchy,* chaps. 1, 4, 5, pp. 46, 134, 147. Arnold was also indebted to Cicero and the Stoic theory of natural law . . . It is true that Arnold sometimes uses "things as they are" to mean as they "objectively exist" or "as they are in fact," in contrast with how they appear to a prejudiced mind.

[61] *Plato,* pp. 156-7. As the quotation suggests, Pater found the beginning of the modern, relative spirit in Montaigne.

awareness that traditional beliefs and institutions are no longer adequate to embody contemporary life; and the representatives of the modern spirit, "the would-be remodellers of the old traditional European order," are "the invokers of reason against custom." For them the end of the intellectual journey is not doubt but reconstruction.[62]

Pater and Arnold face each other across the gulf between two basic conceptions of the human mind that opened up between 1865 and 1875. By 1877, at the house party given by W. H. Mallock where "culture, faith, and philosophy" are discussed in a new "Republic," the Paters have become a society, still small but destined to rise to fame, or notoriety, in the nineties. Mr. Herbert, who speaks for the mid-Victorians (he is Ruskin) berates the younger generation because, in the face of conflicting opinions, they persuade themselves "that neither opinion is of much moment—that the question cannot be decided absolutely—that it should not be decided absolutely." [63] This is as true of morality as of everything else. "There is no recognised rule of life anywhere," comments Mr. Leslie. "Every one who does right at all only does what is right in his own eyes. All society, it seems, is going to pieces." To which another guest replies:

"I," said Mr. Rose, "look upon social dissolution as the true condition of the most perfect life. For the centre of life is the individual, and it is only through dissolution that the individual can re-emerge. All the warrings of endless doubts, all the questionings of matter and of spirit, which I have myself known, I value only because, remembering the weariness of them, I take a profounder and more exquisite pleasure in the colour of a crocus, the pulsations of a chord of music, or a picture of Sandro Botticelli's." [64]

Mr. Rose, I need hardly say, is Pater—a caricature of Pater. A decade later Canon Liddon, who like Arnold and Ruskin was a mid-Victorian, observed that "a morbidly active imagination

---

[62] "Heine," *Essays in Criticism, First Series,* pp. 185, 189–90. Though I develop it somewhat differently, this contrast between Pater and Arnold was suggested to me by Graham Hough, *The Last Romantics,* pp. 134–41.

[63] W. H. Mallock, *The New Republic, or, Culture, Faith, and Philosophy in an English Country House,* p. 279.

[64] Pages 54–5.

which cannot acquiesce in the idea of fixed and unalterable truth" had become a malady of modern society.[65]

Though the Victorians were certain that truth existed and the mind could discover it, they found themselves involved in two forms of doubt: either what is sometimes called negative skepticism, when the judgment is suspended between alternate conclusions, one of which is considered true; or the affirmation of a belief which they only half believed—and half doubted. Both types of insecurity are present in the important passage from Mill's diary quoted earlier: "Scarcely any one, in the more educated classes seems to have any opinions [because he sees "too many sides to every question"] or to place any real faith in those which he professes to have." [66]

When Alfred North Whitehead spoke of the nineteenth century as being disturbed by the conflicting claims of incompatible doctrines, he pointed out that Cardinal Newman in his *Apologia pro Vita Sua* found it a peculiarity of Pusey, the great Anglican ecclesiastic, that "he was haunted by no intellectual perplexities." "In this respect," Whitehead continued, "Pusey recalls Milton, Pope, Wordsworth, as in contrast with Tennyson, Clough, Matthew Arnold, and Newman himself." [67] A letter of George Eliot's, written in 1839, gives a characteristic illustration of this new state of mind, and with reference to a topic which for Newman was especially baffling:

I think no one feels more difficulty in coming to a decision on controverted matters than myself. . . . The other day Montaigne's motto came to my mind (it is mentioned by Pascal) as an appropriate one for me,—"Que sais-je?"—beneath a pair of balances, though, by

---

[65] Quoted by R. H. Hutton, *Aspects of Religious and Scientific Thought,* p. 17. For a similar account of "the intellectual revolution of our time," which he sees beginning somewhat later, viz. "about 1890," see H. Stuart Hughes, *An Essay for Our Times* (New York, 1950), pp. 15–17. . . .

[66] Reference in note 46, above. In discussions of the period, both contemporary and modern, the word "doubt" is sometimes used to mean religious unbelief. In this book I restrict it to the two definitions just given, which apply to all areas of thought, but especially religious thought, and use "religious skepticism," "unbelief," "agnosticism," or "atheism" for outright disbelief in a divine reality.

[67] *Science and the Modern World,* p. 120.

the by, it is an ambiguous one, and may be taken in a sense that I desire to reprobate. . . . I use it in a limited sense as a representation of my oscillating judgment. On no subject do I veer to all points of the compass more frequently than on the nature of the visible Church. I am powerfully attracted in a certain direction, but when I am about to settle there, counter-assertions shake me from my position.[68]

Nothing could better describe the negative skepticism of the time, including, as it does, the rejection of the positive skepticism which Pater drew from the same passage in Montaigne.[69] It was not, of course, limited to religion. In the forties Disraeli found society "in the midst of a convulsion in which the very principles of our political and social systems are called in question," and created a hero in its image—"confused, perplexed," his mind "a chaos"; but his spirit sustained "by a profound, however vague, conviction, that there are still great truths, if we could but work them out." [70] In the same years, worried because the condition-of-England problem was "shaking many old beliefs, and leading him whither he knew not," Tom Brown at Oxford plunged into works on political economy, then consulted an Anglo-Catholic friend about High Church teaching on social questions, and finally read *Past and Present*—and so filled his head "full of a set of contradictory notions and beliefs." By the time he graduated, reading and discussion had combined to drag him into "perplexities, and doubts, and dreams, and struggles." [71] The Victorian plight was summed up by Clough in a poem which deals with still another area of doubt, the nature of man: *Is* he a human automaton?

> Oh say it, all who think it,
> Look straight, and never blink it!
> If it is so, let it be so,

---

[68] J. W. Cross, *George Eliot's Life as Related in Her Letters and Journals,* *1,* 41, letter to Miss Lewis, May 20, 1839.

[69] For the Victorian view of Montaigne, see John Sterling's essay in the *Westminster Review,* 29 (1838), 321–52, reprinted in his *Essays and Tales,* *1,* 129–87.

[70] *Coningsby,* in *Works, 12,* chap. 23, pp. 196–7.

[71] Thomas Hughes, *Tom Brown at Oxford* (which describes the university when Hughes was there from 1842 to 1845), chaps. 35 and 50, pp. 415–19, 572.

And we will all agree so;
But the plot has counterplot,
It may be, and yet be not.[72]

It must not be supposed, however, that the normal state of the
Victorian mind was one of indecision or suspended judgment.
The confidence in reason or intuition and the powerful will to
believe made doubt itself unstable. It came and went. Individuals
passed through it. Mill confessed in 1833 that "I am often in a
state almost of scepticism, and have no theory of Human Life at
all, or seem to have conflicting theories, or a theory which does
not amount to a belief"; but he added at once, "This is only a
recent state, and, as I well know, a passing one, and my convictions will be firmer." [73] Passing but recurrent. What he says of his
own transition (from his early Benthamism through doubt to his
later liberalism) applies in general to all the mid-Victorian intellectuals. For reasons we shall have to consider, Carlyle, Newman, Disraeli, Froude, Eliot, Arnold—none was any more content
than Mill to remain "confused and unsettled." [74] All like him
succeeded in weaving new ideas and old dogmas into a fresh
pattern of thought.

Not until the sixties does a settled state of baffled judgment
and a mind empty of beliefs begin to appear. It was then, when
the *Origin of Species* and *Essays and Reviews* intensified the difficulties of decision, especially in religion, while at the same
time positive skepticism was emerging, that Frances Cobbe was
struck by a new disposition "to accept as a finality that condition
of hesitation and uncertainty which in the nature of things
should be one of transition." [75] Such a condition, as we might

---

[72] *Poems*, p. 44, from an untitled poem beginning, "Is it true, ye gods,
who treat us."

[73] *Letters, 1*, 48–9.

[74] *Autobiography*, chap. 5, pp. 132–3. . . .

[75] *Fraser's Magazine*, 69 (1864), 491. A few years later Henry Sidgwick
(*Henry Sidgwick: A Memoir*, p. 158) detected signs that "an age of
general indecisiveness" seemed to be commencing; and Symonds (Horatio
F. Brown, *John Addington Symonds*, pp. 316–17) referred to "the *habitual*
condition of scepticism" in which the soul is denuded of "moral ideas and
fixed principles," and went on to say that nowadays a man "is *always* saying
like Montaigne: 'Ni comme ceci, ni comme cela, ni même autrement'; or

expect, is habitual in the society of Mallock's *New Republic,*
where "nobody knows what to believe, and most people believe
nothing,"[76] but it did not exist a generation earlier. It had only
afflicted individuals for shorter or longer intervals. Most of the
time the Victorian mind contained beliefs and not doubts—but
the beliefs were shaky.[77]

What *is* constantly present, therefore, is the fear or suspicion,
or simply the vague uneasy feeling, that one was not sure he
believed what he believed. I do not mean that no one had any
strong beliefs. The traditional morality was firmly held by almost
everyone until the seventies and by a vast majority until after
World War I; and there were certainly many people whose religious or political convictions remained unshaken. But the more
one studies the period, the more certain he is that most Victorians were aptly described by Mill himself in *The Spirit of
the Age:* "The men of the present day rather incline to an opinion than embrace it; few . . . have full confidence in their own
convictions"; or, in a variant phrase, people "have no strong or
deep-rooted convictions at all."[78] How could it have been otherwise in a period of dissolving creeds and clashing theories? If
one's formal doubts were sooner or later discarded for one creed
or another, the taint of doubt remained. A prayer attributed to
the Victorians is a witty distortion of the truth: "O God—if there
is a God—save my soul—if I have a soul." Like Spencer in later

---

again, 'Peut-être oui, peut-être non, peut-être ni l'un ni l'autre.' " The italics
are mine.

[76] Page 50. Cf. Harrison, *Autobiographic Memoirs, 1,* 24, in 1882;
Beatrice Webb, *My Apprenticeship,* p. 165, in 1884 (and cf. pp. 49–50);
Mark Rutherford, *Mark Rutherford's Deliverance,* pp. 28, 75–6, in 1885.

[77] This was particularly true of religious beliefs; and in calling the period
one of doubt, I do not mean to imply that it was one of religious skepticism.
On the contrary, Christian faith was characteristic of the frame of mind. If
most Victorians had reservations about one or more theological doctrines,
they instinctively looked for the hand of God in the events of life;
interpreted success as the reward for virtue, or suffering as the punishment
for sin. They thought of death quite literally as a reunion with the loved
ones who had gone ahead. The churches were crowded; Bibles (on
chains!) were placed in railroad stations; sermons outsold novels. But here,
too, as in other areas, belief was shaky.

[78] *The Spirit of the Age,* pp. 12, 13. These remarks were made in 1831,
but the quotation from his diary given above . . . shows that he would
have thought them entirely applicable in 1854.

life (and the example is significant, since no one could seem more certain or dogmatic), one clung to his dogmas, old or new or a mixture of both, "but without confident faith." [79] Or like Tennyson. In the representative poem of the age, the key words are "trust," "hope," "guess":

> Behold, we know not anything;
> I can but trust that good shall fall
> At last—far off—at last, to all.

> I trust I have not wasted breath:
> I think we are not wholly brain,
> Magnetic mockeries.

> The Power in darkness whom we guess.[80]

In Memoriam is not a poem of belief or of unbelief. It is a poem of doubt, that is, of doubtful beliefs. In our generation, Kingsley noted, "few of us deeply believe anything." [81]

The two outstanding features of their world which most impressed the Victorians are now before us. No one could escape them. No one could take them, as we can take them now, with the indifference or the neutrality adopted toward the customary. Everyone in all classes to some degree felt their impact. We might well expect, therefore, that the major Victorian attitudes would have been mainly determined by the powerful influence (as much from the reaction they provoked as from their positive effect) of these two things, one or both of which are implicit in every reference to "the age of transition"—bourgeois industrial society and widespread doubt about the nature of man, society, and the universe. In the analysis that follows this is the central thread in a pattern planned to include, in due relation to it, other important influences, especially that of the so-called Puritan or Evangelical revival.[82]

At the threshold stand two emotional attitudes, in the broad

---

[79] Beatrice Webb, *My Apprenticeship*, p. 32.
[80] *In Memoriam* (1850), secs. 54, 120, 124.
[81] *Letters and Memories*, 1, 113 (unabridged ed., 1, 141).
[82] Elie Halévy's well-known thesis (a typical statement is in the "Conclusion" to his *England in 1815*) that Victorian culture was the child

sense of pleasure-pain responses, which were bound to occur in a period of conscious and radical change, and which were nourished by many of the same social and intellectual developments. The Victorians reacted to their age with hope and dismay, optimism and anxiety.

---

of Evangelicalism and Industrialism has been widely adopted; indeed, this has been the only general key to the period. Valuable as it is, I think it gives too much importance in the total picture to the Puritan revival, however central that was for a few attitudes, mainly moral earnestness (though even there other factors must be reckoned with . . .) and it ignores the widespread and demonstrable influence of doubt upon the Victorian frame of mind.

"Victorianism"

Oh, so, when modern things are thrust
By death below the coffin lid,
Our liberal sons will spurn our dust
And wonder what it was we did.

—TENNYSON

JEROME HAMILTON BUCKLEY

By the time of Prince Albert's death in 1861, many of the Manchester liberals had come to regard the monarchy as merely the relic of an unprogressive age which had not yet learned the advantages of a complete *laissez faire*. Five years later, when Victoria had long since retired from public life, John Bright addressed a great rally of British reformers, some of whom were prepared to demand the queen's abdication. As suggested president of the new republic, Bright was earnestly confident of his cause. Still, he felt it only right during the course of his remarks to repudiate the libels that his more zealous followers had passed upon their widowed sovereign. But the mere mention of Victoria's name brought an immediate and not altogether expected response: of one accord the republican audience arose to sing with fervent heart and voice,

> God save our gracious Queen,
> Long live our noble Queen,
> God save the Queen! [1]

[1] For the anecdote, see Frank Hardie, *The Political Influence of Queen Victoria* (London, 1935), p. 206.

From Jerome Hamilton Buckley, *The Victorian Temper* (Cambridge, Mass.: Harvard University Press, 1951), pp. 1–13.

Victoria indeed outlived most of Bright's republicans by many years. She lived long—long enough to see her name indissolubly linked to a remarkable century's culture. Yet if "Victoria" had once been able to awaken a distinct and uniform impression in the minds of one assembly, the age which bears her name has since been subject to diverse and divided judgment. Already by the 1890's "Victorian" had become a favorite derogatory epithet to a generation which, ironically enough, was spending lavishly of its pounds and poetry to celebrate Victoria's Diamond Jubilee. And into the twentieth century "Victorianism," defined ambiguously if at all, persisted, a shield for the conservative and a target for the modernist.

Any cultural period suffers distortion from a generalized indictment, however speciously formulated. But the outlines of the Victorian era blur beyond recognition in the confusion of contradictory charges. The Victorians, we are told, were "a poor, blind, complacent people"; [2] yet they were torn by doubt, spiritually bewildered,[3] lost in a troubled universe. They were crass materialists, wholly absorbed in the present, quite unconcerned "with abstract verities and eternal values"; [4] but they were also excessively religious, lamentably idealistic, nostalgic for the past,[5] and ready to forgo present delights for the vision of a world beyond. Despite their slavish "conformity," [6] their purblind respect for convention, they were, we learn, "rugged individualists," given to "doing as one likes," [7] heedless of culture, careless of a great tradition; they were iconoclasts who wor-

---

[2] The charge is stated ironically by Arnold Bennett (*The Old Wives' Tale*, chap. I), but is seriously repeated in various forms; cf. H. H. Asquith, *Some Aspects of the Victorian Age* (Oxford, 1918), p. 6, or an incidental remark by an art critic in the *New Yorker*, Jan. 26, 1946, p. 58.

[3] Cf. H. V. Routh, "The true sign of the times was spiritual isolation" (*Towards the Twentieth Century*, New York, 1937, p. ix); or see W. C. Frierson, *The English Novel in Transition* (Norman, Okla., 1942), p. 36.

[4] H. J. and Hugh Massingham, eds., *The Great Victorians* (Garden City, 1932), p. 11; or, for a more extravagant judgment, see E. B. Burgum, "Victorianism," *Sewanee Review*, XXXVI (1928), 282, 286.

[5] Cf. Routh, *Towards the Twentieth Century*, p. 45.

[6] Cf. Osbert Sitwell, *Sober Truth* (London, 1930), p. 22, or A. C. Ward, *Twentieth-Century Literature* (New York, 1940), pp. 2–3.

[7] Arnold's charge freely echoed by the neo-humanists, who often dismiss Arnold himself along with his lost generation.

shiped the idols of authority. They were, besides, at once sentimental humanitarians and hard-boiled proponents of free
enterprise. Politically, they were governed by narrow insular
prejudice, but swayed by dark imperialistic designs. Intellectually and emotionally, they believed in progress, denied original
sin, and affirmed the death of the Devil; yet by temperament
they were patently Manichaeans to whom living was a desperate
struggle between the force of good and the power of darkness.[8]
While they professed "manliness," they yielded to feminine
standards; if they emancipated woman from age-old bondage,
they also robbed her of a vital place in society.[9] Though they
were sexually inhibited [10] and even failed to consider the existence of physical love, they begat incredibly large families and
flaunted in their verses a morbidly overdeveloped erotic sensibility.[11] Their art constitutes a shameless record of both hypocrisy and ingenuousness. And their literature remains too
purposeful, propagandistic, didactic, with too palpable a design
upon the reader; yet it is clearly so romantic, aesthetic, "escapist,"
that it carries to posterity but a tale of little meaning.

Since most of such charges represent personal reaction rather
than objective analysis, the terms "Victorian" and "Victorianism"
have acquired the vaguest of emotional connotations. They have
become what Ruskin chose to call "masked words droning and
skulking about us." While the social historian [12] of the Victorian
age who is able to withhold opinion is forever aware of intrinsic
complexities, the critic intent upon cultural evaluation is constantly betrayed into premature judgment. And it is the aggre-
gate of these judgments that obscures definition. Many are
agreed that in Victorianism inheres a single tragic flaw which

---

[8] Contrast Routh, *Towards the Twentieth Century*, p. 74, with William
Gaunt, *The Aesthetic Adventure* (New York, 1945), p. 237.

[9] Cf. Edith Batho and Bonamy Dobrée, *The Victorians and After*
(London, 1938), p. 81; contrast G. M. Trevelyan, *English Social History*
(New York, 1942), p. 521: "The last thirty years of Victoria's reign . . .
the real period of the 'emancipation of women' in England."

[10] Cf. Batho and Dobrée, *Victorians and After*, p. 37, or Florence B.
Lennon, *Victoria through the Looking-Glass* (New York, 1945), *passim.*

[11] See Mario Praz, *The Romantic Agony* (London, 1933).

[12] Observe the wise cautions of Trevelyan, *English Social History*, p. 509,
and of G. M. Young, *Victorian England* (London, 1936), p. 150.

vitiates all its sounder impulses. But to one it is a moral hypocrisy,[13] to another a deliberate sentimentalism,[14] to a third a social
snobbery.[15] An eminent debunker [16] laments the total failure of
the critical faculty. And a sensitive student of abnormal psychology detects in all Victorian life "a manifestation of the anal
complex [17] operating upon the group psyche." Yet all the subtleties of oversimplification merely confuse; "Victorianism" remains obscure; we approach no nearer the Victorian essence.

But whatever its central defect, the age, we gather, must in
some hidden way have been deeply pernicious. Apparently so
persuaded, not a few essayists have attempted to salvage their
favorite Victorian authors from the contamination of an unfortunate background. Lewis Carroll has been recently depicted as
a frustrated professor attacking "those jungles of nonsense which
were merely the daily life" of cultured adults "in the now legendary reign of Victoria"; and his biographer advises us that we
may safely "call the *Alice* books art, and the entire Victorian age
a neurosis." [18] From a similar point of view, the Brownings may
be commended for having reared their son Pen with intelligence
and sympathy, for "neither Robert nor Elizabeth Browning were
in any way typical Victorian parents." [19] Even Tennyson, who is
somewhat more difficult to dissociate from his milieu, finds an
apologist who contends that the Laureate, having resisted the
"rigid dogma" of his time, may speak to an inquiring modernity,
"in spite of all his Victorianism." [20]

---

[13] See Bonamy Dobrée, "Addison," *Essays in Biography* (London, 1925),
p. 206. Addison seems to Dobrée sufficiently hypocritical to merit the title,
"the first Victorian."

[14] Lascelles Abercrombie, for instance, in a generally judicious estimate
of Tennyson, speaks of "that false emphasis of feeling which is the peculiar
vice of the Victorian age"; see *Revaluations* (London, 1931), p. 63.

[15] See O. F. Christie, *The Transition from Aristocracy* (London, 1927),
p. 108; here the historian indulges in generalization.

[16] Lytton Strachey, still the liveliest of the iconoclasts; see esp. "A
Victorian Critic" (Arnold), *Characters and Commentaries* (New York,
1933).

[17] See Anna Kavan (author of the distinguished fiction, *Asylum Piece*),
"Back to Victoria," *Horizon*, XIII (1946), 65.

[18] See Lennon, *Victoria through the Looking-Glass*, p. 5.

[19] Isabel C. Clarke, *Elizabeth Barrett Browning* (London, 1929), p. 241.

[20] See William H. Swift, "Tennyson in the Twentieth Century," *Search*

It has been possible to recognize the manifold dissatisfactions and rebellions of Carlyle, Dickens, Ruskin, Morris, Samuel Butler, and at the same time to insist that "the note of revolt is not characteristic of the Victorian Age." [21] By definition, the cultural leader must advance beyond his less gifted contemporaries in grasping the problem of his time, but he can scarcely be considered a leader at all if he stands entirely out of relation to those who lag behind. It is, therefore, by no means clear how reasonably we may dogmatize about the acquiescence of the Victorian era, when many of its most representative and influential writers appear restive or refractory. At any rate, we are hardly to be convinced by criticism like that of the British scholar who, writing in the year of the Munich appeasement, condemns Victorian smugness, with the conviction that Englishmen of 1938 have "scarcely a trace of complacency left." [22]

Whether or not, then, their entire age was spiritually apathetic, the most articulate Victorians were, like wakeful minds in any generation, quite prepared to assail omnipresent stupidity and vicious self-satisfaction. Often, to reinforce their assault on the forts of folly, they resorted to the same sort of oversimplified indictment that has since been turned against them. Almost always, they were able to muster their attack with a vigor of statement compared to which latter-day polemics pale into gentle censure. John Morley, for instance, could ally impassioned eloquence to reasoned principle in his denunciation of Victorian England as "a community where political forms, from the monarchy down to the popular chamber, are mainly hollow shams disguising the coarse supremacy of wealth, where religion is mainly official and political, and is ever ready to dissever itself alike from the spirit of justice, the spirit of charity, and the spirit of truth, and where literature does not as a rule permit itself to discuss serious subjects frankly and worthily—a community, in short, where the great aim of all classes and orders with power is by dint of rigorous silence, fast shutting of the eyes,

---

Quarterly, III (1933), 343; cf. also C. H. O. Scaife, *The Poetry of Alfred Tennyson* (London, 1930), p. 96.

[21] See Asquith, *Aspects of Victorian Age,* p. 13.

[22] Batho and Dobrée, *Victorians and After,* p. 36.

and stern stopping of the ears, somehow to keep the social pyramid on its apex, with the fatal result of preserving for England its glorious fame as a paradise for the well-to-do, a purgatory for the able, and a hell for the poor." [23]

If Morley, by reason of his relationship to the positivist radicals of the seventies, seems too clearly biased a witness, we may turn to a comparatively calm early Victorian chronicler who makes no claim to peculiar insight. Reporting with statistical exactitude on the industrial advance of his generation, George Richardson Porter paused to caution a complacent reader against undue optimism. "It must be owned," he wrote, "that our multiplied abodes of want, of wretchedness, and of crime—our town populations huddled together in ill-ventilated and undrained courts and cellars—our numerous workhouses filled to overflowing with the children of want—and our prisons (scarcely less numerous) overloaded with the votaries of crime, do indeed but too sadly and too strongly attest that all is not as it should be with us as regards this most important branch of human progress." [24] Beside strictures so disillusioned and so vehement, twentieth-century anti-Victorianism seems imaginatively stale and rhetorically flabby. The Victorians are still their own severest critics, possessed of an amazing capacity for detachment, a singular command of invective, and . . . an unequaled talent for parody. "Victorianism" was undoubtedly, at least in part, a monster created by rebellious spirits and bequeathed to a posterity which all too frequently is content to regard the spirits as the monster's children.

Violent and vituperative as it frequently was, Victorian self-criticism found direction in the implicit sense that the faults it assailed were remediable by individual and collective reform. For the Victorians were quite unable to view their long era as a static entity, a unique whole to be described by a single sweeping formula. The doctrine of organic development was so thoroughly diffused throughout nineteenth-century science and philosophy that no serious thinker could escape its implications.

---

[23] See Morley, *Critical Miscellanies* (London, 1923), pp. 74–75.
[24] G. R. Porter, *The Progress of the Nation* (London, 1851), p. 631.

Whether or not the thoughts of men were widening with the process of the suns, there were everywhere evidences of continual growth and decay. Wistfully Frederic Harrison looked to the joys of a vanished past; early Victorian life, he felt sure, must have been pleasanter than existence in the seventies, for certainly Dickens and Thackeray "tell us of a livelier, jollier age than that recorded in *Middlemarch* and *Fors Clavigera*." [25] In a more sanguine mood, Walter Besant chronicled the incalculable changes between the accession of Victoria and the Golden Jubilee. He lingered over quaint customs long outmoded, as if contemplating the strangeness of a remote antiquity; for in 1887 he could find scant similarity to early Victorian tastes, no parallel, for instance, to the rules of etiquette acceptable fifty years before:

Never ask a lady any questions about anything whatever.

If you have drunk wine with every one at the table and wish for more, wait till the cloth is removed.

Never permit the sanctity of the drawing-room to be violated by a boot.[26]

If many changes were wrought by deliberate reformers fighting old prejudices, many also, like the shift in standards of deportment, resulted from the gradual operation of hidden social forces.

All in all, the Victorian period achieved little of the stability we have learned to associate with a semimythical neoclassic culture. It moved from form to form, and nothing stood. Almost every Victorian thesis produced its own antithesis, as a ceaseless dialectic worked out its designs. Throughout the period there were vast differences between rural and urban society; the fields of the agrarian South were, as Mrs. Gaskell suggested, a far cry from the smoky cities of the industrial North. And between the towns themselves sharp distinctions could be drawn; the London of Oscar Wilde had little in common with the Birmingham of Joseph Chamberlain. Besides, the "climate of opinion" varied from year to year, from decade to decade; the seventies was perhaps as distant from the eighties as we imagine the twenties

[25] See Harrison, *Autobiographic Memoirs,* 2 vols. (London, 1911), II, 313.

[26] Quoted by Walter Besant, *Fifty Years Ago* (New York, n.d.), p. 124.

of our own century remote from the thirties. The Victorian age as a whole was forced to adapt itself to new values as old traditions crumbled; and the term "Victorian" is, therefore, egregiously abused when invoked to describe attitudes that the Victorians inherited, modified, or discarded.

Viewed in its long perspective, nineteenth-century culture appears entirely relative to the manifold developments of a changing society. Yet within the Victorian period itself, "Victorianism" may well have been a necessary postulate, a distinct absolute deduced from a vague composite of social and aesthetic values which creative thinkers felt compelled to dismiss, in order to clear the way for radical innovation. And to the Edwardians the fiction may have served an essential purpose in assisting towards fresh objectives, until such a time as those objectives were attained and the generation of Virginia Woolf and James Joyce might devise the myth of "Edwardianism." Ultimately the debunking of things Victorian became an amusing pastime rather than a meaningful criticism; the distortion of a past culture represented little more than the evasion of a present problem. Havelock Ellis, who in 1890 had attacked all that seemed to him false within the Victorian world, lived to find "the gesture that was once a vital reaction to real things" becoming at last "a stale and empty trick." [27]

Now that half a century has elapsed since Victoria's death, facile repudiation of the Victorian era seems, in truth, quite as outmoded as the attitudes we can no longer recapture. But the sentimentalization that in some quarters has replaced it is scarcely more constructive. The interests of modern design are not appreciably furthered by the self-conscious revival of baroque styles or the rediscovery of bric-a-brac which has acquired the charm of the antique. We can understand the significant backgrounds of contemporary thought only by transcending indiscriminate praise or blame. Collective guilt, we have learned, is never easy to determine; and value-judgments are best confined to specific creeds and individual works of art.

Working inductively, distrustful of "masked words" and slanted

---

[27] Havelock Ellis, *The New Spirit* (1890), preface to the 1926 edition (Boston, 1926), p. xii.

evidence, the historian might discover the sources of the precise concepts upon which less objective interpreters have based their general indictment. The idea of progress, for instance, an idea which admittedly had considerable currency during the Victorian period, might be related to a broader cultural context. It might be seen as an outgrowth of Cartesian philosophy, receiving its major extension among the *philosophes* of eighteenth-century France, passing with variations through the anarchism of Godwin and the poetry of Shelley towards the socialism of Saint-Simon and the positivism of Comte, until with Herbert Spencer came the assumption that progress and evolution moved consistently in the same direction. Or within the age alone, it might be linked to the Victorian's awareness of his very real social advance. The notion of perfectibility would seem to have some immediate sanction at a time when men were devising a system of education on a broad democratic basis, establishing the rights of free speech and trade unionism, progressively extending the franchise, reshaping their entire legal code, and discovering the principles of a medical science by which the sum of human suffering might be immeasurably reduced.

It might then be debated whether the idea of progress was not as much an incentive to further reform as a cause of stupefying satisfaction with the advances already achieved. Yet a cursory review of Victorian opinion indicates that the idea, whatever its effect upon those who embraced it, was much less widely accepted than we have been led to believe. Huxley, who was at least as articulate as Spencer, insisted that evolutionary change not seldom ran counter to ethical improvement. And Tennyson, whose early visions of the future have too readily convicted his generation of blind optimism, attained by 1886 a thoroughly disillusioned view of the "glooming alleys" where "Progress halts on palsied feet" and a sense of the disaster involved in the failure of social adaptation to keep pace with scientific discovery; if Tennyson held to a modified faith in evolution, he recognized the possibility of regression:

Forward then, but still remember how the course of time will swerve,
Crook and turn upon itself in many a backward-streaming curve.[28]

---

[28] Tennyson, "Locksley Hall Sixty Years After" (1886).

The Victorian temper is thus not to be adequately gauged in terms of a concept which flourished long before 1837 and was subject to important qualification from 1850 onwards.

Many of the specific values associated with the anomaly known as "Victorianism" have, like the idea of progress, partial basis in objective evidence; and the inconsistency of the generalizations itself testifies to the bewildering complexity of the era. It is almost impossible to reduce a culture so various to a common denominator; and conflict, indeed, may emerge as the only unity in a great diversity. Yet it is not difficult to find certain doctrines perhaps opposing each other but recurring with an insistency which suggests the breadth of their influence. Probably the most prominent of these, in the early Victorian period at any rate, are Evangelical religion and Benthamite philosophy,[29] both pre-Victorian in origin and both vigorously questioned throughout the nineteenth century. To the one has been ascribed the sententious hypocrisy of Mr. Podsnap; to the other, the uncompromising factualism of Mr. Gradgrind. But apart from their baneful effects, which are to some extent problematical, each encouraged a sense of social responsibility which did much to mitigate the miseries of an expanding industrialism; each contributed, even to its bitterest enemies, something of its earnestness and fixity of vision.

If hardheaded Benthamism was ultimately undermined by the reservations and subtleties of the greatest utilitarian, its zeal for practical reform infected many who found Mill's hedonistic paradox more ingenious than convincing. And if Evangelical restraints and dogmas slowly dissolved under the scrutiny of critical intelligence, the old thirst for righteousness animated so reluctant a heretic as George Eliot, so willful an agnostic as John Morley. Whether actuated by self-interest or Christian principle, moral duty remained for most a categorical imperative. With all the assurance of his brother's orthodoxy, F. W. Newman the freethinker could insist that "all social action, all national cohesion, all reverence for law, all sanctity in rule, is founded upon man's moral conscience."[30] For a few social purpose

---

[29] See below, Chapter VI ["God and Mammon"].
[30] F. W. Newman, *Causes of Atheism* (Ramsgate, 1871), p. 12.

seemed at one time effectively to coalesce with ethical premise in the short-lived Religion of Humanity. But even to fervent atheists like Charles Bradlaugh the demand for moral sanction and the claims of social justice seemed inescapable. Craving adjustment amid the peril of change, representative Victorians, at least until the seventies, sought either in the radiance of God or in the dim consciousness of man some spiritual absolute by which to interpret and control their material advance; whatever misdirections they may frequently have followed, their impulse was in essence deeply religious.[31]

Prince Albert, we are told, was much concerned with art, though unfortunately he felt it to lie "somewhere between religion and hygiene." [32] Now, if for "hygiene" we might substitute "the general health of the body politic," Prince Albert's view of art would differ little from the first principles of any considerable mid-Victorian aesthetician. The "morality of art"—its religious content—lay in its relationship to the full experience and its power to speak to mankind in the language of universal emotion. For it was the artist's first duty to communicate, and the substance of his message was necessarily of social and, therefore, moral significance. To Ruskin it was clear that the student of art gained the deepest insight into the totality of human affairs. And to Arnold it seemed natural that the critic of books should be first and last a critic of society. The "moral aesthetic" was by no means a Victorian invention; it rested on the major premises of almost every classical aesthetic theory. Yet it bore special relevance to Victorian needs. Confronted with the unprecedented developments of nineteenth-century culture, an emerging middle class with the meagerest intellectual traditions behind it strove desperately to achieve standards of judgment. The early Victorian poet, sometimes no more certain than his contemporaries, was expected to furnish instruction as well as amusement. He could fulfill his vital function in society only by passing dramatic commentary upon the conflicts of his time. Often like Tennyson he had first to relinquish a personal prejudice for a

---

[31] Cf. R. C. K. Ensor, *England, 1870–1914* (Oxford, 1936), p. 137.

[32] See Clive Bell, "Victorian Taste," in R. S. Lambert, ed., *Art in England* (Pelican Books, 1938), p. 45.

more disinterested aesthetic. But usually he came in the end
to feel his renunciation morally—and socially—essential. At all
events, out of his sacrifice was born a considerable didactic
literature.

In its many-sided concern with manners and morals, the Victorian era was not unlike the Elizabethan age, when conduct-
books, pamphlets, plays, sermons, poems explored the problems
of degree in an expanding economy. Both periods brought to the
present a deep sense of the national past, based upon high
scholarship and eager research. Both shared the excitement of
vital education. Far from sinking beneath the weight of its
"moral," their art at its best followed new experience beyond
the bounds of thought. In the years after 1850 novelists and
poets exploited the forgotten "local color" of every English county
to produce a kind of nineteenth-century *Poly-Olbion*.[33] Like the
Elizabethans, the Victorians embarked on their own voyages of
discovery. To the far corners of the unknown traveled "manly"
adventurers—Layard to buried Nineveh, Livingstone to the dark
heart of Africa, Richard Burton to Brazil and Tanganyika and the
Great Salt Lake in a valiant effort to live his unexpurgated
Arabian nights.

But whether at home or abroad, many a Victorian captured
the almost Elizabethan exuberance that led Hurrell Froude to
exclaim on the launching of the Oxford Movement in 1833:
"What fun it is living in such times as these! How could one now
go back to the times of old Tory humbug!" [34] A tireless emotional
energy carried Carlyle through continents of passionate prose,
just as a physical stamina impelled the somewhat calmer Leslie
Stephen to tramp the fifty miles from Cambridge to London on
a hot day.[35] Like the Elizabethans, the high Victorians valued a
manifold competence; Ruskin like Bacon took all knowledge to

---

[33] A comparison suggested by Oliver Elton, *A Survey of English
Literature, 1780–1880,* 4 vols. (New York, 1920), III, 3.

[34] Quoted by John Henry Overton, *The Church in England,* 2 vols.
(London, 1897), II, 324–325.

[35] See F. W. Knickerbocker, *Free Minds* (Cambridge: Harvard University
Press, 1943), p. 29.

be his province, and whether or not, as Whistler suggested, he failed to master his specific subject, he left his mark on many others. Not without some reason, then, did John Addington Symonds conclude that "the English Renaissance of the sixteenth century became renascent in the nineteenth." [36]

Yet it will not do to press the parallel too far. Symonds himself detected in the Victorian period, whatever its buoyancy and promise, elements of "world fatigue" which were, he felt, quite alien to the Elizabethan temper. Certainly the desperate unbelief that permeates so much of Arnold's verse and wracks so little of his prose arises from distinctly Victorian cultural conditions, a sad contemplation of withering faith and an unprecedented fear of encroaching materialism. The paralysis of doubt that is said to have gripped Arnold's generation is far removed from the divided aims of a disillusioned Hamlet. Even if, as seems likely, both conflicts have been overstated, the very real crosscurrents of Victorian assent and denial are scarcely "Elizabethan" in source or direction.

Victorian society was forever subject to tensions which militated against complete spontaneity and singleness of purpose. It experienced in various forms the self-consciousness that is at once the strange disease of modern life and the genesis of analytic science. It learned to fear its own ardors, to distrust the falsehood of extremes. Whenever artist or philosopher was betrayed by the intensity of his conviction, Victorian parody served to restore a lost perspective; laughter prodded eccentric genius into an awareness of common reality. Despite the resounding clash of individual wills, there was until late in Victoria's reign a desire for cultural synthesis urgent enough to inspire from even the most rebellious many a concession to an established social morality. It was often as if the discords were hushed by a half-heard imperious command, "Hark, the dominant's persistence till it must be answered to!" Again and again the poet dreamed of a remote harmony which might catch up diverse themes into a

---

[36] See Symonds, *Essays Speculative and Suggestive*, 2 vols. (London, 1890), II, 274.

larger pattern, a meaningful Victorian counterpoint. Tennyson prayed for his whole generation a prayer which might be echoed by Victorians of vastly different intellectual persuasion:

> Let knowledge grow from more to more,
>   But more of reverence in us dwell;
>   That mind and soul according well,
> May make one music as before.

For all his sharp censure of Victorian culture, even John Morley came to feel that the prayer had been at times richly fulfilled; in the best effort of his age he saw "mind and soul according well." In 1921, nearly fifty years after the first appearance of his essay *On Compromise,* he added a few words by way of epilogue, a Victorian's final answer to a skeptical posterity. "Whatever we may say of Europe between Waterloo and Sedan," he wrote, "in our country at least it was an epoch of hearts uplifted with hope, and brains active with sober and manly reason for the common good. Some ages are marked as sentimental, others stand conspicuous as rational. The Victorian age was happier than most in the flow of both these currents into a common stream of vigorous and effective talent. New truths were welcomed in free minds, and free minds make brave men." Though later critics might charge the Victorians with divorcing intellect and feeling, the liaison was in fact well sustained into the 1870's, and the process of separation was, as we shall see, prolonged and painful. By 1884, when Ruskin sensed a great "storm cloud of the nineteenth century" blotting out the sun and breaking an old "harmony," English culture, heedless of his mid-Victorian warnings, was entering upon a new phase of its development.

The Victorian Mood: A Reappraisal

MARIO PRAZ

There are two different ways of looking at the past, and they correspond to the two different ways in which we can use binoculars, or rather opera glasses, since "all the world's a stage." If we look from one end, our forefathers appear very remote and quaint, but if we look from the other, they seem so near that we might mingle with them with no sense of surprise. After so many books written in our century have shown us how absurd the Victorians were, and how *stupide* the *dix-neuvième siècle* was, historians of the cast of Professor Jerome Hamilton Buckley have invited us to look through the other end of the opera glasses and to see the past as very similar to the present in its essentials. In *The Victorian Temper* [1] Professor Buckley sets out to prove that one cannot talk of the Victorian period in the manner that has become current in the first half of our century; that there existed at the time a quantity of frequently divergent tendencies; that far from presenting a homogeneous bourgeois aspect, self-satisfied, sentimental, and firmly rooted on unshakable foundations, the Victorian epoch was a period of extreme restlessness, in which nothing was more stable than in the most dynamic period of English history, the Elizabethan—in a word, the more one

---

[1] (Cambridge: Harvard University Press, 1951).

From Guy S. Métraux and François Crouzet, eds., *The Nineteenth Century World: Readings in the History of Mankind* (New York: The New American Library, Inc., 1963), pp. 19–42.

analyzes the Victorian temper, the more one finds it elusive, and the idea of Victorian family life as acquiescent and dull, unduly sanctimonious and alarmingly repressed, with an austere father dominating an abject household with impervious piety (the idea one gathers from Samuel Butler's *The Way of All Flesh*) "appears to have been largely a figment of the post-Victorian literary imagination."

A survey of recent historical literature (one is tempted to say "fiction," since history is recognized as possessing some of the characteristics of creative work and of presenting, like fiction, though in a different degree, a mixture of observation—i.e., of science and art) shows that it is possible to prove anything: that Tiberius and Nero were not the tyrants ancient historians have represented to us from their biased point of view, that Richard III was a benevolent king, that James II was anything but a bigoted autocrat, that the Inquisition was a compassionate and enlightened tribunal, that the French Revolution was a predominantly aristocratic revolt, that the Bourbons of Naples and the House of Hapsburg were model dynasties—there is enough to give rise to skepticism about history and historians were it not for the thought that all this is rendered possible by the ambivalence typical of most human phenomena, so that there is no bright color that has not a pale one as its complement; and for the fact that in the field of history, as in any other field, one perpetually runs the risk of missing the forest for the trees. What matters is the kind of tree that impresses its character on the wood, and a man who maintains that a garden in Europe is a tropical garden because of one or two rickety palm trees growing there would hardly be taken seriously. Professor Buckley's contention is true to the extent that men have always been the same, under Semiramis as well as under Queen Victoria, but is at the same time false when, laying undue stress on a quantity of tendencies destined to a brief life (who, nowadays remembers the Spasmodic School of poets of the eighteen fifties?), he proceeds to deny the existence of a Victorian temper distinct from that of the preceding and following periods. In a garden, if I may be allowed to pursue the botanical simile, there will always be a variety of flowers, but those command attention which yield the prevailing scent. Now if, in crossing the Victorian garden, there lingers in our noses a specific odor we shall remember, are we to say that our impression is false and that we ought to have taken into account also other flowers that no doubt blossomed there, though scentless and unseen? A garden is no *hortus siccus* where all the plants are deprived of scent, dead samples of a herbal.

The inner history of a period is liable to misconceptions because the essence of ideas is subtle and deceptive: the imponderable plays a great role in philosophy as well as in psychology. All things considered, one is led to wonder whether we should not be on safer ground in studying the temper of a period from its externals—more or less as Alain Robbe-Grillet and *l'école du regard* write their novels, pretending to push psychology aside, and concentrating on a minute description of objects and surroundings. Let the monuments of the past speak for themselves —and by monuments I do not only mean a triumphal arch or a cathedral, but also a humble utensil or a fashionable knickknack. Thackeray sought the spirit of the past not so much in official histories as in works of fiction and caricatures; Hogarth and Fielding, in his opinion, give a much better idea of the manners of the age than the Court Gazette. Turning the pages of fashion magazines of the nineteenth century, such as the *Journal des Dames, La Mode, Ackermann's Repository*, the *Gallery of Fashion*, or looking at the fashion plates of *Le Bon Genre* and *La Mésangère*, a superficial observer will only feel astonished or amused at the variety of costumes and at the so-called vagaries of fashion; but a philosopher will decipher there, as in hieroglyphs of indisputable meaning, deeper and weightier historical phenomena than may be inferred from a study of state documents or plans of campaigns. Diplomatic battles are won and lost, wars end in victory or disaster, territories change hands, empires thrive and decay, nay, they follow each other with the same aspirations and symbols, as Prince Karl Schwarzenberg has shown in his illuminating survey of the idea of world sovereignty throughout the ages:[2] the conquerors always present the same

---

[2] *Adler und Drache* (Vienna & Munich: Verlag Herold, 1958).

profile, whether they are called Alexander, or Caesar, or Frederic II, or Napoleon, the wars unleash the same passions and invariably show how thin is the veneer of civilization, and as for politics, Machiavelli's treatise is still up-to-date. But magazines of fashion, the frivolous fashion plates, have something even more curious to tell us.

Let us first take paintings into consideration. Even Professor Buckley admits that the Victorian taste in painting was peculiar. Painting in the Victorian era possessed the same bourgeois characteristics as Biedermeier painting in the rest of Europe, only more so; thus it may be taken as an illustration of the kind of taste that prevailed throughout the greater part of the century, notwithstanding the new tendencies (impressionism) that arose in France and failed to win public recognition until the century was nearing its end.

Victorian painting was dominated by a principle of narrow-minded, though occasionally charming verisimilitude, by a taste for anecdote, for genre, for the edifying and pathetic story, social propaganda, costume documentation, and the rehearsal of past history that most of the time was merely a parade in fancy dress. Few periods in the history of painting have been more homogeneous than Victorian art, which was no more than a corollary of minor Dutch art, singularly motionless even when it presumed to be revolutionary (as in the Pre-Raphaelites), showing no interest in those discoveries that were just then bringing French art to the fore (the English artists who went to Paris in order to rid themselves of the native academic tradition saw no further than Bastien-Lepage's *plein-air* naturalism, which in its turn was academic).

It is easier to form a general impression from a gallery of paintings or a collection of photographs of them than from reading the contents of an entire library. Now the Victorian scene, such as we see it in a pictorial record (for instance, in Graham Reynolds's *Painters of the Victorian Scene*),[3] is the quintessence of Victorianism in the current sense of the word with which Professor Buckley joins issue. If, as is generally assumed, there is

---

[3] (London: Batsford, 1953).

an interdependence between art, literature, and society, a country which had that kind of painting must have had moral principles and standards of taste, works of poetry and fiction typically bourgeois and Biedermeier, even if some isolated thinker expressed himself in a different language. Victorian painting begins with a Scot, Wilkie, and ends more or less with an Anglicized Frenchman, Tissot. The former was a painter of popular customs, the latter of the costumes of the smart set: in any case, the unifying factor of their paintings is a subject, a story, rather than a chromatic research, though Wilkie discloses the Flemish origins of his art through the brown—the color of a Stradivarius —dominating his genre pieces inspired by Brouwer and Teniers, and Tissot betrays some faint echoes of the impressionist in his water reflections and sun effects. The majority of Victorian painters are reporters of contemporary life, small-beer chroniclers who reproduce objects in all their details with an almost hallucinatory intensity, which appeals not only to our curiosity but occasionally to something deeper, our very emotions. Just look at a series of three scenes, Augustus Leopold Egg's *Past and Present.* In the first, in a heavy middle-class dining room, a stunned man sits near a table and crumples a letter with his left hand; a woman stretched on the floor wrings her hands; the elder of the two little girls busy in building a castle of playing cards on a chair turns in dismay, while the castle is on the point of collapse. Like the castle of playing cards, so a family has collapsed, because the crumpled letter has revealed to the husband the infidelity of his wife. On the walls of the room hang two equally symbolical paintings: *The Fall* and *The Abandoned* (representing a shipwreck). Hogarth had taught this manner of moral painting, but with a touch of humor. The other two paintings by Egg represent the same moment, five years later; that it is the same hour of the same night is made evident by the moon accompanied by a thin cloud visible in each painting. In one the adulteress, reduced to beggary, with a barefoot child in her arms, turns a haggard face to the serene sky from under the arches on the bank of the Thames (behind her, on the wall, posters speak of pleasure excursions to Paris—the seat of Vice—and of two theatrical performances with telltale titles: *Victims* and *A Cure for*

Love); in the third picture, from inside a bedroom the elder
daughter of the first painting, in mourning for her father, looks at
the moon and cloud, while the younger one, in her nightgown,
sobs on her knees. Here is one of a thousand instances of the pathetic bourgeois moral illustrated not only by Victorian paintings,
but by painting in the same vein throughout Europe. Tragedies
of unlawful love, the pleasures of family life, sweethearts who
meet again too late after many years, heart-rending departures
and cheerful returns, the last day in the old home, a young sailor
who sobs on the tomb of his mother, who has died during his
voyage, a schoolmistress consumed with homesickness (on the
piano the score of "Home, Sweet Home"). "Tears, Idle Tears";
but also crowded scenes by Frith and Hicks, the Derby Day,
the Ramsgate Sands, the Railway Station, the General Post Office
one minute to six, Billingsgate Market. Pictures one could read
like easy puzzles (not always easy: for instance William Frederick Yeames's *Defendant and Counsel,* showing a lady cross-ex-
amined by a barrister, was a "problem picture," which left many
in suspense about the story behind it), and a record of the life
of the middle class in its spectacular and melodramatic aspects:
those were the main themes of the enormous output of genre
painting that flooded England and Europe during the nineteenth
century, and that is nowadays considered as mere period illustration, apart from a few artists of outstanding merit. It is a pictorial
counterpart of the fiction of the period, with its increasing interest in the lower classes and everyday life, in the tragedies of
humble folk and scenes of crowds, almost invariably with a moral
or social lesson to impart.

In the latter part of the eighteenth century painters had represented peasants and country scenes mainly because these
were picturesque subjects: George Morland's softened realism
was in keeping with the idealization of country life prevailing
at the court of Marie Antoinette. About 1782 peasant girls and
little beggars were considered picturesque. In the nineteenth
century, when great artists like Géricault and Courbet in France,
or Venezianov in Russia, treated subjects from country life, the
approach was entirely different: the hardness of that life is not
concealed, ugliness is not avoided insomuch as it is expressive of

character, and still, notwithstanding the realistic treatment, a certain dignity is discovered in popular types, particularly by Venezianov, for whom the lesson of classicism had not been in vain. To account for these new tendencies it is enough to recall the two outstanding events that close the eighteenth century and set the tone of the nineteenth: the romantic movement, with its stress on the individual and on characteristic features as a criterion for beauty, and the French Revolution, which, whatever were its origins—whether it was by a mismanagement of the situation on the part of the educated classes that at a certain moment the rabble took control, or whether the moment was ripe, and not only in France, for the people to make their voices heard—had among its effects the recognition of the dignity of man, whatever his social background, and, a bit later in the century, the dignity of labor. The French Revolution, also, broke a spell (though one may say that it had been broken already by the Puritan revolution in England); it showed that the person of the sovereign was not sacred and that a mass of desperate people and barricades could win the day. It was the first earthquake whose repercussions occurred throughout the century (1830, 1848) and beyond, when the long-delayed explosion in Russia (1917) changed the face of the world to an even greater extent than had the French Revolution. The nineteenth century had thus had two fairies of ambiguous significance presiding at its birth: Belief in (and Fear of) Revolution and Respect for (and Exaltation of) the Individual. Only in our present century have we seen where these two fairies or inspirations were ultimately going to lead: the era of totalitarian regimes was the fatal outcome of those premises.

The nineteenth century, though not unaware of those dangers, preferred on the whole to ignore them. While Carlyle exalted the heroes, novelists more and more concentrated their attention on humble folk, painters little by little discarded the cult of history as the only worthy muse and painted scenes of everyday life and poor people instead of saints and warriors. The Industrial Revolution, the new scientific discoveries, Darwin and Lyell, and Biblical criticism disturbed some Victorians (e.g., Tennyson, A. H. Clough). At first they tried to cajole machinery into esthetic

shapes: locomotives were decorated with elements from Greek
or Gothic art, railway stations were built like Gothic cathedrals.
Eventually the machines were going to get out of control, as
were the masses bred by the Industrial Revolution, but this happened only in our century. In the mid-nineteenth century only a
distant rumble could be perceived; painters were astonished by
the new means of locomotion, and trains and interiors of railway
carriages frequently formed the subject of paintings. In novels
the locomotive occasionally held the role of the time-hallowed
deus ex machina. In Dickens's *Dombey and Son* a would-be se-
ducer, pursued by the husband of the intended victim, is run
over by a train and his "mutilated fragments" are cast into the
air; in Anthony Trollope's *Prime Minister* (1875–76) an adven-
turer of Portuguese-Jewish extraction, Ferdinand Lopez, who has
ruined himself and the daughter of a good family he has succeeded in conquering, hurls himself under an express train at the
Tenway Junction (Trollope's description of this crowded station
shows a thoroughness worthy of Frith), and his body is likewise
scattered in bloody bits. And everybody remembers the death of
Anna Karenina. This new *deus ex machina* was what could be
expected from an age awakened to the prodigies of machinery.
In our time, the automobile accident has taken the place of the
locomotive in a number of novels.

The nineteenth century, as is well known, marked the triumph
of middle-class ideals. England, which was ahead of the rest of
Europe at the time in both industrial development and social
history, offers the perfect picture of a situation that elsewhere
in Europe was blurred by political disturbances from which England was exempt. Those middle-class ideals had started asserting
themselves two centuries before, and the Victorian era represented only their final phase, in which the main characteristics
had become coarser, and supreme maturity was approaching decay. Macaulay is a less fine Addison, Thackeray possesses certain of Miss Austen's qualities, without her subtlety, Dickens is
an inferior Fielding; Puritanism, which during the seventeenth
century had been a force, was now lying, as James Laver says in
his introduction to *Victorian Vista* [4] "like the carcass of a great

---

[4] (London: Hulton Press, 1954).

ideal across the chest of the English people." No doubt there were in the Victorian era people of elevated moral feeling, but the current morals of the period have a touch of caricature that no historical perspective will be able to place in a better light: from the prim petticoat Cupid was made to wear in a valentine to a certain bedroom episode, but "without the bed," in one of Charlotte Brontë's novels; from the ridiculous taboos in consequence of which one could not talk of legs, whether ladies' or table (and tables were hidden under a cover just as ladies were smothered in clothes calculated to prevent their feet from being seen) to their methods of education (of the sadistic kind of *Struwwel Peter*) of which we have a fair sample in Mary Martha Sherwood's *The Fairchild Family,* when Mr. Fairchild takes his children to see the body of a man hanged in chains in order to teach them what is the end of those who hate their fellow men; we find another instance in Augustus Hare's *The Story of My Life,* when the author tells that, as a child, he was offered by his mother the most delicious puddings instead of his ordinary uninteresting fare, with the injunction not to touch them but to carry them off to some poor person in the village.

The coarsening of the middle-class ideals is particularly evidenced by the arts: one need only have a look at the *Official Descriptive and Illustrated Catalogue of the Great Exhibition* 1851 to become convinced that the same kind of taste that prevailed in England was typical also of the foreign states whose exhibits are illustrated in the third volume of that catalog. Industrial progress had destroyed fine craftsmanship by introducing mechanization and mass production, a fact of which Arthur Hugh Clough was well aware in the early fifties (in 1853–4, while he was in America, he wrote in a review of Charles Eliot Norton's *Considerations on Some Recent Social Theories:* "The crying evil, as it appears to us, of the present system of unrestricted competition, is not so much the distress of the workmen as the extreme slovenliness and badness of their work. The joy and satisfaction of making really good things is destroyed by the criminal eagerness to make them suit the market. The love of art, which, quite as much as virtue, is its own reward, used in the old times to penetrate down as far as to the meanest manufacture, of kettles, for example, and pots": similar remarks had already been made by Ruskin in the best of his *Seven Lamps of Architecture,* 1849, "The Lamp of Life"). Traditional styles (Gothic, Renaissance, neoclassical) still provided the models the new technical processes were only capable of travestying, whereas a style had not yet been evolved that could avail itself of the new materials and processes, except for a single case, Paxton's Crystal Palace, the first instance of a functional building whose lucky emergence was due to contingent reasons (the necessity of having the building completed within a narrow margin of time led to the employment of a gardener instead of a proper architect).[5] We have already seen how revealing of the prevailing bourgeois taste genre painting could be. Hardly less revealing are the conversation pieces, those portraits of family groups whose vogue had started with the heyday of bourgeois culture, in seventeenth-century Holland. The single portrait of the aristocratic tradition had then found a powerful competitor in those family scenes that stressed the intimate character of the relationships of the subjects, thus consigning them to the sentimental remembrance of posterity. The second half of the eighteenth century had been the golden age of the English conversation piece, reaching a grace and distinction, both in the attitudes of the figures and in the details of the interiors, that found a verbal counterpart in Jane Austen's novels. But during the Victorian period a didactic and sentimental bias became apparent in the conversation pieces just at the time they were about to be supplanted by photography. Thus for instance Sir Edwin Landseer is not content with representing Lady Emily Peel with her favorite dogs: he must show her in the act of upbraiding one of her pets for having upset a flowerpot, while another dog looks as if he were interceding for the culprit.

---

[5] Of course, it can be maintained that the railroad station was the first type of building expected to solve new problems functionally. Unfortunately, throughout the nineteenth century, railroad stations seemed to be particularly designed, in consequence of a mistaken sense of dignity and stateliness, to reflect the picturesque eclecticism of the period: thus the façade of Euston Station, London, was conceived as Doric propylaea, St. Pancras as a kind of Châtelet, etc. Only toward the end of the century did functional lines begin to assert themselves, whereas the Crystal Palace was unashamedly functional all of a sudden. On the evolution of railroad-station architecture and nineteenth-century taste, see Carrol L. V. Meeks, *The Railroad Station: An Architectural History* (New Haven: Yale University Press, 1956).

Every picture had to tell a story, and it had to be an edifying story. The recipes of Victorian paintings astonish us no less than the endless lists of courses of their meals: we wonder how they could digest those meals and those pictures. The result was the same: apoplexy. The apoplexy of art in the Victorian period is a fact that a moderate quantity of amusing genre paintings is unable to conceal.

James Laver tells us that Frith and Mulready are again appreciated nowadays, but these are but raindrops in comparison with the flood of paintings produced at the time, which no esthetic theory of the future will ever rehabilitate. A period that found Landseer's *Baptismal Font* mystical and profound (emblematical sheep and lambs of the gospel that typify every taint of sin from that of the youngest life to the deepest dye of the blackest sheep, throng around the font in order to be cleansed by the Savior, while doves have alighted on the edge of the font, and in the sky appear the colors of the rainbow), Alma Tadema's *Sappho* "a very gem of classical art," and Burne-Jone's languorous women "quite too utter," i.e. stunning, not to speak of shaggy dogs gazing mournfully at the coffins of their dead masters, angelic children, a bloom upon their cheeks like that of wax fruit, giving away their dolls to ragamuffins, wives of fishermen, or mothers of prodigals eternally peering out of windows into the darkness, or lighting moderator oil lamps to guide the wanderers' return, old women in church, gamblers' wives, thatched cottages, dying children, and the legions of historical paintings that rehearse famous episodes with a realism worthy of Madame Tussaud. A period whose taste can be sampled in this kind of painting seems to offer an ideal field of research to the sociologist rather than to the art historian. This taste was widespread in the Europe of the time, and is still found lingering in Russia, with the necessary adaptations suggested by the new social structure.

Equally, if not more, revealing of the temper of the nineteenth century are the interiors. The taste for the picturesque, in the first decade of the century, was still contained within the bounds of a somewhat pedantic classicism that, in obedience to reason, prescribed an interior decoration suited to the spirit and occupation of the inhabitant, so that, for instance, hunting attributes were required for the house of a lover of venery, helmets, swords, and Winged Victories were the proper decorations of the bed of a military man, and so on (according to a rational principle as old as Lomazzo's *Trattato dell'arte della pittura,* 1585). But around 1815 a new mood sets in, soon giving shape to the typical Biedermeier interior, which was to dominate throughout the rest of the century. In the *Confession d'un enfant du siècle* Musset deplores the interiors of the thirties "in which furniture of all periods and countries is mixed together. Our age is shapeless. We have failed to stamp the character of our age on our houses, our gardens, or anything else . . . . The houses of the wealthy are collections of curios: the antique, the Gothic, the taste of the Renaissance and that of Louis XIII, everything is thrown in as in a hotch-potch. In a word, we have something of every century except of our own. This has never happened before. Eclecticism is our badge: we lay hands on everything we can get hold of: this for the sake of its beauty, that because of its comfortableness, that other because of its antiquity, and yet another thanks to its ugliness; so that we live only on wrecks, as if the end of the world was at hand." Far from failing to stamp the character of their age on interior decoration, the men of the nineteenth century made their houses a perfect mirror of their souls, with their minute accumulation of details, their stuffy feeling in consequence of the overwhelming drapery, and, at the same time (which seems contradictory), their desperate craving for flowers and the presence of nature, either in painted landscapes or in stuffed birds. We see the same characteristics in feminine fashions, suggesting both repression and (imperfect) sublimation. The room, or the body, is protected from the outside world by curtains, hangings, flounces, etc., but shapes of the outside world made harmless and idyllic by their emblematic value are impressed on the very protections.

The exuberance of a Victorian, or Biedermeier interior has possibly another reason, which has been indicated by Walter Benjamin [6] in the dissociation between the surroundings in which

---

[6] *Schriften,* Frankfurt, Suhrkamp Verlag, 1955, Vol. I, p. 414, "Louis-Philippe oder der Interieur."

one works—the office, with its flat, prosy, workaday character—and the haven of comfort and relaxation, the home, which is meant to foster dream and make-believe. "For the private man the interior is his universe. He collects there what is distant and what is past. His drawing room is like a box in the theater of the world." As Wemmick said to Pip in Dickens's *Great Expectations* (Chap. xxxvi) speaking of his home in Walworth: "Walworth is one place, and this office is another. . . . They must not be confounded together. My Walworth sentiments must be taken at Walworth; none but my official sentiments can be taken in this office." His house was "the Castle." "On arriving before the battlements," writes Pip (Chap. xxxvii), "I found the Union Jack flying and the drawbridge up, but undeterred by this show of defiance and resistance, I rang at the gate, and was admitted in a most pacific manner by the Aged [Wemmick's father]." A hypothetical drawbridge was in front of most Biedermeier houses, and not only the external approach, but the interior decoration often reminded one of the Middle Ages.

Emphasis on the interior begins to be noticed in the latter part of the eighteenth century, in portraits and genre pictures by Boilly, Marguerite Gérard, Martin Drolling in France, but most of all in Germany and Denmark. At the same time a new genre appears: the interior for its own sake, reproduced in all its details, without the presence of human beings, one of the first examples of this kind being a reproduction of a room in the Prinz Max Palais in Dresden, 1776, once in the now no longer existing Karl Haberstock collection.[7] The painter who best expressed this new mood was G. F. Kersting (1783–1847), who in a number of scenes full of *Stimmung* "painted the *Heimat* in which the man of his time moves, in which he is really at home." [8] The pattern of all these paintings is always the same: a single figure, a man at his desk, or a girl in front of a mirror or embroidering at her frame, are seen in their simple surroundings, near a window that only in one case allows a glimpse of the scene outside: they gen-

---

[7] See plate XVIII in A. Feulner, *Kunstgeschichte des Möbels* (Berlin: Propyläen Verlag, 1927).

[8] Richard Benz and Arthur Schneider, *Die Kunst der deutschen Romantik* (Munich: 1939).

erally turn their heads away, so that they do not command the chief attention of the onlookers, which is first of all attracted by the room itself, with its few pieces of furniture and the play of light and shade caused by the daylight coming through the window, or by a lamp at night: what the painter wants to convey is the sense of the interior, its *Gemütlichkeit*, its *Stimmung*. This is a different kind of feeling from that conveyed by romantic painters, such as Friedrich and Runge, whose chief interest was the distance, the infinity of the surrounding world: Kersting concentrates on what is near; [9] like Wordsworth in the *Ode to Duty*, he seems to be "tired" of the "unchartered freedom" and to "long for a repose that ever is the same." This sense of a quiet permanent haven breathes from his interiors: the world that matters is found within the compass of four walls; the painter seems to say with Blake, though with a different application: "Hold Infinity in the palm of your hand, and Eternity in an hour." Why yearn for infinity when happiness is so near at hand? Why ask of the Spirit of the Wind to bear one like a swift cloud over the universe, rivaling with him in uncontrollableness and impetuosity, when staying at home one can feel master of a diminutive universe of familiar objects, and find contentment in rehearsing their delightful inventory? In the Hamburg Kunsthalle there is a family keepsake painted by Julius Oldach (1804–1830) for the silver wedding of his parents: medallion portraits of the members of the family are accompanied by vignettes in which everyday episodes of family life are affectionately commemorated. There were never so many conversation pieces and interiors painted as in the Biedermeier period in the Germanic countries. At the beginning of the century France seemed to be following the same road, with Garneray, Loeilliot, and other painters of interiors, but Biedermeier themes soon receded into the background in that country agitated by romantic ambitions, social dreams, and cravings for the exotic and the rare. The artists there rebelled against middle-class ideals to an extent

---

[9] For this section of the essay I am partly indebted to a dissertation of Fritz Laufer, *Das Interieur in der europäischen Malerei des 19. Jahrhunderts*, which has been published only in part in Zurich in 1960 (Buchdruckerei Schippert & Co.).

unknown to other European nations. But in England to set against a Carlyle and an Arnold one has a legion of writers who acquiesced in the Victorian compromise, even Dickens, whom some critics have represented as a radical, even Thackeray, who was a mild critic of that society. The banner of revolution continued to be raised in France throughout the nineteenth century in politics (1830, 1848, the Commune of 1871), in morals (Baudelaire, Flaubert, even Lautréamont), in art (the impressionists), so that Delacroix's famous painting *La Liberté guidant le peuple* may be taken as an emblem of the French spirit in the nineteenth century, whereas, if one should search for appropriate emblems describing the prevailing temper of England and the Germanic countries in the same period, one would think perhaps of the tune of "Home, Sweet Home," of Dickens's Christmas spirit, and of Uhde's painting "Stille Nacht, heilige Nacht." The term "still life" is appropriate in more than one sense to the vast quantity of interiors that were painted, mostly in the Germanic countries, during the nineteenth century. They are as telltale as the religious paintings of the Middle Ages or the portraits of courtiers, warriors, humanists, and fair ladies of the Italian Renaissance. They celebrate the pleasures of the home, a nonmystical *hortus conclusus,* and pride of possession. During the course of the century the interiors become more and more crowded. One has only to look at the collections of water colors preserved at Charlottenburg, Sans Souci, the Oranje Nassau Museum at The Hague (Album of Queen Sophia), or the Chigi Album (at l'Ariccia, Rome) containing views of the rooms occupied by the family Wittgenstein in several parts of Europe, including Russia, from 1834 to 1843. This latter album, for instance, gives a fair idea of the kind of life the Princes Wittgenstein and their likes led in that nineteenth-century Europe in which the aristocracy, notwithstanding the French Revolution, still enjoyed a considerable prestige and held a monopoly of leisure and pastimes that nowadays, in a reduced and popularized form, are shared by all and sundry (today summer resorts and tours to distant countries are accessible to the masses). Turning the leaves of this album one seems to listen still to the impassible carillon of the Versailles clock, which continued to

strike after Marie Antoinette had appeared to the crowd for the
last time on the scaffold, or to that other carillon of the cathedral
of Saint Peter and Saint Paul, which played "God save the
Czar!" when the Russian revolution had already swept away the
Czar and a vast number of noble families like the Wittgenstein.

In the interiors of the previous centuries the furnishings still
bore evident signs of being destined to certain purposes: this is
evident in the scanty pieces of furniture of a medieval or Renaissance room; it was only under Louis XIV that a distinction came
to be made between furniture meant only for show (destined
to the court) and furniture with a specific function in a bourgeois
family; but when in the eighteenth century the aristocracy preferred *maisons de plaisance* and *hôtels* to stately palaces, when
in court apartments variety, comfort, and cheerfulness seemed
desirable, there began the golden age of interior decoration
with the merging of the aristocratic and the bourgeois taste, and
the creation of a large number of new types of furniture designed to meet the various demands of convenience and comfort:
the bookcase, different kinds of tables, each having a special
function (such as folding tables, dumb servants, library tables,
etc.), and sofas and chairs with attractive names (the *bergère*,
the *marquise*, the *duchesse*, the *turquoise*, the *veilleuse*, etc.).
But even with all this variety the eighteenth-century interior
was not redundant; this can hardly be said of the Biedermeier
interior with its fondness for superfluous ornament and particularly with its determination, amounting to sheer mania, to dissimulate the practical use of furniture under covers, drapery,
hangings, to litter with china and knickknacks every available
surface, and to hide the walls under rows of paintings reaching
up to the ceiling. This wish to dissimulate the practical use of
furniture together with a prevalence of decorative elements over
the functional ones tended to transform the Biedermeier interior
into a temple of art; it generally succeeded only in transforming
it into a sepulchral chamber in which all the possible specimens
of earthly possessions should be heaped together for the afterlife
of the occupant. The presence of many objects was unexplained
and puzzling; thus the Biedermeier interior became mysterious.
It also became sinister. No wonder Benjamin could see a connec-

tion with the detective story.[10] The inventor of the detective story, Poe, also wrote the *Philosophy of Furniture*. It is only at the close of the century that an attempt was made to put an end to the shapelessness resulting from this rank abuse of arbitrary decoration; and *art nouveau* was born not really as the last escape of art besieged by an increasingly mechanized world, as Benjamin maintains; it was, rather, an attempt to convert technique into art by subjecting ferroconcrete devices to an Ovidian metamorphosis into vegetable shapes, a kind of inversion of the myth according to which Gothic architecture was supposed to derive from an alley in a forest. The vegetation was only short-lived, however; the steel core asserted itself with that stiffening of *art nouveau* that took place in Holland. The reduction to essentials and bare geometrical forms in De Stijl heralded what nowadays we call the modern taste.

Let us now consider the most frivolous of the external phenomena of the nineteenth century: fashion. Let us look at a collection of fashion magazines of the early nineteenth century, or better still, at that series of amiable cartoons that goes under the title of *Le Bon Genre*, covering the first twenty years of the century, and let us try to see in it something more than the headdresses *à la Titus* or *à la Caracalla*, or those ladies' silk shoes, so fragile that a shoemaker is reported as having replied to a lady who complained that her pair had curled up: "Madame a marché." One thing strikes us, even more than the muslins and the Greek tunics of the ladies: men's and women's clothes, when seen together, do not jar: gay colors enliven both—nay, at the beginning of the century, the variety of colors of men's clothes catches the eye among the almost general whiteness of feminine garments. True, men's breeches are usually white—white, too, is

---

[10] Benjamin, *op. cit.*, pp. 415–16: "The interior is not only the universe, but the case of the private individual. To inhabit means to leave traces. These become more evident in the interior. Covers and protections are invented, any amount of sheathing and casing, which help the traces of daily use to disappear. Also the traces of the inhabitant disappear in the interior. The detective story is born which hunts after these traces. The *Philosophy of Furniture* and the detective stories show Poe as the first physiognomist of the interior. The delinquents in the early detective novels are neither *gentlemen* nor *apaches,* but private middle-class people."

the voluminous tie the convolutions of whose elaborate knots were taught in special treatises—and top hats are as a rule gray or black, but look at the showy or pastel colors of the frockcoats and waistcoats. Bottle-green, blue, purple, puce coats, red waist-coats with red or yellow trimmings, or striped white and red, or bright yellow, or blue with red flowers; and even pistachio-colored frockcoats, and sky-blue, light-brown, autumn-tinted breeches. A dandy, Brummell, dresses in a much less showy way, aiming at exquisiteness in the cut and the details; his costume, compared with that of the average fop, is as blank verse is to rhymed couplets; but Brummell, in this army of fashion, makes the impression of the *Petit Caporal* with his faultless gray frock-coat in the midst of the general staff of his field marshals, as gaudy as tropical birds. Color, then, at the beginning of the century, had not been forsaken by the male sex; women and men harmonized in the same vivid palette.

Let us now take a conversation piece of the midcentury. A photograph of 1860 shows us the imperial court at Fontainebleau; the ladies are seated on the steps, the photograph does not reveal the colors of their dresses, but we may guess at them; we have only to consult a fashion magazine to learn them. The men are lined up behind them; and finally, on the water of the little lake, Napoleon III is seen with the Prince Impérial in a small boat. All the men, the Emperor included, wear dark frockcoats, and all the men wear black ties. Or let us take another photo-graph (in the Cromer Collection) that represents a group of German noblemen: the men wear, all of them, dark frockcoats, dark ties, and the two ladies are dressed in gay silks (one of them wears a dress with a Scotch pattern, possibly red and white stripes on a green ground). Why is there such uniformity in the men as against the gay variety of their costumes at the beginning of the century? Why, conversely, have women's dresses gained in eccentricity in comparison with the early nineteenth century? Why do their swelling petticoats and gay bonnets look so bizarre to us? Why have men's fashions become crystallized? Few phenomena are so clearly indicative of a whole social revolution. Thorstein Veblen in his *Theory of the Leisure Class* has fur-nished the explanation with his laws based on the principle of sumptuosity as indicative of belonging to a social upper class.

Feminine fashions have always obeyed, and continue to obey these laws. Thus for instance the silk shoes of the *Premier Empire,* calculated to clothe the foot, but not for walking, illustrate the law of conspicuous leisure; the thin Greek tunics of the same period, which leave the body almost bare, illustrate the law of conspicuous outrage and also that of conspicuous leisure insofar as they do not take climatic conditions into consideration: underwear under the light dress was reduced to a minimum for the sake of the figure, thus exposing the smart ladies to the risk of catching pneumonia. On the other hand the cumbersome dresses that became fashionable toward the middle of the century hampered the movements in conformity with the same principle, to demonstrate the complete incapacity of the person wearing them to lead an active life.

Masculine dress at the beginning of the nineteenth century conformed to the same criteria: tight-fitting breeches and high boots bore witness to the habit of riding, an aristocratic activity; on the other hand, collars devised to give the wearer the elegant appearance of being strangled are an indication of conspicuous leisure: this may actually sound contradictory, because leisure and comfort can hardly be associated with strangulation; the point is not this, but rather the impression conveyed of being utterly unfit for mechanical activity. The dandy is a martyr, a flower impaled on a stick: Brummell is known to have had himself carried in a sedan chair right up to the threshold of the house where the party he was coming to bless with his presence was taking place: there he would be laid down immaculate, intact.

With the onset of the Industrial Revolution in the thirties, however, the marks of inefficiency, of absolute indolence cease to be for men indications of belonging to a wealthy class. The industrialist is often wealthier than the man who lives on his income; an industrious life ceased to be synonymous with a care-ridden, feverish life; it was no longer dishonorable. It was enough for a man to wear the distinctive signs of the class that handled money to show that he took part not in the actual production of goods, but in the distribution of wealth. Hence the dark suit, the cylindrical hat, spotless linen, and a carefully rolled umbrella. Up to the beginning of the century masculine dress had been that of the gallant, of the man whose chief occupation was to court the ladies; by midcentury it became that of the financier, of the man managing public money.[11] His sober attire can be traced back to the severe style of the Puritans; this link in fashion may confirm the opinion of those who have seen the origins of modern capitalism in the Puritan conception of life. Naturally enough, modern masculine attire established itself in the country in which the industrial system first developed— England—which incidentally was also the country of the Puritan revolution; and the London fashion has set the standard for masculine dress up to the present day. The evolution of the masculine collar provides a good illustration of the transition from the ideal of the gallant or the Cavalier (to use the term antithetical to Puritan in seventeenth-century England) to the ideal of the financier: collars become lower and lower during the course of the century, and, apart from sporadic returns to the high, strangling collar, evolve toward the low, soft collar of our days. For a time, though, there remained for military men the gorgeous dress, full of futilities, which has in common with feminine costume its conformity with the law of conspicuous consumption, and the preservation of atrophied elements that had once had a practical purpose, preserved like idle emblems for no other reason than that they are emptied of present usefulness. These uniforms, magnificent as they were for a parade in peacetime, proved impractical and even dangerous to soldiers in time of war. The charge of the Light Brigade, which in recent years has formed the subject of a deservedly famous book by Cecil Woodham-Smith (*The Reason Why*), might serve for the Victorian period as one of those typical episodes John Aubrey picked up in order to give in brief the essence of a character. Six hundred horsemen, in consequence of a confused and misunderstood order, charged in the valley of death in perfect parade style, with no other prospect than being mowed down by the Russian cannons; Lord Cardigan, galloping in front of all, offered himself alone to the astonished Russians, dressed in his splendid uniform glittering with gold braid, heroic and grotesque like

---

[11] See Quentin Bell, *On Human Finery* (London: Hogarth Press, 1947).

somebody facing a public meeting naked: these are the symptomatic signs of a period and a society that, under the veneer of
a debased enlightenment, were harboring a confusion of principles and purposes that eventually had to come to a head.

Uniforms gradually lost their gorgeousness in the course of the
nineteenth century, and two world wars have since hastened
the process, so that in our time the uniform of a high officer, with
its iron or earth color, is but the sublimation of the mechanic's
overall. But the revolution in masculine attire we have just
discussed is only one aspect of the general decay of the picturesque that the industrial age brought about in the outward
appearance of the world.

Let us remember what England was like at the beginning of
the nineteenth century: it was the time of thoroughbreds, horse
races, boxing matches (a sport that found no Pindar for its
singer, but only the pen of an essayist, Hazlitt), of Manton's
dueling pistols, of clippers, the supreme achievement of sailing,
and of the stagecoaches celebrated by De Quincey. And all
these things bore a certain resemblance to each other, just as
Beau Brummell, perfect from his boots to his elaborate tie and
top hat, bore a resemblance to the Corinthian columns just then
multiplying in crescents and squares (the tie corresponded to the
capital, the top hat to the abacus); all these things were marked
by the same type of slender, resilient elegance, so that a pistol
and a horse had a similar profile, both slim and austere, and
the clipper that crossed the Britain-ruled oceans, and the stagecoach that rolled at the unheard-of speed of fourteen miles an
hour on roads perfected by MacAdam, were fruits of the same
taste, manifestations of the same spirit. Perhaps one had to go
back to the ancient world, Pericles' Greece, or to Renaissance
Italy, to find a like harmony of style penetrating everything.
Think only of the stagecoach, which, with its body supported
by springs and its spidery wheels, was no less elegant than the
horses, possessing a shape as typical of the equilibrium of the
period—a balance resulting from slim though robust joints—as
the arrogant, ballistic line of modern automobiles (shapes of
torpedoes and sharks) is typical of our age. To make the body
of the stagecoach even more human, its flanks were decorated

with the stars of the four orders of knighthood, almost as if it were the breast of a uniform—actually, it had the gorgeous colors of a uniform, with yellow prevailing. Finally, it must be borne in mind that the education of a dandy (or "gay young bloods," as they were called) was not considered complete until he knew how to drive four-in-hand to perfection, as a rule on the Brighton Road, which was peopled, from beginning to end, with "fashionables" before whom the gentleman-coachman could display his skill. Amateurs, among them the famous Count d'Orsay, had formed the *Four-in-hand Club,* whose rule was "to drive like coachmen but to look like gentlemen." Rural England was still intact, with the added magnificence of the country houses: horses had never been more beautiful, coaches had reached a supreme grace of design, masculine attire was simple and exquisite. But, as always in the course of history, the achievement of perfection is the forerunner of catastrophe. Coaches and sailing ships reached perfection at the very moment the application of steampower to transportation marked their end. When in 1838 Parliament passed the law that authorized the conveyance of mail by railway, the fate of the mail coach— and of many other things—was sealed.

It may be that nowadays we are approaching a new kind of equilibrium: the machine is inexorably taking control of all aspects of life, from industrial design to painting and architecture; poetry can be machine-made, music electronic. But the period between the destruction of the old harmony and the advent of the new one (diabolical as it may appear to *laudatores temporis acti*) was accompanied by a decay of old standards and clumsy—even ludicrous—attempts to cope with the new reality, together with a rank growth of nostalgic revivals of old styles and a pathetic heaping up of "fragments shored" against the century's "ruins." [12] I take the nineteenth century to be such a period of *âge ingrat,* of laborious transition. This manifestly implies an adverse judgment on many of the manifestations that passed for art in the nineteenth century, and it could not be otherwise, at least so far as concerns the art that best expresses

---

[12] T. S. Eliot, *The Waste Land,* V (New York: Boni & Liveright, 1922).

the temper of a period, namely architecture, though there have been recent attempts [13] to revaluate Victorian buildings. The confused scene offered by nineteenth-century architecture is a mirror of the times. But the very restlessness that proved inimical to architecture was a salutary ferment in the social field. The progressive ascent of the working classes is too well known a fact to need rehearsing here. The emancipation of women is another of the achievements of the nineteenth century.

The average idea of a woman's position in society at the beginning of the Victorian age is fairly represented by the following: [14] "The peculiar province of a Woman is to tend with patient assiduity around the bed of sickness; to watch the feeble steps of infancy; to communicate to the young the elements of knowledge, and bless with their smiles those of their friends who are declining in the vale of tears." Woman was still the angel-like creature of the Provençal and the *stil nuovo* poets, but translated into bourgeois terms—a cherub or a seraph who had a crinoline for wings, behind which the body was angelically invisible. Like books of the romantic period, she was cased in an *à la cathédrale* binding. This Gothic woman found in sickness and death two magnificent occasions to display her pent-up exuberance. The mourning ceremonial was never more elaborate and subtly graduated with innumerable shades as in Victorian England. And abroad, too: etiquette prescribed that the apartments of the widow of the Duc de Berry at the Pavillon de Marsan should all be hung with black; black veils hid the mirrors and gildings, and yellow wax candles completed the sepulchral decoration, reminding us of the ingenuity of the Greek sophist who, having lost his wife, did not want to see anything white around him and was attended by black servants, and of the funereal device of the seventeenth-century Spanish knight, who, not content with hanging his walls with black, burned black candles and had recourse to other lugubrious inventions recalling the House of Sorrow of the Indian emperor

[13] See Henry Russell Hitchcock, *Architecture, Nineteenth and Twentieth Centuries*, Pelican History of Art Series (Harmondsworth: Penguin, 1958).
[14] C. Willett Cunnington, *Feminine Attitudes in the Nineteenth Century* (London: Heinemann, 1935), p. 73.

Montezuma. There is little doubt that Victorian ladies often ac-
centuated their passive role with a touch of masochism. Even if
there is some exaggeration in speaking of "the orgy of sadism in
the upper-middle class during the late '60's and '70's," as C.
Willett Cunnington does, an admission like the one he quotes of
a lady, to the effect that "tight-lacing produces delicious sensations, half pleasure, half pain," is telltale enough.

Women's education had its grotesque aspects: they were taught
to do exquisite embroidery, but not to make their own dresses,
to paint wax or shell flowers, to gild plaster casts, to learn how to
walk gracefully down carriage steps, to learn Italian because it
was useful for singing—and singing was an accomplishment that
no young lady could neglect, as if, according to an ancestral
idea, the chief task of a woman was to restore the hunter or the
warrior on his coming home from his hard day; in a word, as one
of them said, women were taught everything in the inverse
ratio to its importance. However this is also the period in which
the feminist movement, started at the time of the French Revolution by Godwin's future wife, Mary Wollstonecraft (her *Vindi-
cation of the Rights of Women* was published in 1792), began to
exert an influence on the great Victorian novelists' conception of
woman. The wedge by which the feminist movement penetrated into Victorian society was philanthropy: it took advantage
of the prevailing idea of the role of women we have illustrated
already. The philanthropic missions, which consolidated around
1850, provided an occupation for middle-class women who felt
the emptiness of their lives and the futility of an education of
the type hinted at above. A first stage of voluntary philanthropy
was succeeded by another in which the service of employed
women was paid with a salary; schools were founded to prepare
women for their missions in hospitals and schools, in workhouses
and reformatories: professionals took the place of amateurs, and
a great step forward was accomplished with the admission of
women to the Social Science Association in 1857. Octavia Hill created model houses for the poor, asking them to pay small rents
in order to educate them to a proper sense of dignity; Harriet
Martineau organized charity according to a scientific program at
Ambleside. The profession of governess, typical at first of desti-

tute young ladies of good family, became organized in the Association for the Promotion of the Employment of Women (1857). The first university colleges for women were founded: Queen's College for Women (1848) and Bedford College (1849). The profession of governess came to the limelight in the novel chiefly with Thackeray's Becky Sharp and Charlotte Brontë's Jane Eyre. These governesses were not beautiful; Becky was pale with red hair, Jane was small and plain, and with all that they were successful. Not only governesses, but the most interesting women in Victorian fiction—for instance, in Trollope's novels—were far from beautiful. This certainly points to a gradual prevalence of the feminine point of view and to a revenge women were taking against the traditional man-made conception of woman as an adorable brainless doll. After the working woman, the seamstresses and governesses, who appeared in so many best sellers of the 1840's and '50's, it was the turn of the nurses led by the peerless Florence Nightingale during the Crimean War. In 1858 women laid siege to the medical profession; Mrs. Lynn Linton was the first woman journalist to receive a salary; little by little the profession of actress came to be considered with respect, whereas before a woman who exhibited herself in public was looked upon as little better than a prostitute. As the position of woman in society changed gradually in the Victorian scene,[15] so in other respects too that scene was far from static; its tone changed sensibly after the death of the Prince Consort (1861), with his ideal of domestic purity, and the appearance of the Prince of Wales, the future gay monarch Edward VII. It changed not only in the sense of a more frank and open discussion of problems of morality and immorality, but chiefly because of the increasing importance unmarried women gained in English society.

Another aspect of education that strikes us as very remote from our system is the education of Victorian boys: those who were educated in colleges were still obliged to write Latin epigrams on various subjects, just as their forefathers had in the

---

[15] See Patricia Thomson, *The Victorian Heroine, A Changing Ideal,* 1837–1873 (London and New York: Oxford University Press, 1956), from whom I have derived most details on the emancipation of women.

seventeenth century, and with a seventeenth-century insistence
on wit. Methods of education at Eton and Winchester, where
cruelty, bullying, and caning were of common occurrence, are
apt to shock us, who have been made wise by Freud and his
disclosures about the origins of repressions and neuroses. We
ought rather to be surprised that by those elementary ways of
enforcing discipline a type of young man should be produced
"of utter integrity and courage, complacent, a little priggish,
kind but insensitive and inexpressive," [16] in fact, the typical
nineteenth-century Englishman who called his father "sir" and
was ready to take up "the white man's burden." For better or for
worse, those young men helped to create an empire; whereas
the modern systems, in their anxiety not to breed repressions in
the young, have seen, among their results, a frightening increase
in juvenile delinquency all over the world. So, before pronounc-
ing those Victorian methods of education strange, we ought to
reflect whether our posterity may not consider our own methods
even stranger. And what can be said for education may perhaps
be extended to other fields: if Victorian painting seems to us so
peculiar, what will posterity think of the abstract painting of
our own? And if the nineteenth century deserves the epithet of
stupide, may not our own century deserve an even harsher
epithet—such as, for instance, insane?

---

[16] Marion Lochhead, *Young Victorians* (London: Murray, 1959), p. 25.

II

Religion and Science

ASA BRIGGS
Religion and Science

NOEL ANNAN
Science, Religion, and the Critical Mind

NORTHROP FRYE
*The Problem of Spiritual Authority in the
Nineteenth Century*

Religion and Science

ASA BRIGGS

Although there were signs in the late eighteenth century that the pursuit of scientific enquiry and experiment upset those churchmen who were afraid of 'human presumption', deviation from Biblical orthodoxy, and intellectual 'Jacobinism', most early nineteenth-century scientists believed that there was a more confident link between science and morality than there was between morality and art. Some of them talked in familiar terms, as Paley had done, of Divine Design in the pattern of the Universe; others employed new theories of catastrophic geology to 'prove' the Flood [1] or, when these had been discounted, looked for manifestations of God's 'government' in the history of the natural world. 'Truth is always delightful to an uncorrupted mind', the Cambridge scientist, Professor Adam Sedgwick, wrote in 1845, 'and it is most delightful when it reaches us in the form of some great abstraction which links together the material and moral parts of nature.' [2] It was thought proper to extend the in-

---

[1] This was the view put forward by the most eminent English geologist, Professor William Buckland, in 1820. 'The grand fact of *an universal* deluge . . . is proved on grounds so decisive and incontrovertible, that had we never heard of such an event from scripture. . . . Geology of itself must have called in the assistance of some such catastrophe.' *Vindiciae Geologicae* (1820), pp. 23–4.

[2] *Edinburgh Review*, vol. LXXXII, p. 56.

From Asa Briggs, *The Age of Improvement* (London: Longmans, Green & Co. Limited, 1959; New York: David McKay Co., Inc., 1959), pp. 479–488. Footnotes have been renumbered.

fluence of science outside the laboratory and the study. The universities might prefer the classics, but in the popular education of mechanics and artisans in institutes and night schools, scientific as well as technical instruction was often included; an appreciation of Truth, it was believed, would make the workers not only better workers but better men. 'Science teaches us', Brougham wrote, 'to look on all earthly objects as insignificant and below our notice except the pursuit of knowledge and the cultivation of virtue—that is to say, the strict performance of our duty in every relation of society.' [3] The lessons drawn from science left many working men unmoved, but they had a special appeal for the middle classes who found in geology in particular a science which could account for their wealth—thick coal seams—and could enliven their leisure hours through the favourite Victorian pursuit of collecting fossils and shells. The British Association for the Advancement of Science was founded in 1831, largely as a result of the activities of geologists, with the twofold purpose of increasing public interest in useful knowledge and of inspiring scientific discovery.

Emphasis by scientists on the social and moral as well as the intellectual or utilitarian rôle of science was in many ways extremely unwise, for by the time of the revolutions of 1848 it had been demonstrated that 'science' might teach the wrong lessons as well as the right ones, and that there were bound to be difficulties in reconciling scientific conclusions with those of revealed religion. The enormous success of an avowedly popular book, Robert Chambers's *Vestiges of Creation* (1844),[4] alarmed orthodox scientists themselves. In his volume Chambers began with the solar system and ended with man; just as 'gravitation' was the 'one final comprehensive law' relating to inorganic life, so 'development' was the one great law relating to organic life. Organic forms had not been created in fixed groups at the be-

---

[3] Quoted in G. C. Gillispie's extremely interesting and original study *Genesis and Geology* (1951), p. 195.

[4] It was published anonymously, went through four editions between 1844 and 1845 and eleven editions by 1860. One theory was that it had been written by Prince Albert. In fact, Chambers was a self-made man with a passion for popularizing all kinds of knowledge. He was a 'precursor' of Smiles as well as of the popular evolutionists.

ginning of the world, but had chronologically progressed, and 'man, considered zoologically, and without regard to the distinct character assigned to him by theology, simply takes his place as the type of all types of the animal kingdom'. Established scientists were the first to attack the *Vestiges*. Sedgwick believed, for example, that Chambers had 'annulled all distinction between physical and moral', and that the framework of natural theology which Chambers had retained was completely artificial. Yet although scientists were able to point out scores of serious academic and scientific shortcomings in Chambers's work, they could not 'muzzle' a thesis which appealed both to poets like Tennyson and to secularist working men.

Before Darwin gave a responsible scientist's answer in 1859 to the problem of the descent of man, the work of other responsible scientists was raising difficulties for those people who placed a simple trust in the infallibility of the Biblical record. Sir Charles Lyell, whose three-volume *Principles of Geology* (1830–3) destroyed the dramatic geological case for the Flood, had made it equally difficult to believe in the simple Biblical view that the world was created in 4004 B.C. His book created much popular interest but little scandal, for it was unimpeachably scholarly, and Lyell himself was extremely tactful and reserved, as conscious of his social as of his scientific rôle. He believed in man's absolute uniqueness and the immutability of other species, but had come to the conclusion that Mosaic chronology was 'an incubus on our science'.[5] This was a most important conclusion, for it not only altered the whole sense of time span, but left less and less of the record of the past to be explained in terms of supernatural intervention. In private circles in the '40s and '50s it was well known that most distinguished scientists, whatever their public utterances, agreed with Lyell that it was impossible to hold to a strictly literal interpretation of the Old Testament. Not only was the earth far older than the Bible suggested but, just as serious, the order of creation of the various living forms described in *Genesis* did not correspond with the order

---

[5] K. M. Lyell, *Life, Letters and Journals of Sir Charles Lyell* (1881), vol. I, p. 328.

in which the creatures appeared in the rocks. At this point archaeology lent its aid to geology and natural history. In 1857 the first remains of Neanderthal man came to light, and the discovery of stone implements and other objects demonstrated conclusively that long before the time of Biblically-placed Adam there were beings on earth to whom the name of 'man' could not be denied.

Darwin's *Origin of Species* 'from the standpoint of the providentialist interpretation of nature . . . was a *coup de grâce* rather than an entering wedge'.[6] For years before 1859 the cautious, cultivated, retiring, and sickly Darwin was collecting facts about evolution—he wrote out a long and coherent statement of 231 pages in 1844 which included nearly every detail of the final theory—but he shrank from writing a book on a subject which he knew would cause great controversy. It was only when he read an article by A. R. Wallace in the *Annals of Natural History* in 1855 that he began to feel that it would be vexing 'if anyone were to publish my doctrines before me'[7]; the further revelation of the nature of Wallace's work and the pressure of his friends led him into producing *The Origin of Species*, one of the most important books of the nineteenth century,[8] a book based on the accumulation of a mass of detailed and carefully checked information.

It began with a brief but shattering introduction which stated simply that 'the view which most naturalists until recently entertained, and which I formerly entertained—that each species has been independently created—is erroneous'. Species were not immutable. Hereditary modification was possible under human control—the first part of the book was devoted to careful conclusions drawn from horse-breeding and pigeon fancying—and stood out as the main theme of natural history, the doctrine of Malthus applied to 'the whole animal and vegetable kingdoms'. During a relentless 'struggle for existence', 'natural selection' had determined the future of living creatures 'under the complex and

---

[6] Gillispie, *op. cit.*, p. 220.

[7] Quoted W. Irvine, *Apes, Angels and Victorians* (1955), p. 80.

[8] A joint paper summarizing both his own and Wallace's views was read before the Linnean Society in July 1858 and published in that society's *Journal of Proceedings* (*Zoology*), vol. III, August 1858.

sometimes varying conditions of life'. In the final paragraphs of peroration, with their stormy note of optimism, Darwin claimed that there was 'grandeur' in his new view of life. 'Whilst this planet has gone cycling on according to the fixed laws of gravity,' he concluded in a sentence reminiscent of Chambers, 'from so simple a beginning endless forms most beautiful and most wonderful have been, and are being, evolved'.

Darwin's sense of beauty did not impress a large number of his influential contemporaries. The most dangerous of his critics were not the Biblical fundamentalists—they had been shocked by so many scientific writings before 1859 that *The Origin of Species* was merely the latest and biggest blow—but those scientists who felt that Darwin had destroyed the much-treasured link between morality and science. The theory of spontaneous 'natural selection', they believed, substituted accident—or perhaps mechanism—for intelligent purpose in the world of nature. It was this aspect of Darwin's theory which T. H. Huxley, Darwin's great protagonist, claimed was new in 1859.[9] Darwin made little attempt to resolve the dilemma between chance and design; instead, he took the view that when he used the word 'spontaneous' he merely meant that he was ignorant of the causes of that which he so termed. His 'ignorance' on what after all was a key point in Victorian argument was as upsetting as his positive conclusions. It was his old Cambridge geology professor, Sedgwick, who had predicted a brilliant scientific future for him, who wrote that Darwin had revealed 'demoralized understanding' and had done his best to plunge humanity into 'a lower grade of degradation' than any yet recorded. Reverting to the argument he had advanced against Chambers, he maintained that 'there is a moral or metaphysical part of nature as well as a physical' and that a man who denied this was 'deep in the mire of fallacy'. In conclusion he objected to the manner of Darwin's conclusion, particularly the appeal to 'the rising generation'.[10]

Huxley, bold, brilliant, and pugnacious, did much to publicize

[9] See F. Darwin (ed.), *The Life and Letters of Charles Darwin* (3rd edn. 1887), vol. I, ch. V. In this chapter Professor Huxley describes the contemporary reactions to the *Origin of Species*.

[10] See Gillispie, *op. cit.*, p. 217; Irvine, *op. cit.*, p. 113.

Darwin's thesis and to defend it against more old-fashioned scientists. He spoke the new language of the 'rising generation', compared Darwin with Galileo and Newton, and warned his countrymen that 'the origin of species' was not the first, and would not be the last, of 'the great questions born in science, which will demand settlement from this generation. The general mind is seething strangely, and to those who watch the signs of the times, it seems plain that this nineteenth century will see revolutions of thought and practice as great as those which the sixteenth welcomed.' [11]

There was not the slightest doubt, Huxley later said, that if a general council of the Church scientific had been held in 1860 Darwin's views would have been condemned by an overwhelming majority. As it was, it was not the Church scientific but the Christian Church militant and non-militant which was quickest to give an opinion. Bishops, parish clergy, journalists, and laymen almost all condemned that part of Darwinism which they thought they understood, and only a few priests of the Church of England, notably Charles Kingsley,[12] showed any sympathy with the new picture of evolution by natural selection. Darwin's main ecclesiastical antagonist was Bishop Wilberforce of Oxford who at a famous meeting of the British Association at Oxford in 1860 asked Huxley with studied politeness whether 'it was through his grandfather or his grandmother that he claimed his descent from a monkey'. The ecclesiastical case often rose to no higher a level than this, but in reality the divided Church of England was shaken by the impact of the new views in a way that a more authoritarian body would not have been, and there was no single effective answer which any Churchman could make at that time, with any hope of securing general agreement. Throughout the 1860s and '70s Christianity as 'a system of ideas, aspirations and practices' was facing a far graver challenge than the Church of England had faced as an ecclesiastical institution in the 'Church in danger' days of the mid-1830s.

---

[11] Quoted F. Darwin, *op. cit.*, vol. I, p. 283.
[12] 'Now they have got rid of an interfering God', Kingsley wrote to Darwin, 'a master-magician as I call it—they have to choose between the absolute empire of accident and a living, immanent, ever-working God.'

The challenge from science was not the only one, and there was in fact an important intellectual link between the problems of the 1830s and those of the 1860s. Ever since the early Tractarians began to examine the *origins* of ecclesiastical authority, many Anglicans were drawn into a study of history which might lead them out of the Church of England either into the Roman communion or out of Christianity altogether. The two Newman brothers—John Henry and Francis—typified the choice. Pulled in the two opposing directions, the first passed from Protestantism to Roman Catholicism, becoming a cardinal in 1879, while the second moved from Protestantism into a religious 'modernism' which stopped short at the confused boundaries of agnosticism. 'It is as if', Basil Willey has written in a most illuminating image, 'two rivers, taking their rise in the same dividing range, should yet be so deflected by some minute original irregularity of level, so that one pours its waters into the Mediterranean, the other into the German ocean.' [13] Germany was the great centre of Biblical criticism, but before German influence helped to provide a scholarly foundation for a new English view of the Bible as a historical document and of Jesus as a historical figure, sensitive English intellectuals were already feeling a sense of insecurity in the traditional Christianity of their fathers, particularly Evangelical Christianity. 'Whether or not Anglicanism leads to Rome', John Henry Newman was writing in 1840, 'so far is *clear as day* that Protestantism leads to infidelity.' [14]

George Eliot was an interesting representative of one team of travellers along Francis Newman's road. She began researching into the origins of Christianity in 1831 when she was living a quiet provincial life among English Calvinists and hovering in her own mind between the Evangelical and Tractarian arguments. One of the books she read was Charles Hennell's *An Inquiry Concerning the Origin of Christianity* (1838) which represented an English, rather than a German, tradition of rationalist enquiry. With Hennell and Charles Bray, a prosperous Coventry

---

[13] B. Willey, *More Nineteenth-century Studies* (1956), p. 11.
[14] Quoted M. Ward, *Young Mr. Newman* (1952), p. 360.

ribbon manufacturer, as her guides, she soon came to the conclusion that miraculous interventions do not occur in the course of nature, and on the basis of that conclusion she abandoned all her belief in the doctrines of Christianity and in the need for Church attendance. From 1844 to 1846 she was translating *Leben Jesu*, a German rationalist study by D. F. Strauss which talked of the 'Christ Myth' and treated Christianity entirely as a historical product.[15] It was thus through a study of human history and not through natural history that George Eliot and many of her contemporaries reached a position where they could no longer accept the Bible or the Church as sources of authority. Their position was clearly defined long before the publication of *The Origin of Species*.

There was another element in the English 'rationalist' protest. John Stuart Mill's *System of Logic* (1843) influenced intellectuals in the universities, and it in turn was influenced by Auguste Comte's new sociology. According to Comte and his English disciples, the Positivists, of whom the most able was Frederic Harrison,[16] society had a history of its own, an ordered course going through three stages of growth—the theological, the metaphysical, and the positive or scientific. In this last stage the Christian religion would give way to the religion of humanity, a genuine religion, demanding acts of worship, but completely free from the superstitions of the past. While Mill, influenced by Comte, pleaded for a clash and conflict of opinions out of which new truths, like new species, would emerge, Harrison and his friends pointed to the inevitable emergence of a moral system superior to that of Christianity. Not all the rebels against traditional Christianity were so optimistic. Like the scientists, they could either view the process of human change with eager

---

[15] For the details of George Eliot's early intellectual development and its relevance to her later career, see J. Bennett, *George Eliot* (1948).

[16] Harrison's college tutor, Richard Congreve, was the first Positivist preacher in England; he was a pupil of Dr. Arnold of Rugby. Harrison admitted that it was the Positivist view of history which was the first feature in its philosophy to appeal to him (*Memories and Thoughts* (1906), p. 15). Mill too was influenced by the 'connected view of the natural order of human progress' (*Autobiography* (1873), ch. V).

anticipation or they could contemplate it with alarm—and even with despair.

George Eliot, as an artist, and T. H. Huxley as a scientist, agreed with the Comtists that the abandonment of Christianity did not mean the abandonment of 'morality'. They believed instead that they had to be good for good's sake not God's, to cultivate broad human sympathies, and to find a moral 'aim' or 'object' in life. George Eliot held that 'in proportion as the thoughts of men and women are removed from the earth on which they live, are diverted from their own mutual relations and responsibilities of which they alone know anything to an invisible world which can only be apprehended by belief, they are led to neglect their duty to each other [and] to squander their strength in vain speculations'.[17] Huxley had no doubt that 'the ledger of the Almighty is strictly kept and every one of us has the balance of his operations paid over to him of every minute of his existence'.[18]

For those who did not abandon Christianity, though they often went through religious crises and experienced intense moments of 'honest doubt', three ways were open—complete indifference to the impact of science on older views of life and history, an attempt to adapt Christian argument to new challenges, and an obedience to the full authority of the Roman Catholic Church. The first choice was the most frequent, and there were enough disputes within the Church of England on matters of religious observance and discipline in the 1850s and '60s to keep conventional ecclesiastical energies active and passions alive. The world of *Barchester Towers* (1857) was far more satisfying to a large section of the clergy than the world of *The Origin of Species*. Those people who chose the second way were in an extremely difficult position, meeting with great hostility from both Evangelicals and Tractarians alike. When in 1860—the year of the foundation of the High Church English Church Union—seven talented members of the Church pro-

---

[17] Quoted Bennett, *op. cit.*, p. 25.
[18] L. Huxley (ed.), *Life and Letters of Thomas Henry Huxley* (1900), vol. I, pp. 219–20.

duced a volume of essays designed to cast off 'incrustations' from Christianity and to bring out the 'eternal import' of religion, they were attacked as 'Seven against Christ' by both Pusey and Shaftesbury.[19] Their essays were, in fact, reasonably mild and thoughtful attempts to 'reconcile intellectual persons to Christianity'.[20] Only one of the essayists referred to Darwin (very favourably), although there were frequent references to Biblical criticism, appeals to theologians to stop clinging to out-of-date theories of 'God's procedure towards man', and demands for further discussion by churchmen of contemporary intellectual issues. 'It is a stifling of the true Christian life', one of the most-criticized writers declared, 'both in the individual and in the Church, to require of many men a unanimity in speculative doctrine, which is unattainable, and a uniformity of historical belief, which can never exist.' [21]

For all the mildness of most of the seven writers, two of them were condemned officially by the Court of Arches and suspended from their offices for a year. All of them were rebuked by Bishop Wilberforce with as little subtlety as he had shown in his rebuke to Darwin. At the same time they were all sharply criticized by secularists and Positivists for not going far enough. It was Frederic Harrison and not Wilberforce who remarked that their views were 'incompatible with the religious belief of the mass of the Christian public, and the broad principles on which the Protestantism of Englishmen rests'.[22]

The third choice is best represented by John Henry Newman, although his methods of argument and the quality of his thinking

---

[19] *Essays and Reviews* (1860). The seven writers included Frederick Temple, Headmaster of Rugby and later Archbishop of Canterbury, Mark Pattison, and Benjamin Jowett, later Master of Balliol College, Oxford. The *Quarterly Review* of January 1861, which included Bishop Wilberforce's attack on the book, went through five editions.

[20] E. A. Abbott and L. Campbell (ed.) *Life and Letters of Benjamin Jowett* (1897 edn.), vol. I, p. 345.

[21] H. B. Wilson, 'The National Council', *loc. cit.*

[22] *Westminster Review*, October 1860. Kingsley's anti-intellectual reaction was typical of those who did not want to think too much. 'Do not darken your mind with intellectual puzzles', he told his curate, '[they] may breed disbelief, but can never breed vital religion, or practical usefulness.' *Letters and Memories of His Life* (ed. F. Kingsley, 1877), vol. II, pp. 103–4.

were quite exceptional. In his *Apologia Pro Vita Sua* (1864), Newman described the Roman Catholic Church as a 'port after a rough sea' and added that from the time that he became a Catholic he never had one doubt. 'Ten thousand difficulties do not make one doubt.' Even before he became a Catholic, however, he had reacted strongly against attempts to relate the existence of God, as Paley did, to the Divine Design of the Universe and had come to the conclusion that the religious apologetics of the day discussed the wrong problems in the wrong way. He was neither surprised by Darwin's theory of evolution nor shocked by it, preferring to ground his faith not in 'mutilated and defective evidence' but in 'a right state of heart'. His *Grammar of Assent* (1870) rejected all ideas of a 'balance of arguments' to control and fix man's minds, and he was thus able to by-pass not only the immediate problems of his age but the technique of free discussion and enquiry which the leading spokesmen of his age considered the necessary means to increase understanding. Harrison believed that Newman's brother Francis much surpassed him in 'mental versatility' and that 'the central ideas of the Cardinal's philosophy are so wild and incongruous that we can only account for them as intellectual "faults" (in the geological sense), abysmal fractures produced by a truly "seismic" act of the will',[23] but what Harrison craved for was what John Henry Newman considered basically unprofitable— the meeting of brain with brain, Christians, atheists, Positivists and 'agnostics' (the word was coined by Huxley in 1870) all together. It was a craving which has little appeal in the mid-twentieth century, but it was satisfied for a time by the remarkable Metaphysical Society, set up in London in 1869, which really did bring many of the great men of the age together to discuss the central philosophical problems of the day.

For Huxley—and he should have the last word as a scientist— it was just as necessary as it was for the orthodox Anglican theologians that one side should win the debate between science and religion. He had no doubt which side it would be. After a struggle of 'unknown duration', which would have as its 'side issues vast

---

[23] *Realities and Ideals* (1908), p. 393.

political and social troubles', 'free thought' would conquer and organize itself 'into one coherent system, embracing human life and the world as one harmonious whole'. It would need generations, however, to complete the task, and 'those who further it most will be those who teach men to rest in no lie, and to rest in no verbal delusions'. In the middle of the vast political and social troubles which followed the end of the period of mid-Victorian equilibrium, Huxley's prophecy already began to date. The conflict between science and religion petered out, giving way to new debates about the nature not of the the Universe but of society. At the same time, the verbal delusions persisted, the mid-Victorian quest for 'ultimate truths' was followed by a period of flirtation with every form of historical and moral relativism, and, above all, the sheer indifference to the issues raised by both Huxley and Wilberforce increased.

Science, Religion, and the Critical Mind

NOEL ANNAN

Science is a word for ever changing its meaning in popular imagination. It still conjures up for us, as it did for the Victorians, the romance of man making discoveries and taming Nature, and like them we take pride in our scientific geniuses. They were also proud of their artisans, as we admire technologists, for translating the scientific discoveries into marketable products. But we realize, as they did not, that the development of science and technology rests on a vast base of institutions. We realize what technological effort is required to transform the brain-child of a team of university or industrial or government research scientists into a mass-produced product; what ingenuity and organization is required to market such products; and what complex investment by banks and corporations is needed to finance new projects. We know how scientific invention is for ever changing the structure of industry and transport—still more the welfare, culture, and way of life—of both highly industrialized and under-developed countries. Today science is part of politics. For better or for worse nation-states have begun to invest in science and technology and to organize them as part of the national power complex.

I

A century ago no such picture could have formed in the minds

From Philip Appleman, William A. Madden, and Michael Wolff, eds., *1859: Entering an Age of Crisis* (Bloomington: Indiana University Press, 1959), pp. 31–50.

of the Victorians. Mr. Haines* tells in his essay of a country in which science had scarcely begun to be taught, and individual initiative and the demand of the market were expected to supply engineers as well as engineering. That even by 1859 science was still neglected in education was partly due to the difficulty of reforming institutions in an age still rigidly respectful of the law and of vested interests. When a Fellowship at Oxford or Cambridge was regarded as a private chattel, to deprive a man of which would be an act of pillage and the abrogation of the sacred rights of property, how could educational or other resources be re-allocated to take account of the needs of science? Education, moreover, was connected with the idea of a governing class, and the reformers in the 'fifties were thinking in terms of examinations which would test the abilities of a future Indian Civil Servant rather than of training wage-earning technicians or creating a band of physicists or chemists in universities.[1]

Science, then as now, was feared. Today while we see in it the hope of human welfare, we fear it as the agent of our destruction. But it is not the subject itself but the use to which nation-states put it that we fear. In 1859 the Victorians were hardly beginning to take account of the political and international implications of science, but they were deeply suspicious of its effect upon individuals. Science was suspected of being a moral danger. Ruskin pointed to one type of corruption—the corruption of the craftsman. Newman, and after him Matthew Arnold, pointed to another—the impoverishment of the individual's mind if he were permitted to specialize in science and set aside the liberal arts. But in the popular imagination the greatest danger seemed to be whether science was going to contradict the whole tradition of European thought by substituting a totally different account of what life on this planet had been, was, and ought to be. How could the findings of science be reconciled with

---

* [In the course of his essay, Professor Annan refers to four other contributions to *1859: Entering an Age of Crisis:* "Darwin and Clerical Orthodoxy" by Basil Willey; "The Limits of Religious Thought: The Theological Controversy" by R. V. Sampson; "Darwin, Pater, and a Crisis in Criticism" by Philip Appleman; "Technology and Liberal Education" by George Haines, IV.]

[1] W. A. Leigh, *Augustus Austen Leigh* (1906), pp. 133–134.

the history, the morality, the ideals, and the faith of Christian England? The situation was similar to that in the twelfth and thirteenth centuries, when men were forced to reconcile Aristotle to Christian theology. And this time no Aquinas was born to resolve the crisis.

The *Origin of Species* was not, of course, the sole great dissolver of faith in mid-Victorian England, and we would misinterpret the age if we saw it as such. To see the celebrated controversy between science and religion a century ago in perspective we must stand back from the 'fifties and relate Darwin's book to a tradition of thought already long developed. The *Origin of Species* was simply another stage in the development of the positivist tradition—a tradition that owed something to Bacon but first took shape in the writings of Hobbes, Locke, and Newton. For over two centuries it was to be the most consistently powerful intellectual movement in England. Its most original philosopher, Hume, might expose its limitations; the governing class might prefer pragmatic reform and Burkean principles to Benthamism; the Romantic poets and seers from Blake to Yeats pilloried its methods and conclusions. But positivism called the tune and forced other modes of thought to dance to it.

Positivism was both a method and a disposition of mind. It claimed to be scientific because it applied to human behaviour the methods of inductive and deductive reasoning that Newton had hallowed. The interplay of these methods (which John Stuart Mill sketched in his *System of Logic*) was put forward as the soundest way of discovering truth about all subjects. Today we think of knowledge as a set of different subjects, each with its own discipline; but when in 1852 Cambridge, responding to demands to broaden its curriculum, instituted the Natural Sciences and the Moral Science Triposes, the names reflected the implicit assumption that knowledge was a unity. In the nineteenth century, moreover, science meant pre-eminently the discovery of new laws: great immutable hypotheses necessarily replete with profound cosmological implications. There was nothing new in such extrapolation. From Newton's laws not only had a new physical universe been constructed; psychology and even economics and religion were infused with Newtonian inferences. And so, as each new scientific law in Victorian times was propounded, men tried to apply it to society or the universe. Tennyson, whose sensibility was so acutely tuned to the dilemmas of his generation, was of course doing this when he immortalised in *In Memoriam* the relation of thermodynamics to the ancient tale of the loving purposes of God towards man.

There was every reason why such ideas should take root easily. The eighteenth-century tradition of rationalism had assumed that the words "scientific" and "rational" were synonyms. The business of living in society—of choosing between right and wrong, of choosing your objectives, of choosing between different courses of action, of choosing the means to achieve your goals—was described as a rational, and, as men grew wiser, a scientific process. It was irrational to prefer pain to pleasure; it was ascetic or unnatural to aim at unattainable goals; it was superstitious to perform actions, such as rituals, which were not directed towards a specific end. Circumstances, "other people," and the situation in which you found yourself of course influenced your conduct. But you could prevent circumstances dictating to you by acquiring facts about your situation and inferring—scientifically—from them how best to act. What prevented men from doing this? What impeded the march of mind and the progress of civilization? Ignorance, false doctrine, and anachronistic institutions. Here the positivist disposition of mind deeply disturbed the conservatives and the orthodox: they were faced by something much more sweeping and alarming than a movement for political reform.

At the same time positivists recognized that the social sciences could not hold a candle to the natural sciences when it came to making claims that incontrovertible truths had been discovered. The basic premise about society—that its health and wealth rested on the pursuit of rational self-interest—was said to be implicit in Nature herself and to be confirmed by the most striking achievement in all the social sciences—the body of related conclusions about human behaviour constructed by the classical economists. And yet, difficult as it was to refute these conclusions, the abstract and deductive nature of the argument detracted from its prestige. The conclusions of Bentham or

Comte or Buckle were not demonstrable to the same degree as those of Lyell. Lyell's work contained hypotheses in plenty but they rested on facts. Was there a branch of knowledge about human beings that could produce facts of comparable strength and validity?

There was indeed. History had suddenly become a much more impressive study and had acquired a new status. The critical study of sources which the Germans introduced became a science in itself and the material on which the conclusions of yesterday were based was exposed, at the worst as surmise, gossip, travellers' tales, and myth, and at the best as documents which carried a meaning for the original writer and his contemporaries quite different from the meaning which had traditionally been assigned to them by the churches and other self-interested parties. The techniques which Barthold Niebuhr had used on Livy began to be applied to the Bible, and it was these techniques, not the general philosophy of the individual historian, that impressed the English clerisy. Strauss, for example, was no eighteenth-century rationalist: his purpose was to expose the shallowness of the old-fashioned rationalist attack on the Bible: but his Idealist interpretation of Roman-Jewish history was insignificant beside the spectacle of his remorseless examination of every fact, every parable, and every incident in the Gospels. This new scientific treatment of evidence put Biblical history outside the orbit of any but professional scholars, and as a result bewildered and enraged the mass of the clergy in mid-Victorian England.

There was, then, a disposition of mind towards interpreting all natural and human phenomena in positivist terms; and it was continually gaining strength. No single thinker ever set out its assumptions and conclusions in their entirety (though Mill came nearer to it than any). Yet already by the 1830's the study of man could not be undertaken analytically without reference to utilitarianism, classical economics, and associationist psychology; and by the 'fifties the positivist interpretation of the history of man began to take a more formidable shape. Lyell's geology was all grist to the positivist mill, and the idea of development— the idea that the world and all that is in it has radically changed over the centuries and that nothing, not even our knowledge of God, is given once and for all and is immutable—was current long before 1859. Darwin confirmed more rigorously what positivism had for long asserted—that the history of the world is the history of progress and that there was no need of supernatural intervention during the ages to account for whatever had happened. The descent of man was incorporated into the positivist cosmology and the picture painted by the new scholars of Natural History was set up to mock the old picture of Creation which the churches implicitly upheld.

And yet we should be equally wrong to minimise the shock made by the publication of the *Origin of Species*. No doubt Francis Newman, George Eliot, and others had lost their faith because they found Christian morality as preached by the churches deficient. No doubt J. A. Froude and Baden Powell were more affected by the Higher Criticism of the Bible than by science. No doubt Lecky or Herbert Spencer or Clough or W. R. Greg or Matthew Arnold or Browning or dozens of other mid-Victorians who moved on their different paths away from belief in dogmatic Christianity were impelled by many reasons. But Darwin remains a crucial name and 1859 a crucial year. The *Origin of Species* became the foundation of a new history of the world. Colenso's statistical enquiry into the arithmetic of the Pentateuch, which so enraged his brother bishops, was influenced by Darwinism as well as by the Higher Criticism. The issue was not simply whether scholars might re-interpret the Bible but whether the beloved story of man's Creation and the Flood was rubbish. Darwin not only offended the Fundamentalists among all Christian communions (and how numerous they were Mr. Willey's essay indicates) but all those attuned to believing in a world in which God was continually at work in a material way—in a world which He planned. Was Natural Selection part of God's design? It might indeed seem so to men who saw the principle at work in the ruthless competition of the early Industrial Revolution in which the weakest capitalists went to the wall and only a prodigious effort of Self-Help on Smilesian lines could lift a man out of the squalor of the slums. But if this seemed morally repulsive, was not Huxley right in claiming that man's sole hope lay in "combatting the cosmic process" and defeating by his own efforts the blind determinism of evolution? A great chasm seemed to have opened between God and Nature. Darwin introduced the idea that *chance* begot order in the world, and today, whether in atomic physics or in the genetical properties of the nucleic acids, chance still rules in terms of any single individual particle, however much the laws of mathematical probability work in respect of any groups of particles. To the Victorians the metaphysical significance of this situation seemed of appalling importance. As Mr. Willey shows, it seemed to many of them that God had been banished from the world and that the new account of Creation foretold a spiritual and moral destiny for the human race incompatible with the story of God's dealings with man as depicted in the Bible. Belief in Divine intervention in the affairs of men was widespread and disasters in Nature were often held to be instances of God's justly provoked wrath. How could this be if mechanistic blind chance alone prevailed in the order of Nature? Despite the fact that Darwin denied that he intended to trespass on theological pastures, and despite the fact that he was to dissociate his work from Herbert Spencer's adaptation of the principle of evolution, the churches fell upon him. The rumpus perhaps was inevitable, but it turned out to be singularly unfortunate for the churches. As sometimes happens when the established order in society decides to force an issue and crush a lone danger, the dissident suddenly appears to gather strength from the soil itself and emerges as the leader of an army triumphant with banners flying.

The year 1859 was also the year in which Mill published his essay *On Liberty*. In it Mill confused two distinct propositions, but he confused them with incomparable power and fervour. He argued that all repression and restraint is bad because it frustrates human beings, and can be justified only if it can clearly be shown to prevent a demonstrably greater evil; and that only in a free society can men discover the truth and cherish it. The two propositions are not identical, but small wonder that later, with Darwin's experience before their eyes, the new English intelligentsia was convinced that they were. This intelligentsia, which was gaining power as it filled the Civil Service at home and in the colonies, which was providing teachers in the universities and Public Schools, which was editing and contributing to the growing numbers of periodicals that were such a stimulus to Victorian intellectual life, and which was establishing links in the governing class itself but was in no way dependent on aristocratic patronage, was in no mood to be called to order by bishops and country clergymen. When Darwin made his well known comment that Lyell's support for the *Origin of Species* was heroic in view of his age and his position in society, he underlined one of the main theses in Mill's book: the search for truth and hence the means of progress were being impeded not by the laws but by social pressures, such as the risk of losing respectability, or the pillorying and petty persecution of men in the ancient universities, or the requirement that men should be reticent or even prove their soundness by a prudent display of unction. Sometimes today we detect a strained note, an unattractive overemphasis, in the protestations of the mid-Victorian rationalists, but their plea for intellectual freedom was justified and carried all before it, not solely from the rightness of their cause, but because the treatment of Darwin's work was a simple touchstone. That is why 1859 marked a new phase in the development of positivism and led to the outburst of anti-clerical and rationalist books and articles in the 'seventies and to the secularisation of intellectual life.

II

Undoubtedly the churches had become more sharply opposed to science than they had been a century before. Odd as it may sound to speak of an alliance between religion and rationalism in the time of Hume and Gibbon, the theology of Natural Religion was not unsuccessful in harmonising Revelation and Nature. It confidently assumed that the world of spirit and matter were as one, and rested this assumption on verifiable observation. A hundred years after Bishop Butler published his *Analogy* the evidence no longer seemed so clear. The teleological explanation of Nature and the argument from design no longer carried weight. Yet of the dozen other factors that one could mention, which led to the conflict of science and religion, none is as important as the rise of Evangelicalism. The movement that began with Wesley and revived both the Nonconformist communions and the Anglican Church scorned the value of evidences and proofs and wagered all on the conviction of faith. The question was no longer, "How do we believe?" but "Do you believe?" It reduced the Christian religion to "God's scheme of salvation," an historical-theological account of the Fall, of man's universal need for redemption, of Christ's atoning sacrifice, of man's justification in God's sight by faith in this sacrifice, and of an after-life of reward or punishment. It told this story in simple, literal, and personal terms. The transcendent Father, majestic in wrathful justice, could be propitiated by belief in Jesu, the Son, the pitying Saviour, the sinner's friend—an intensely personal and corporeal God. Evangelicalism transformed practical religion and the nation's morality. By the very simplicity of its Christian message it affected the lives of many people who underwent an intense religious experience—even the lives of many of those who disliked the Evangelicals. But this same simplicity rendered it terribly vulnerable to the new weapons in the positivist armoury; and it is not, I think, an exaggeration to see Victorian theology in retrospect as a tireless, and at times almost desperate, attempt to overcome the appalling weaknesses which this simple faith presented to positivist criticism.

It was vulnerable on so many counts. The piercing Evangelical emphasis upon the figure of Jesus was one, and strange as it may seem, this emphasis is theologically dangerous. Theologians are sophisticated men. They are well aware of the dangers of allowing Christians to suppose that the utterances and actions of the Jesus of the Gospels are the main source of a Christian knowledge of God. For centuries they had relied on the constructions of the Early Fathers and the mediaeval Schoolmen to explain how the figure of Jesus was the Word and how through the doctrine of the Trinity He was related both to the Person of God and to humanity. But the human-divine Jesus of Galilee, through whom Evangelicalism stirred the popular imagination, became an historical, rather than a theological, Person. And suddenly the Churches were faced with a new Revelation: the deductive painstaking reconstructions of the historical figure of

Jesus produced by the critical study of the Bible. The quest for
the historical Jesus had begun. Those who denounced it were
fighting a losing battle. Those like the Broad Churchmen who
welcomed it were brought up short against the darker eschato-
logical sayings of Christ; they met these difficulties by depicting
Christ as a teacher of morality and, in so doing, they often almost
humanised away His divinity.

The Broad Churchmen anxiously stressed the higher morality
of the Christian faith because Evangelical doctrine had made
serious men doubt it. The Evangelical love of personalized
religion had led them to treat the Atonement, according to Frances Cobbe, as a "huge commercial transaction between God
and man" in which one acquired "a saving interest in the Blood
of Jesus";[2] or alternatively it was described in terms of a spectacular trial at the Old Bailey. In 1856 McLeod Campbell published his *The Nature of the Atonement*, in which he tried to
avoid the moral difficulty of God appearing to punish Christ by
substituting vicarious repentance for vicarious suffering. But
such a technical theological study was hardly likely to satisfy
those who were revolted by the injustice of the doctrine when
presented in its journalistic form and by the equanimity with
which so many Churchmen viewed the doctrine of Eternal Punishment.

Furthermore the popular notion of God visiting His punish-
ments upon His erring peoples, so current in a generation that
liked to speak of "judgments" falling upon individuals or nations
(or even on wicked cities such as Paris), appeared increasingly
simple-minded as historiography (whether mechanistic or Idealist) gave other explanations of the rise or fall of civilisations.
We have to remember how many were the parsons and the
devout whose own brand of proof was to collect scraps of learning that coincided with their convictions and serve them up
piping hot: or who used Scripture almost cabalistically and
wrenched Old Testament prophesies out of their context.[3] This
kind of Biblical interpretation, common among all denomina-

---

[2] F. P. Cobbe, *Broken Lights* (1865), pp. 36–37.
[3] See E. M. Forster, *Marianne Thornton* (1956), pp. 162–163.

tions, made some theologians try to discard allegory. But they at once came up against historical evidence and were asked to explain how precisely God, when He appeared as Christ, put off his attributes of omniscience while retaining those of omnipotence.

What sign, then, was there at this time of an intellectual challenge by the Church to positivism? Among the first Liberal Anglicans, Dr. Arnold and Hare were dead, Thirlwall and Whately preserved episcopal silence, Stanley was a spent force, Jowett was being sniped at in Oxford; and in retrospect the contributions to *Essays and Reviews* show a lack of intellectual vigour and originality. The Tractarian party lay in ruins, its energies now flowing into ecclesiology and ritualism, and its leaders, such as Pusey, as obstinate in their rejection of the new learning as their Evangelical opponents. There was, of course, the solution to these scientific and historical difficulties that the great Tractarian apostate offered: not to come to terms with them at all—to scorn the Protestant reliance on Biblical facts and triumphantly to turn Hume's scepticism upon the rationalists themselves and to argue that all reasoning rested on inferences of little or lesser probability. In 1859 Newman, in his *Lectures and Essays on University Subjects,* admitted that at times Catholics in the past had been led to question the findings of Copernicus or Galileo or other scientists; but that "after a little time" the Church "had never been led formally to explain the [sacred] texts in question or to give them an authoritative sense which modern science may question." [4] Newman denied that there could ever be a conflict between dogma and science: he quoted Macaulay's dictum that no discovery in science could ever affect the arguments for or against Transubstantiation.[5] To those who asked what grounds there were for being dogmatic about religion if its dogmas were incapable of being verified, Newman answered that the truth of Revelation had been attested by great minds and the onus of proof lay on those "who

[4] J. H. Newman, *Lectures and Essays on University Subjects* (1859), pp. 278–280.

[5] Newman, pp. 234–236.

are introducing into the world what the whole world feels to be
a paradox." [6] But whatever Newman wrote at this time was ignored. John Bull dismissed him as a sophist and in 1859 he was
at the nadir of his influence. The Church of Rome was distant
towards its notable convert. It, too, needed to accommodate itself to evolution and Newman had hoped (without success) that
it would adopt his *Essay on Development* as its guide: but the
Roman Church has not favoured in recent times selecting one
particular apologist and resting its case upon his reasoning. It
prefers to state as its main argument that reason and faith can
never conflict; and where conflict exists, the wrong social and
moral conclusions must have been drawn from the study of man
or nature. It was to this argument that Newman had turned in
1859, but it was not until 1865 when he published the *Apologia*
and Manning became Archbishop of Westminster that there
was a sign of a significant counterattack from that quarter.

In 1859 the new defender of the faith was a man whose cast
of mind was the antithesis of Newman's sensitive intelligence.
He did not play with the paradoxes of scepticism but rather
destroyed rational theology with logic. The previous year Henry
Longueville Mansel, a witty Oxford High Church Tory, had delivered the Bampton Lectures in which he demolished the
grounds for believing that reason could tell us anything about
the contents of either revealed or natural religion. The human
mind was an inadequate instrument with which to acquire a
knowledge of God. That was why Christian Revelation had to
be accepted in its entirety. To pick and choose between different parts of it, to allege that this or that doctrine was especially
difficult or unacceptable was folly: when all was strictly incom-
prehensible, why should any part be more or less easy to swal-
low? Such boldness brought its reward. Hailed at the time as an
intellectual triumph, the lectures were pulverised by Mill in
1865 in his *Examination of Sir William Hamilton's Philosophy*.
Mansel (who had edited Hamilton's *Metaphysics* in 1859) replied
—and his reply showed the future economist Alfred Marshall, who

---

[6] Newman, p. 309.

had just taken his degree at Cambridge, "how much there was to be defended."[7]

But in 1859 Mansel had had to defend himself against an attack from another quarter, and Mr. Sampson's essay analyses the conflict between Mansel and F. D. Maurice. It was a really important debate because it marked a turning point in Anglican theology. To J. B. Mozley Maurice "had not a clear idea in his head"; to Jowett he was "misty and confused"; and Mansel exposed his two main weaknesses, a lack of respect for language and an inability to perceive logical connections.[8] Maurice would never admit that in saying something new he was deviating from the old because he saw theology as a polygonal body of truth and not as a multitude of lines which if orthodox were parallel and met in infinity, and if schismatic cut across the parallels. Often he was more old-fashioned than those he criticised: he accepted Genesis as history and spoke of the history of mankind as having lasted for six thousand years.[9]

Yet by 1907 C. F. G. Masterman was already calling him the greatest thinker of the English Church in the nineteenth century. He was an innovator. Until Maurice theology was still a *propositional* excerise: not conducted, of course, with the same rigour the scholastics used, nor appealing with such a ponderous display of learning to the doctors of the church as had seventeenth-century divines, but nevertheless still a branch of learning which relied on making logical connections between different dogmas, doctrines, or propositions which were contained within a rigid metaphysical system. Maurice held that a theologian's task is not to construct systems but to study the nature and being of God and His revelation to men. He did much to free English theology from its slavish obsession with the doctrine of the Atonement. In place of universal depravity he set the conception that the whole human race had been adopted by God, however sinful individual members of it might be. He related religion to society, not in the sense that Feuerbach and the anthropologists were

---

[7] J. M. Keynes, *Essays in Biography* (1933), p. 163.
[8] A. R. Vidler, *Witness to the Light* (New York, 1948), pp. 4–5.
[9] Vidler, p. 34.

doing, but in the terms of a theologian who used traditional theological language. Language was half of his quarrel with Mansel: he was saying that if the language of philosophy brought Mansel to the barren conclusion that men could not know God and could only repeat certain formulas of the faith about Him, then philosophy was not a suitable language in which to study God. He tried to divorce theology from positivism. Indeed the core of his dispute in 1838 with Pusey over baptism lay in the fact that Pusey thought of baptism as an event in a child's life and not a symbol of God's relation to man: it did not confer a blessing upon an individual, it was a statement that mankind was permanently reconciled to God. What, too, was his well-known criticism of the doctrine of Eternal Punishment—that eternal has nothing to do with time—but another indication that he was taking the language of theology out of range of the language of positivism?

Maurice was not quite alone. On the second Sunday after Epiphany in 1859, at Cambridge, B. F. Westcott preached a sermon before the university on the miracle at Cana in which he maintained that miracles were not a proof but rather a part of Revelation, since they were not to be thought of as facts but as symbols of the Word.[10] Westcott was then not yet thirty-five and at the beginning of a career in which he was, like Maurice, to teach that Scripture should never be interpreted in literal terms. Seen in retrospect the work of the Cambridge trio, Westcott, Lightfoot, and Hort, together with that of Maurice, was far more important in the development of theology than the immediate response in 1860 of the Broad Churchmen in *Essays and Reviews*, for their work led to the infinitely more revolutionary book, *Lux Mundi*, which appeared in 1889 and which echoed biological evolution by its acceptance of the doctrine of Immanence. Nothing, it was argued in this book, was ever new. God always used what men previously had thought to reveal Himself anew; and He made use of all created beings, infidels as well

---

[10] B. F. Westcott, *Characteristics of the Gospel Miracles* (Cambridge, 1859), pp. 3–4.

as Christians, to make His message plain. But Immanence was no more than an echo of Darwin. *Lux Mundi* was another landmark in setting the language of theology quite apart from the language of positivism.

III

The most obvious effect of science upon religion was thus to change the character of theology and hence the character of Christianity itself in England. There were other curious byproducts. The development of brain physiology made men speculate whether the mind could exist independent of the brain. On a lower level the lively interest in ghosts exhibited by all classes in society was partly due to the mid-Victorian demand that the truth of all supernatural occurrences, and religion itself, must rest on factual evidence. Then, too, began to flourish sects which used scientific terminology—Christian Science, Theosophy, Spiritualism, and the British Israelites. Their emergence coincided with the rise of a large, leisured, ill-educated middle class in which women were becoming more emancipated and more inclined to show their independence of thought—and how better could they do this in that age of ceaseless religious debate than to embrace a "modern" church, which eschewed the old theology and cashed in on the growing prestige of science?

A less obvious, yet far more important, offspring of Darwin's work was the way in which it revolutionised our ideas of Space and Time. It is difficult for us to conceive how fast men's *imagination* in those days was bound by Europe and European history. For almost a century geology and archaeology had been extending the length of world history and as early as 1836 Boucher de Perthes had argued that mankind and extinct mammals were contemporaries. But not until 1859 was this hypothesis accepted by scholars, such as Falconer and Prestwich, and it was to take many more years before such notions were emotionally accepted. The story of mankind was stamped upon the Victorian imagination in the same images as Ghiberti chose for his reliefs on the golden doors of the Baptistry in Florence. It needed to be supplemented only by the story of Greece and Rome, and the rest was the history of Christian Europe, the centre of the world, which brought the blessings of its civilisation to other continents and rescued them from barbarism.

Darwin upset this tidy and self-contained cosmos. He created a vast new time-sequence in which man played a minute part. He linked man to Nature, and organic matter to inorganic matter, in an unbreakable chain. He gave impetus to the rise of anthropology and soon the history of pre-history man was being written. McLennan and Tylor were evolutionists and interested in showing how savage customs and beliefs could eventually evolve into civilised shape, but they could not help bringing to men's minds simultaneously the idea that at different periods in time people had lived in societies with widely different systems of values and beliefs, these in turn being affected by their economy and status and kinship systems. If this was true of the past, it was equally true of the present. Different cultures could flourish simultaneously. Thus the idea of relativism gained fresh currency.

It had, of course, been given currency by Montesquieu; and relativism was implicit in Romanticism. For long the old positivist assumption that men were much the same in every age—though, to be sure, they were progressing from barbarism to enlightenment—held it in check. When Darwin published his book few doubted that the culture of the present was superior to that of the past, and the culture of England surpassed all others in the present. Yet even among the most noted apostles of progress one could find passages which recognised the separate existence and validity of past cultures. There was Macaulay's famous third chapter. There were the Liberal Anglican historians, who had learnt the theory of cyclical change from Vico, and emphasised that different societies were ruled by different codes of conduct. It had even begun to be fashionable to idealise the past: the cult of the Middle Ages was well under way. And in 1859 FitzGerald published the *Rubáiyát*.

Here was the voice of a totally distinct culture propounding different values and proceeding from different assumptions. Who are we to say, FitzGerald seemed to ask, that the civilisation that is held suspended in this poem, is inferior to ours? The

Rubáiyát should prepare us for an important modification in the Victorian tradition. Within a few years the Victorians had discovered Hellenism. Both Jowett and Pater wrote on Plato: the difference between them is immense. Jowett followed Dr. Arnold in reconciling the classics to the Christian tradition: Pater, Swinburne, and later Hellenists, such as Lowes Dickinson, opposed the culture of Greece to Christianity. At the same time Pater and Symons painted the culture of the Renaissance. No doubt today these pictures seem to portray a Greece that never was and a Renaissance which (so it is foolishly said) never existed. But they recognised that glorious cultures, in some ways superior to our own, had flourished in the past and must be judged in the light of their own standards. Thus a dichotomy in judgment was set up, and this is the subject of Mr. Appleman's essay, which shows how Darwin's influence reaches out into criticism. Pater had read his Darwin and his work illustrates the dichotomy, which is still alive today. Are we to judge things historically, in relation to their age and to the stage of evolution which they have reached? Or are we to judge them against the standard of our own sensibility—or against the culture of our own age—or against perennial standards of what is good and bad? And, if the last, by what right do we assert that these standards are perennial?

IV

When A. W. Benn published in 1906 his *History of English Rationalism in the Nineteenth Century,* he concluded that the work of positivism had been done: little remained now except to wait for the great structure of Christianity, riddled and undermined, to collapse. But Benn's vision of the unbroken ranks of the Victorian positivist army marching into the future faded, not because of any religious revival, but because the ranks broke.

They broke because the Victorian belief in the unity of truth vanished. In the first half of the twentieth century it became less and less possible to relate one kind of intellectual inquiry to another by means of an all-embracing method, or language, or conceptual system. The *desire* to do so, of course, remained, and the continual recruitment to—and defections from—Marxism has shown how strong the desire and the consequent disillusionment have been. The old positivist contention that all questions ultimately were scientific questions and hence could all be answered in the same terms was challenged by the new philosophy of linguistic analysis. Linguistic philosophy, it is true, began by removing religion from the logic of reason: but today it also asserts that there is no difference between the statements of those who deny the truth of religion and those who assert it. The kind of questions which religion answers are unanswerable, but they are not, as Ayer once argued, nonsensical questions.[11] The urgency with which people ask these questions suggests that the answers which religion gives help some people to *accept* the world just as the explanations which science gives help others to *understand* it. Nowadays it is more difficult to attack the religious for believing in individual propositions: they accept complete notions, and all that can be asserted is that others reject them. Religion deals with the hidden and with what can never be seen, whereas in Victorian times it was thought such things could be seen if only man had a large enough microscope or a less sinful nature. The language of modern literary criticism has also helped to dissolve Victorian positivism: its theory of tradition, its emphasis on modes and levels of argument, and its assertion that the validity of a work of art depends not on its "truth" but on the intensity and seriousness of the artist's vision which create a kind of internal logic in the work of art itself, implicitly reject the existence of a single method of eliciting truth.

The revolution in language and logic led to a change in the status of science. Science bowed itself off the stage. Victorian science was determinist science, and scientists were thought to proceed by collecting facts and inferring general laws from these facts. Today scientists are thought rather to invent hypotheses, test them, retain them until they are shown to be false, and abandon only those which *are* shown to be false. Nor do we believe that the world can be made comprehensible only if every true proposition is also logically necessary. The very complexity of science has also dissolved the metaphysical conclusions of

---

[11] A. J. Ayer, *Language, Truth and Logic* (1946), p. 115.

many nineteenth-century scientists. The operations of science, multiplying and sub-dividing at immense speed each quinquennium, no longer permit scientists to make large-scale generalisations about the nature of the universe or of human personality. A Jeans or a Carrel or a Hoyle may dogmatise from physics or physiology that God does or does not exist, but no one seriously contends that such conclusions derive from the scientific method itself. The man who attempts to deduce moral or cosmological significance from Heisenberg's principle of indeterminacy or from the left-handed universe of Lee and Yang is in for a rough passage. The linguistic philosophers no doubt struck at the arguments which derived God from morality or ethics from psychology, and in rejecting the old theories of objective ethics they have rejected what was a favourite defence of Victorian orthodox Christianity. But the same philosophers have made especially devastating analyses of the efforts of scientists, such as T. H. Huxley or his grandson Julian Huxley, to derive an ethical theory from evolution. The ruthless separation of factual or descriptive statements from normative statements has undermined any pretensions which thoughtful scientists may cherish to tell us that science ordains that men should behave in any particular fashion.

The other main breach in the old positivism was made by modern sociology. Whereas the Victorian positivists held that actions which were not directed towards a specific end, such as rituals, were irrational, Weber and Durkheim showed that ritual played a part in many different kinds of social behaviour and that religion fulfilled certain functions in society. They gave no comfort to the Victorian rationalists who predicted that as reason spread her wings, religion must necessarily moult. Certainly they were ominously neutral concerning the "truth" of religion; but they turned rather to examine not whether beliefs were true but what role they performed in society. Simultaneously the rise of clinical psychoanalysis immensely complicated the idea of "reasonable" behaviour in the individual. Henceforth there was always a challenge to so-called scientific political theories, whether Marxist or utilitarian, which purported to deduce from studying social relationships or individual psychology how society should be organised and to what goal or goals it should be moving. It is true that it was long before the full implications of the new sociology were recognised. Many writers in the first half of the twentieth century asserted that social problems could in fact be submitted to "scientific" examination: and when this had been done, their "solution" would then be clear. There was much talk of blundering politicians being reduced to the level of public relations officers and of scientists and administrators becoming the real rulers in society. Traditions, customs, and institutions in their present form were asserted to be impedimenta deliberately used to delay the march of science; and the very real advances which had been made in applying statistical and other scientific techniques to social problems admitted of a neutral, correct, scientific solution. These notions were popularised by sociologists such as Lester Ward and scientists such as J. D. Bernal. But today in the West this kind of scientism is a spent force.

In retrospect the Victorian agnostics scarcely seem to deserve the name: they knew so many things. But one of their predictions has come true. Many professing Christians are today in their beliefs agnostic in the Victorian sense. The word "orthodox" has been drained of meaning. Most Christians today, no less than rationalists, eschew dogma. Theology is no longer a series of interlocking propositions and, in its most abstract forms, it tries to dissociate itself as far as possible from reasoning about phenomena. Tillich's famous statement, "It is as atheistic to affirm the existence of God as it is to deny it" is a measure of the change.[12] Assertions about the Divine must be made, if they are to be accurate, in non-worldly language; and since this is impossible, the words such as Love or Spirit, which we use, are almost more misleading than to use none at all. To speculate about a transcendental God is to denigrate God by bringing Him onto the same level of existence as ourselves. A Mansel come to judgment! Ambiguity is today the essence of dogma: a dogma is valuable if it carries a variety of meanings—just as Empson twenty years ago diagnosed his seven types of ambiguity in poetry. Words about the Divine, therefore, are but a feeble analogy to what is

---

[12] Paul Tillich, *Systematic Theology* (1953), I, 263.

Divine. The Christian scheme of creation and salvation cannot accordingly be pinned down to the beliefs which were defined in popular terms and were current during the past nineteen centuries, partly because they were purely an analogy and partly because they are always evolving and changing their shape; and it is argued that while the great Christian dogmas may be said always to have *contained* the full truth, that truth is never in any age fully *explicit*. Some theologians, such as Reinhold Niebuhr, who are aware of the emphasis which literary critics and sociologists place on symbolism, interpret scripture freely in terms of allegory: others, such as Bultmann, want to strip the New Testament of its myths and destroy the ancient cosmology of Heaven and Hell in order to free Christianity from the accusation that its cosmology is intended in any sense to represent what God has really willed the universe to be.

Protestant theologians have moved away from the propositional religion of the mid-Victorians in two other ways. They are prepared to rely on metaphysicians and anti-rationalist thinkers for the logical structure of their theologies. Kant, whose work was in 1859 so strange and so suspect among English clergymen, was the first foreign philosopher to comfort theologians by providing a new basis for distinguishing between scientific and moral reasoning. Today the chasm between the languages which rationalists and theologians use has grown even wider owing to the use which theologians make of Kierkegaard, Heidegger, and existentialist philosophy. It is asserted, for instance, that no criticism of Tillich's epistemology affects his thought since it rests on an analysis of Being, not of Knowledge, and therefore that there is no point of contact between him and his rationalist critics.[13] Rationalists today often discover that their opponents do not assert what rationalists think that they are asserting, and that they can therefore give no precise meaning to what is asserted.

The use which Christians make of history has also changed. In mid-Victorian times the Churches were engaged on the quest for the historical Jesus—a search which was organised, as it were,

[13] *Religion and Culture,* ed. Walter Leibrecht (New York, 1959), pp. 3 and 355 n.

on positivist terms. The quest ended in a mire of hypotheses. Many Biblical scholars accordingly shifted their ground and argued that the New Testament was not a record of historical facts providing evidence for what happened in Galilee, but a repository of the worship of the primitive Church; and they follow Westcott's hint in his sermon in 1859 that the miracle at Cana, for example, is an allegory of Christ's relation to the water of the Mosaic Law which is transformed by Him into the wine of the new Law of the Spirit. Other scholars, such as Niebuhr or Butterfield, follow Novalis in saying that all history is an evangel to the truth of Christianity. It is a record of the universality of sin in which all men of all countries are alike involved in the curse of Nazism and Communism and of the brutal inhumanity of the age in which we live and for which we are responsible. To try to gloss over this catastrophic human depravity by practising a religion of good works, of social service and of community chests—the religion of organisation man—is futile.

Such immense activity in re-interpreting theology must be regarded quizzically by the Church of Rome. In 1859 Roman Catholicism was only beginning to emerge as an intellectual force in England. Today it would claim that its stand on all these questions remains *quod semper, quod ubique, quod ab [Ecclesia] creditum est.* Pascal, Bossuet, and the great seventeenth-century apologists gave answers to most of the problems of accommodating Roman Catholicism to new learning. Newman's simple lectures in 1859 stated the position clearly enough. Although there may *appear* to be a conflict between science and religion, and even if the hierarchy of the Church speaks strongly and with the full weight of their authority against some innovating scientist, there can be no real conflict: for either the scientific propositions denied are later found to be true and it becomes clear that the hierarchy did not speak in the full sense in which the Church pronounces judgment, or the propositions are found to be masquerading as scientific and are in fact moral and cosmological—in which case the Church is the sole authority on such matters. It is precisely on this clear distinction between what science, using the working hypothesis of the uniformity of Nature, asserts to be for practical purposes true and the moral consequences of pursuing certain courses of action, that the Church of Rome's pronouncements on birth control or on gynaecology are based. In his lecture on "A Form of Infidelity of the Day" Newman warned his audience of the danger that the practical results which continue to be obtained from scientific research were leading men to be impatient of any other kind of thought; whereas Catholic theology alone could give science "meaning."

But it is one thing to say that the logic of science, the scientific method, the new positivism of linguistic analysis and modern sociology, no longer erect a barrier against religion; whether religion still possesses the same power that it had over men's minds is another. How far has society become more secularised in the past hundred years?

As the inheritors of the Industrial Revolution we live in a society which still enjoys the novelty of ever-increasing production and consumption and in which human beings possess an infinitely wider range of choice in the way they spend their leisure hours. A century ago the choices were fewer and religion was for many the main refreshment from work. It had a long lead over other subjects in the art of popularisation; it provided in sermons, books and tracts serious topics for conversation; in its sects it provided lively in-groups with which people could identify themselves; in its hymn-singing, its lectures by missionaries, and its revivalism, it provided entertainment and release from misery for the poor. Some of the working classes felt the influence of religion, the lower middle classes were permeated with it. By belonging to the Nonconformist communions the poor could protest against the church of the ruling class and the rule of squire and parson; and whatever the faults of the Anglican Church in not accommodating itself to the changed conditions of industrialised society, it was trying to perform the functions now undertaken by a dozen government ministries. Victorian culture was one in which religion was a familiar referent and ecclesiastical influence and power was still a reality. Even so there were sectors where religion did not penetrate. Although Marx argued that the working classes turned to salvationist religion because there was no place for them on earth, the "submerged tenth" lived untouched by Christianity. So did a sizeable proportion of upper- and middle-class rakes, Bohemians, demi-mondaines, artists, and *révoltés*. Mudie-Smith and Booth both showed in their surveys how at the end of the century church membership became more and more confined to the middle classes. Part of the losses which the churches today are said to have sustained were never theirs to lose. If it is said that the churches today are themselves secularised, when, if ever, could popular religion withstand the criticism of deeply religious minds? When, if ever, did religion not suffer from the connection between cash and cant and from political compromise and worldly ministers?

And yet it cannot be denied that society is today far more secularised. Some of the causes lie deep in the social changes during the past century. The class war in Europe led the working classes to think of religion as part of the culture of the ruling classes who used the churches to repress them. The sons and grandsons of those who left the churches have not returned. Religion seems only remotely connected to the major political issues of our time; and as governmental techniques have improved men put greater faith in political action to remedy wrongs. Western liberalism envisages a society with many value-systems of which the churches are but one. And whereas the Victorians sought first to regenerate the individual in order to improve society—and hence were concerned for his soul—we approach social problems in a more depersonalised way. "We dimly perceive," writes Norman Birnbaum, "that our disasters are our collective fault. We are individually and collectively helpless before them but a sociological rather than a theological view of causation dominates our thinking about our fate—even if, as is mostly the case, our sociology is false . . . Our social relations are occasional, fragmentary and instrumental: we can conceive no other pattern." [14] Religion, he adds, is a matter of feeling, as well as knowing, and industrialised society represses emotion so that our inner lives are standardised and depleted: dedication,

---

[14] Norman Birnbaum, "An Agnostic Looks at the Church," *Frontier*, II (1959), 8–13.

spiritual inwardness, moral concern, and implication in human tragedy are now as a result almost eradicated. Eradicated or not, the life of the spirit is not associated, as it was almost invariably a hundred years ago, with a religious vocation. This in turn is due to the fact that, when all logical distinctions have been made, it is the impression of life as a whole, and the theories which purport to explain phenomena, that incline men towards or away from belief in religion. Many of the notions which men entertain about the nature and meaning of life are non-Christian: indeed David Lack in his recent work on Darwin continually suggests (even though in logic the antithesis is meaningless) that the conflict between the Christian explanation of life and the theory of natural selection is too striking to be ignored.[15] Similarly speculations about the nature and destiny of man are couched in psychoanalytical or historicist terms which deliberately make no reference to other-wordly concerns. The bright clear light in which Heaven was seen in Victorian times is extinguished, and men see it, if at all, through a glass darkly.

On the other side theologians claim that the first stage of secularism—which was the belief that man was lord of all things—is passing away and being succeeded by the second stage of disillusionment as man finds that he is enslaved by an empty materialism. They point to the fact that three out of five Americans belong to a church, and to a revival of belief among the clerisy in Britain. Part of the difficulty in making an assessment lies in the fact that the religion of the present always radically differs from that of the past yet is always being compared with it: the religion of 1759, for instance, was immensely different from that of 1659. In the end one returns to Newman's assertion that those who deny the truth of Revelation are "introducing into the world what the whole world feels to be a paradox." Do we feel it to be a paradox? That is a question which ultimately each has to answer for himself.

---

[15] David Lack, *Evolutionary Theory and Christian Belief* (1957).

The Problem of Spiritual Authority
in the Nineteenth Century*

NORTHROP FRYE

When it was suggested to me that I should contribute a nine-teenth-century topic to this Rice University semicentennial series, I hesitated, because the nineteenth century is far from being what I hopefully think of, in my furtive non-administrative moments, as my "field." But there is one aspect of Victorian culture that interests me a good deal, and that is the extraor-dinary fertility and suggestiveness of its educational theories. I speak of the problem of spiritual authority, because all educa-tional theory seems to me to be essentially an application of that problem. I hope also that the subject of educational theory will have some relevance to an anniversary program of a university, which should be an appropriate time for considering the func-tion of the university and its relation to the social order.

The source of actual or "temporal" authority in society is sel-dom hard to locate. It is always in the near vicinity of what-ever one pays one's taxes to. As long as it can be believed that might is right, and that the tax-collecting power is not to be questioned, there is no separate problem of spiritual authority.

* [This essay is the published form of a lecture presented at Rice University during its semicentennial celebration, 1962–63.]

From Carroll Camden, ed., *Literary Views: Critical and Historical Essays* (Chicago: University of Chicago Press, 1964), pp. 145–158.

But the thesis that might is right, even when as carefully rationalized as it is in Hobbes, has seldom been regarded as much more than an irresponsible paradox. There has almost certainly never been a period in history when the taxpayer did not try to cheat the publican, and even the desire to cheat raises the question of what kinds of authority may be thought of as overriding the actual one. For self-interest also has a separate authority.

Spiritual authority is usually connected, of course, with religion, God being normally thought of as a sovereign spirit. Our cultural tradition has inherited from the Old Testament a conception of the will of God which may often be in the sharpest possible opposition to the will of man, especially an Egyptian or Babylonian or Philistine will. But if a religion can find an accredited human representative, the two kinds of authority again tend to merge. The medieval theory of the pope's right to temporal power and the post-Renaissance conception of the divine right of kings are examples of an effort to make the spiritual order a guarantee of the stability of the temporal one. As far as the normal workings of the human mind can go, the will of God differs in degree but not in kind from the will of man, and the metaphors applied to it, such as the metaphor of divine "sovereignty," are drawn from the more primitive forms of human society. When Greek philosophers began to frame ethical conceptions of justice and righteousness, they ran into similar problems. Their traditional gods, as they appear in Homer, still had all the arbitrary and whimsical quality of a human aristocracy, and submitting to a human conqueror would not be psychologically very different from praying to Poseidon the irascible earth-shaker. In Christianity the human product of spiritual authority is supposed to be charity, but Christian charity has usually been, down to quite recent times, supported by temporal power, and it may be significant that the word "charity" itself has come to mean chiefly a form of voluntary taxation.

Ordinary social consciousness usually begins in a sense of antithesis between what the ego wants and what society will allow it to have. Hence temporal authority comes to the individual first of all in the form of an external compulsion. In this stage freedom is identified with the ego's side of this antithesis. But education, and more particularly education of the reason, introduces us to a form of necessity or compulsion which is not opposed to freedom but seems to be rather another aspect of it. To assent to the truth of a geometrical demonstration is psychologically a contrast to assenting to the will of a social superior. Hence reason can do what faith, hope, and even love by themselves cannot do: present us with the model or pattern of an authority which appeals to the mind but not to the body, which compels but does not enforce. Such authority confers dignity on the person who accepts it, and such dignity has no context of hierarchy, nobody at whose expense the dignity is achieved.

The nineteenth-century social and political writers in Great Britain had inherited from Milton a conception of spiritual authority of this sort, and a singularly lucid and powerful one. For Milton the source of spiritual authority was revelation from God, more particularly the revelation of the gospel which had spiritualized the law, and delivered those under the gospel from the sense of external constraint. St. Paul tells us that where the spirit of the Lord is, there is liberty, and those under the gospel should do as they like, because what they like to do is the will of God, not the illusory pseudo-acts suggested by passion or selfishness. For Milton, again, the accredited human agent of spiritual authority is the church in the sense of the society of individuals who are under the gospel, among whom the one who has authority is the apostle or saint, which according to Milton is what the New Testament means by an *episcope* or overseer. Such authority clearly has no relevance to magistrates or penal codes. Revelation from God accommodates itself to man primarily in the form of reason. Reason manifests itself in the decisive acts of a free life ("Reason is but choosing," Milton says in *Areopagitica*, annexing Aristotle's conception of *proairesis* of the Christian *logos*), and as revelation is the opposite of mystery, there is no conflict between spiritual authority and reason. A revelation from an infinite mind may transcend the reason of a finite one, but does not contradict or humiliate it.

Human society, as Milton saw it, is conditioned by the inertia of original sin to seek the habitual and customary, to do things

because they have been done before, to make an idol of tradition. The impact of revelation, coming through reason, is always
subversive and revolutionary: it is bound to shake up the
somnambulism of habit and confront it with the eternal opposition of God and fallen man. Such reason is also liberty, which
man does not naturally want, but which God wants him to have.
Purely social changes are, at best, gradual adjustments: genuine
liberty is sudden and apocalyptic: "In state many things at first
are crude and hard to digest, which only time and deliberation
can supple and concoct. But in religion, wherein is no immatur-
ity, nothing out of season, it goes far otherwise. The door of grace
turns upon smooth hinges, wide opening to send out, but soon
shutting to recall the precious offers of mercy to a nation" (*The
Reason of Church Government*). Temporal authority, however
essential, is also provisional, the result of the permanent emer-
gency in human affairs caused by the Fall. It can never be accepted as an end in itself: the reason why it is there is stated
in scripture, and all non-scriptural ways of trying to justify it are
suspect. There is no inherent authority, in other words, in tradition or custom or precedent, on which temporal authority may
rest as a basis. Hence no church which bases its claim to authority
on tradition can be a genuine embodiment of revelation. Milton's
regicide pamphlet, *The Tenure of Kings and Magistrates*, is a
work of extraordinary originality of thought, outlining an early
theory of contract and being one of the earliest efforts to try to
give some functional place to revolution in history. But even
this involves an appeal to precedent, and Milton embarks on an
appeal to precedent with the greatest unwillingness: "But because it is the vulgar folly of men to desert their own reason,
and shutting their eyes, to think they see best with other men's,
I shall show, by such examples as ought to have most weight
with us, what has been done in this case heretofore."

We have, then, in Milton, a spiritual authority with its roots in
revelation and manifesting itself largely in reason, and a temporal authority which is to be acknowledged and obeyed in its
own sphere, but should not be rationalized by arguments drawn
from precedent or custom. Temporal authority is primarily something that is there, whether we like it or not. If we don't like it,

we turn to a conception of spiritual authority and subordinate
the temporal power to it as far as possible, if only in our own
minds. If we do like it or want to defend it, on the other hand,
we tend to see in tradition, custom, habit, in short the process
by which temporal authority came to be, some kind of inherent
right. We may note in passing that if social revolution is not, for
Milton, organically related to precedents, it is not organically
related to the future either. The rebellions of the Jews against
their overlords, as recorded in the Old Testament, had varying
degrees of success, but none were permanently successful. Hence
the significance of such a rebellion is typological, manifesting
the power of the true God for and at the moment. The extent to
which Milton was able to reconcile himself with the failure of the
revolution of his own day is perhaps indicated in *Samson
Agonistes,* where the temporary victory of Samson in destroying
the Philistine temple has this kind of significance.

In the eighteenth century the conception of the natural society
in Bolingbroke and Rousseau brought a new kind of revolutionary
dialectic into social argument. Rousseau thought of man in his
context as a child of nature, and not, as Milton did, in his context
as a child of God whose original state was civilized. It was reason
and nature that were associated in his thought, not reason and
revelation, and the original free and equal society of man was
not something intended for man by God which man irrevocably
lost, but something man still has the power to recapture. Rousseau's thought resembles Milton's only in associating reason and
revolution, and in thinking of reason as essentially the vision in
the light of which the free act is performed. It is with the
counter-revolutionary thought that developed in Britain in opposition to Rousseau, particularly in Burke, that the problem of
spiritual authority in the nineteenth century begins.

For Burke, in almost direct contrast to Milton, the first justification for temporal authority consists in the fact that it is there:
the right underlying its might, therefore, is the process of tradition and precedent that has brought it into being. The social
contract of any society "is collected from the form into which
the particular society has been cast." Any developed society is
found to consist of various classes, and the tendency of each

class is to promote its own interest by acting "merely by their will." This creates tyranny, whether exerted by the king (who is historically a class in himself), by the nobility, or, as in France, by the "people," which means one class or group of people. The source of spiritual authority for Burke, therefore, is to be found, not so much in tradition as such, as in a kind of *telos*, a sense of belonging to a social organism whose health is preserved by maintaining a balance of power among the different organs. The health of the social structure is the end of all social action from any class, and the standard by which such action should be judged. Revolutionary action, which sets free an automatic and unconditioned will, is to society what the cancerous growth of tissue is in the individual. A social organism of this kind is the only genuine form of natural society, for nature is to be thought of as an order that preserves constancy in change by a process of continuous repair. "Thus, by preserving the method of nature in the conduct of the state, in what we improve, we are never wholly new; in what we retain, we are never wholly obsolete."

Two factors in Burke's thought are particularly relevant here. In Milton, the current of liberty, so to speak, normally flows in a deductive direction, from revelation to reason, and from reason to social action. For Burke, liberty can only be preserved by the inductive, empirical, even *ad hoc* procedures of the political action that operates on the basis of what is there: prudence is the greatest of political virtues, and prejudice the only valuable form of deductive thinking. It is the revolutionary action leading to tyranny which is deductive, like the "metaphysical" French Revolution which had begun with a set of major premises about the abstract rights of man, and had then attempted "a decomposition of the whole civil and political mass, for the purpose of originating a new civil order out of the first elements of society." Hence reason, given its full deductive and speculative head, is not an emancipating but a destructive and ultimately enslaving power in politics. Spiritual authority, at least, is something to which we owe loyalty, and loyalty is not primarily rational; hence society is held together by profounder forces than the reason can express or reach.

In the second place, most temporal authority is vested in the ascendant class: this class is faced with a strong revolutionary bid for power coming from further down in society: the maintenance of the health of the social organism, which means the maintenance of spiritual authority, is therefore bound up with preserving the existing rights and privileges of the ascendant class. "We must suppose [society] to be in that state of habitual social discipline, in which the wiser, the more expert, and the more opulent conduct, and by conducting enlighten and protect the weaker, the less knowing, and the less provided with the goods of fortune." Burke goes on to say that "the state of civil society, which necessarily generates this aristocracy, is a state of nature"—that is, once again, the genuine form of natural society. The ascendant class includes the church, as for Burke the church is a continuous social institution, and its spiritual authority is inconceivable without that continuity. Hence Burke says, in what from our present point of view is a key statement of his thought: "Nothing is more certain, than that our manners, our civilization, and all the good things which are connected with manners and with civilization, have, in this European world of ours, depended for ages upon two principles; and were indeed the result of both combined; I mean the spirit of a gentleman, and the spirit of religion."

The ascendant class, therefore, and more particularly the aristocracy, comes to represent an ideal authority, expressed in the term "gentleman," at the point in history at which its effective temporal authority had begun to decline (though of course its privileges and much of its prestige remained for another century). The social function of the aristocracy has always included the art of putting on a show, of dramatizing a way of life. It is natural that America, with no hereditary aristocracy as such, should have invented an *ad hoc* aristocracy out of its entertainers, who attract much the same kind of identification that royal figures do in British countries. In the thought of Carlyle, who has no interest in spiritual authority distinct from temporal authority, and wants only to identify the two, the reactivating of the aristocracy naturally occupies a central place. For Carlyle the "holiness" or radiance of the indwelling divinity in man, which is perceptible in the hero, is the source of an undifferentiated authority which is spiritual and temporal at once.

Yet even Carlyle distinguished the *de jure* authority of the aristocracy from the *de facto* authority of captains of industry and self-made heroes of the Napoleon and Cromwell category. The basis of the distinction seems to be that as *de facto* or temporal authority is essentially active, so *de jure* or spiritual authority has something about it associated with the contemplative. In his chapter on symbolism in *Sartor Resartus* Carlyle sees the heroic personality as an "intrinsic" symbol (that is, one that has value in itself, as distinct from the flag or the cross which are extrinsic and have value only as indicators). As a symbol, the hero is the focus of a community, and the purely *de jure* figure seems to have the most prestige as one. Crowds gather to see the Queen in order to see their own unity as a society reflected in her. Here again there is a link between the recognition of spiritual authority and the dramatic function of an ascendant class.

Samuel Butler also associates spiritual authority with the aristocracy, in a more speculative and paradoxical way. He is, of course, particularly fascinated by the working of the evolutionary process in human society, and his conception of education, traditional as it is in itself, reflects this interest. He points out in *Life and Habit* that no skill is learned thoroughly until it passes through consciousness into the unconscious. It follows that the most profoundly educated people are those who have been born to wealth, leisure, and privilege, and have never been troubled by a conscious idea, which includes a good many of the aristocracy. Thus in *The Way of All Flesh* the hero, Ernest Pontifex, at that time engaged in social work in East London, meets an old classmate named Towneley who is large, handsome, simple-minded, well to do, and altogether admirable. Ernest asks Towneley effusively if he doesn't love the poor: Towneley says no, and gets away as quickly as possible. It could hardly be a briefer encounter, but it is an epiphany for Ernest: spiritual authority has spoken, as unmistakably as it spoke from the burning bush. Ernest considers this situation carefully, and finally decides: "I see it all now. The people like Towneley are the only ones who know anything that is worth knowing, and like that of course I can never be. But to make Towneleys possible, there must be hewers of wood and drawers of water—men, in fact, through whom conscious knowledge must pass before it can reach those who can apply it gracefully and instinctively as the Towneleys can."

We are reminded of the respect paid in *Erewhon* to those who are handsome, healthy, and rich, and how Erewhon considers it a crime to be ill or unfortunate. In Huxley's terms, society's sympathies are with nature, rather than with ethics, even though society itself is an ethical creation. Yet Ernest's solution is still a trifle immature, and *Erewhon* brings us a little closer to Butler's real view of spiritual authority. Most of the Erewhonians, according to Butler, are unthinking, instinctive conservatives, whose values are determined entirely by habit and prejudice: worshippers, as he says, of the goddess Ydgrun. But there is also in Erewhon a small group of "high Ydgrunites," whom the narrator describes as the best people he met in Erewhon. Of them he says: "They were gentlemen in the full sense of the word; and what has one not said in saying this?" The high Ydgrunite would be something like Montaigne, presumably: able to live in and with society, able to see not only the power but the real significance of convention and prejudice, yet remaining intellectually detached from them. Such gentlemen are not only the natural aristocracy but the genuine apostles of society, correcting instinct by reason and reason by instinct, and never allowing the two to make that fatal alliance which is the mark of all bigots, whether reactionary or revolutionary.

The problem of spiritual authority, we see, has as its crucial point the problem of defining the community of such an authority. The writers we have been quoting, all of whom are deeply conservative, associate this community with the ideal aristocracy which the term "gentleman" conveys. For a revolutionary thinker, such as William Morris, spiritual authority would be isolated from society, confined to the small conspiratorial group of those who repudiate its values and are shut out from its benefits. It is perhaps worth noting that Morris's revolutionary ideal, as outlined in the future Utopia depicted in *News from Nowhere*, is the assimilating of the conception of a natural aristocracy to the whole of society. In *News from Nowhere* everybody has the creative versatility and the *sprezzatura* that are the marks of the ideally educated courtier in Castiglione, except that, of course, there is no court and no prince, and no one to serve except one another. They are at once producers and consumers, and as consumers they have the sharply limited and defined quality of a privileged class. "We know what we want," says one of them, "so we make no more than we want." This applies even to the production of human beings: the population has become stabilized, apparently, because people are no longer rutting out of nervous instability, as they do in societies based on exploitation. The curiously childlike quality of Morris's ideal citizens is also significant, for of course the real natural aristocracy, the society of those who are genuinely entitled to leisure and privilege and consuming the goods produced for them by others, are the children.

We have just traced a parabola from the counter-revolutionary polemic of the later Burke to the revolutionary polemic of Morris. The former places spiritual authority in the middle of the ascendant class, or at least its center of gravity is to be found there, and the *Appeal from the New to the Old Whigs* ends in contemptuous ridicule of John Ball, "that reverend patriarch of sedition," who could not find the conception of "gentleman" in the original producing society when Adam delved and Eve span. Morris, in contrast, places spiritual authority for his own time in the small alienated group who are possessed by the ambition of realizing the dream of John Ball. For Morris the Peasants' Revolt was the one brief moment when something like a proletariat appears in British history. In the thought of John Stuart Mill the problem of spiritual authority is located in a much less simplified view of society. For Mill, Burke's continuum of habit and prejudice is the way in which the majority of people live. Being a majority, they are not confined to a single class, and the progress of democracy involves making their will the source of *temporal* authority. As in Burke and Butler, their motivation is instinctive and empirical. Over against them are the smaller group of the liberal opposition, a much more highly individualized group, of whom Mill says that they initiate all wise and noble things.

Mill, somewhat unexpectedly, resembles Hegel in seeing the political opposition of Conservative and Liberal as the symbol of an ideal or intellectual opposition of conservative and liberal attitudes. As the liberal opposition is intellectually always a minority, it has the peculiar problem of getting enough mass support to be effective in a democratic election. Some of Mill's devices, such as a plurality of votes for the educated, are sufficiently desperate to indicate that this is a matter of some difficulty. To grasp the nature of the ideal opposition we have to grasp two principles. First, the majority is always right, for the majority is the source of temporal authority. Second, the majority is always wrong, for it is not the source of spiritual authority. The latter is to be found in the intellectual opposition, for "almost all the greatest men who ever lived have formed part of such an Opposition."

Authority in its two forms, therefore, rests on a paradoxical and illogical tension between majority rule and minority right. The minority are not a class but an elite, and no social epithet like "gentleman" will apply to them. In practice most of them may be gentlemen, but that is not why they belong there. The gentleman behaves according to a social convention, and for Mill the toleration of unconventional or eccentric behavior is the mark of a mature society. What holds this elite together is something intellectual, though it is certainly not intellectual agreement. To put the question in another way, what gives a minority a right? Criminals are a minority, but clearly have no right to be criminals. In the *Essay on Liberty* the right appears to be the ability to contribute something to the area of free thought and discussion which for Mill is the real parliament of man, the ideological debate that is close to being the source of spiritual authority because it supplies the vision for temporal power. To permit freedom of thought is to direct freedom of action, as unrestricted speculation is the best check so far discovered on premature, spasmodic, or panic-stricken action. Here again we run into a Hegelian element in Mill's thought: no idea contributed to this social debate has any real effectiveness unless it contains its own opposite: unless, therefore, the possibility of refuting it is also present. Mill draws our attention to the peculiar importance of Rousseau in challenging the validity of the structure of society itself.

Burke's counter-revolutionary argument was based on a completely inductive conception of political action; Mill's argument attempts to associate his liberal opposition with a more deductive point of view. He remarks for example that "the non-existence of an acknowledged first principle has made ethics not so much a guide as a consecration of men's actual sentiments." The Utilitarian philosophy held his loyalty because it provided a major premise for majority behavior. That people will seek what they consider pleasure and avoid what they consider pain is individually probable and statistically certain. But this purely descriptive principle supplies no standard or value, no way even of distinguishing reality from illusion in the conception of pleasure. In Milton, who in *Areopagitica* presents a similar conception of truth as something arrived at dynamically through the conflict of opinion, the major premises come from scripture. Milton never conceived the possibility of a free society trying to find truth without the aid of scripture. In Mill there is no clear source of the premises of debate of this kind, no set of standards and assumptions that can be taken as given. The absence of such a source may be one reason for his curious attraction toward the most uncongenial types of political dogmatists, including Carlyle and Comte (it would take us too far afield to apply this principle to Harriet Taylor), as though he felt that they held some missing piece he was looking for.

In Newman, on the other hand, the source of spiritual authority is the church catholic: his great strength as a nineteenth-century thinker lay in his unvarying acceptance of that view. At no time in his adult life was Newman ever anything that a Protestant would call a Protestant: his problem was only to decide whether the Anglican or the Roman communion was the genuinely catholic one. He takes our present argument a step further by finding the road to spiritual authority through education. Education for him is partly social and retains the social aim of producing the "gentleman" which we met in Burke and Butler. Even its intellectual characteristic, a disinterested or liberal quality in it which is "its own end," has an analogy with the social ideal which is detachable from the necessity of earning a living. On its intellectual side, liberal education is essentially a discipline of reason, as in Milton, and, as in Mill, it seems to have something to do with a "master view of things," a deductive or synoptic sense of intellectual form which gets one's head above the habit of living: "The principle of real dignity in Knowledge, its worth, its desirableness, considered irrespectively of its results, is this germ within it of a scientific or a philosophical process. This is how it comes to be an end in itself; this is why it admits of being called Liberal."

But the university turns out to be a function of the church, and the education it gives confronts the student with a dilemma: he must either attach himself along with his education to the church or keep his education as a private possession. Recurrently we have come to this point of having to define the community of spiritual authority. The individual can readily be seen to be capable of understanding more than society in general, and hence of possessing standards and values, with an authority superior in kind if not in power. But the conception "gentleman," however interpreted, defines the superior individual rather than the superior group, even granted that one may recognize the individual as one of a group. For Newman only the church provides this community, and of the gentlemen who cannot commit themselves to it he says: "When they do wrong, they feel, not contrition, of which God is the object, but remorse, and a sense of degradation. . . . They are victims of an intense self-contemplation."

In Newman's view of the church there is no place, as there would have to be in Protestant thinkers, including Milton, for a dialogue between scripture and church. The church for Newman is the definitive teacher of doctrine; hence it encloses scripture, and operates on ordinary society very much as the British constitution does in Burke. For Burke the conflict of classes and their interests, in a free society, is settled by a legal compromise which preserves the rights of both parties, and these compromises then form a series of precedents diffusing freedom through society, as the quarrels of king and barons produced Magna Carta and the quarrels of king and Parliament the Bill of Rights. Newman sees church doctrine as developing in a somewhat similar way, being evolved out of the crises of history, defining a dogma here, marking off a heresy there, in an endless pilgrimage toward the City of God. Thus spiritual authority in Newman is, as in Milton, a revelation, but a revelation that has no place for metamorphosis, for the revolutionary and apocalyptic transformation of society.

In Arnold, the conception "culture" is the basis from which we have to start. In using the phrase "spiritual authority" to describe a pervasive problem of nineteenth-century thought, I have been putting unfamiliar conceptions into the minds of some of my writers. For Mill, the problem is not exactly one of *spiritual* authority, and for Butler, it is not exactly a problem of authority. But Arnold is quite explicit about the authoritative nature of culture: "If we look at the world outside us we find a disquieting absence of sure authority. We discover that only in right reason can we get a source of sure authority; and culture brings us towards right reason." The traditional elements of gentleman and liberal education are both involved in Arnold's culture, but Arnold clears up a point about the social location of spiritual authority that has been confusing us so far. We noticed that the more conservative a writer is, the more inclined he is to locate spiritual authority in the middle of actual society, in the place of greatest prestige and prominence. The more radical he is, the more inclined he is to locate it in an opposition, an alien or even excluded group. Something in Arnold—possibly the Romantic poet in him—realizes that the center is the place of greatest isolation. The argument of *Culture and Anarchy* is to the effect that what is of greatest cultural value, such as a university or the established church, is central to society and demands to be placed at the center, in the position of Carlyle's intrinsic symbol. Society itself presents a conflict of class interests, and culture for Arnold operates like law in Burke or doctrine in Newman, as a harmonizing principle creating a new kind of order out of this conflict. Those who support it have to begin by isolating themselves from class conflict, which means isolating themselves from the present structure of society: "Within each of these classes there are a certain number of *aliens,* if we may so call them,— persons who are mainly led, not by their class spirit, but by a general *humane* spirit, by the love of human perfection."

Culture represents an evaluation—the *best* that has been thought and said—and the conception of "best" is bound up with permanence. Class conflict deals with temporary issues, and its arguments are rationalizations based on a temporary situation. Temporal power is based on the ascendancy of one class— here we come back to Milton's conception of temporal power as an interim power. The class qua class is always anticultural: the aristocracy, considered purely as a class, are only barbarians, the middle class only Philistines, the lower class only a populace. Hence it would be the wildest paradox to think of creating a new society through the dictatorship of one class. It is culture that is the genuinely revolutionary force in society, for culture "seeks to do away with classes," and tends to create out of actual society an ideal order of liberty, equality, and fraternity. Culture for Arnold is a whole of which the church forms part, but as culture is not, like church, the name of a specific community, the problem of defining the community of spiritual authority is still with us.

The question of the origin of spiritual authority, and of whether that origin is purely human, partly human, or wholly superhuman has come up at various times in this inquiry. Anyone working out this question in Christian terms, whether Catholic or Protestant, would be likely to say that its origin is out of human reach, though the fact that Christ is at once God, Man, and Logos guarantees the validity of human reason as a means of receiving it, at least up to a point. For Burke and Butler, in different ways, spiritual authority, or whatever is homologous with it, comes to us as a process of nature, a datum or something given, which we may modify but must first of all accept. We have seen that spiritual authority begins in the recognition of truth, and truth usually has about it some quality of the objective, something presented to us. But for a liberal thinker, such as Mill, there can hardly be any real spiritual authority apart from what man himself creates. A revolutionary thinker would go a step further and see in truth itself a human creation which, as man continues to create it, he may also re-create. Marx's second thesis on Feuerbach makes this quite clear: "The question whether objective truth can be attributed to human thinking is not a question of theory, but is a practical question. In practice man must prove the truth, that is, the reality and power, the this-sidedness of his thinking." Arnold's "culture" unites these qualities of the datum and the continuous creation, being a human construct which, so far as it is rooted in the past, possesses an objective authority. This authority, we should note, is not exclusively intellectual, for "many things are not seen in their true nature and as they really are, unless they are seen as beautiful," and the imagination as well as the reason may recognize a monument of its own magnificence.

Wherever we turn in nineteenth-century thought we meet some version of a "drunken boat" construct, where the values of humanity, intelligence, or cultural and social tradition keep tossing precariously in a sort of Noah's ark on top of a menacing and potentially destructive force. This is the relation of the world as idea to the world as will in Schopenhauer, of ethics to evolution in Darwin and Huxley, of the ascendant class to the proletariat in Marx, and, later, of ego to libido and id in Freud. There are also many variants of a "saving remnant" theory, ranging from Coleridge's "clerisy" to various pleas for a new kind of monastic movement (one thinks of the symbolic function of the idealized monastery in the argument of Carlyle's *Past and Present*). Of other metaphors of spiritual authority, two are conspicuous. One is the metaphor of the social human body, whose seat of intelligence and authority ought to be somewhere on top, as it is in the individual body. The other is the thermostat or feedback metaphor which has organized so much social thinking in the last two centuries. In a sense the search for spiritual authority is really the search for a "governor" in the mechanical sense, something that distributes the rhythm of a mechanism without being involved in the mechanism itself. This figure appears in Huxley's *Evolution and Ethics:* "To this extent the general cosmic process begins to be checked by a rudimentary ethical process, which is, strictly speaking, part of the former, just as the 'governor' in a steamengine is part of the mechanism of the engine."

The problem dealt with in this paper could of course be extended over a far wider area of nineteenth-century thought than I am here able to cover. So far as I know, the twentieth century has not added much to the question, which may be one reason why the political axioms and assumptions of the twentieth century are still rooted in the nineteenth. It seems to me, however, appropriate for an audience celebrating a step in the progress of a university to consider whether the university itself may not have a peculiarly close relationship to the question. In particular, the university seems to me to come closer than any other human institution to defining the community of spiritual authority. Newman's view that the university is a function of the church, with theology occupying a central role as the queen of sciences, does not seem to be borne out by the development of universities in the last century. I have no doubt that religion indicates where the ultimate source of spiritual authority is, nor that the churches have an essential function as custodians and interpreters of its tradition. But in the present-day shape of society, so dominated by science and technology, they clearly have only a partial and peripheral role in embodying the spiritual authority of that society.

Arnold comes nearest to seeing the universities in this light, but universities in his day, and more particularly as he conceived them, made it necessary for him to distinguish them from "culture." A century later, we seem to be living our lives on two levels. One is the level of ordinary society, which is in so constant a state of revolution and metamorphosis that it cannot be accepted as the real form of human society at all, but only as the transient appearance of real society. Real society itself can only be the world revealed to us through the study of the arts and sciences, the total body of human achievement out of which the forces come that change ordinary society so rapidly. Of this world the universities are the social embodiment, and they represent what seems to me today the only visible direction in which our higher loyalties and obligations can go.

III

Education and the Spread of Knowledge

WILLIAM S. KNICKERBOCKER
Victorian Education and the Idea of Culture

E. D. H. JOHNSON
The Role of the Artist

RICHARD A. E. BROOKS
The Development of the Historical Mind

RICHARD D. ALTICK
*The Social Background [to the Growth of a Mass
Reading Public]*

Victorian Education
and the Idea of Culture

WILLIAM S. KNICKERBOCKER

"Educate or govern," wrote John Ruskin, "they are one and the same word."

During the sixty-four years of Victoria's reign, a time of hazardous transition, education in England supplemented parliamentary action as a substitute for revolution, for achieving national change without catastrophic violence. The instruction of the masses, the opening of higher education to women, the establishment of educational institutions for workingmen, and the rebirth of spirit in public schools and universities tended to break down the barriers between classes and to bridge chasms between minds. Educational processes quietly radiated, creating an intellectual climate which vastly favored creative attitudes towards renovating the national social order. Victorian education became England's alternative to successive *coups d'etat* manifested by some other European nations.

Utility or culture—which? New educational institutions tended to abandon the humanistic tradition which had been preserved in England since the revival of the classics, to reject traditional literary bases of education, and to substitute the study of science and of technological machines and processes. Emergence of new educational concepts created a conflict. Aggressive

From Joseph E. Baker, ed., *The Reinterpretation of Victorian Literature* (Princeton: Princeton University Press, 1950), pp. 97–129.

attacks upon the study of the classics aroused resistance by traditionally educated scholars who, in the situation thus evoked,
voiced their faith in the formative power of literature, a philosophy of education resident in old established English seats of
learning. They resisted the threat to time-honored ways of life, a
threat engendered by revolutions abroad and by economic uncertainties at home. They met criticism of their own ideals and
the rivalry of newer institutions by militantly recommending the
idea of culture to preserve qualities of character and of human
dignity which radical experimenters were too prone to ignore
or destroy.

Of the two old universities, Oxford more valiantly resisted
innovations, and therefore bore the brunt of the struggle. Cambridge was more elastic, more active in developing its inheritance in stressing physical science, less committed than was
Oxford in devotion to literary studies as the organizing discipline
of higher learning. Defending and extending the idea of culture,
the humanization of man in society, were directly undertaken by
some Oxford humanists, the most notable of whom were Newman,
Arnold, and Ruskin.

I

Unprecedented effects resulted from extending education to
hitherto excluded classes. Indispensably a phase of Victorian
democracy—both stemming from it in the inchoate and spasmodic efforts to instruct the children of the poor and, inversely,
shaping and directing it in the period between the two Reform
Bills (1832 and 1867)—popular education enormously increased
the numbers of those who could read and write, altered the
nature of conditions of authorship and multiplied the phases of
national life hitherto untouched in English literature.

Efforts to instruct the lower classes through teaching poor
children to read the Scriptures and moral tracts (humanitarian
by-products of eighteenth century Methodism) were scattered
and unorganized. From 1700 to 1798, twenty "Charity Schools"
were founded to provide the rudiments of instruction to the poor,
but they too elicited little public interest until they found a
champion in Sarah Trimmer whose *Reflections upon Charity
Schools* (1792) called attention to their inadequacies while

making a plea for their improvement and increase. Maria Edgeworth's *Practical Education* (1798) proceeded further and provided Clapham evangelicals with an educational manual for their humanitarian zeal. For four years (1802 to 1806), Mrs. Trimmer continued her campaign in her magazine *The Guardian of Education.* Some development of the schools resulted from the work of Thomas Stock and Robert Raikes (1780) who succeeded in removing these separated experiments from the wastefulness of amateurism and converting them into the supervised schemes known as "the ragged schools."

Perhaps the intentions of these humanitarians was to rescue children of the lower classes from the blight of gin whose sodden effects were so tellingly depicted by Hogarth. The limited scope of instruction in reading, writing, and a little arithmetic bore fruit in unanticipated results; for once taught to read the poor did not, of course, restrict their reading to the Holy Bible or to pious tracts like Hannah More's *The Shepherd of Salisbury Plain.* They avidly read, in too many instances, whatever came within range of their understanding, including (to the horror of the faithful) infidel and subversive printed matter hawked in the streets—inflaming their sense of discontent with conditions approved by their benefactors. Reaction and suspicion followed as a consequence when Paine's *Rights of Man* and *The Age of Reason* circulated freely among the newly literate poor so that public opinion feared that the mere ability to read was probably more a menace than a blessing—an attitude which became patently evident during the disturbances in England accompanying the progressive violence of the French Revolution. More than one contemporary vigorously questioned, or denounced, all efforts to instruct the poor. Yet extensive popular education as a panacea for the growing problems of ignorance, poverty, and crime lingered in the minds of some who uneasily saw the threatened deterioration of England. Wordsworth, turning to this problem, ventured to descant on its solution in his *Excursion:*

> O for the coming of that glorious time
> When, prizing knowledge as her noblest wealth
> And best protection, this imperial Realm,
> While she exacts obedience, shall admit
> An obligation, on her part, to *teach*

Them who were born to serve her and obey;
Binding herself by statute to secure
For all the children whom her soil maintains
The rudiments of letters, and inform
The mind with moral and religious truth,
Both understood and practiced—so that none
However destitute be left to droop
By timely culture unsustained; or run
Into a wild disorder; or be forced
To drudge through a weary life without the help
Of intellectual implements and tools;
A savage horde among the civilized,
A servile band among the lordly free.[1]

Wordsworth's lines anticipate Victorian faith in the edifying power of educating the masses. In somewhat cumbersome verse, he phrased in idealistic sentences the vision which inspired Bell and Lancaster in establishing free schools for elementary instruction. Their efforts were consolidated in 1811 by the creation of the National Society for Promoting the Education of the Poor and, three years later (1813), the British and Foreign School Society. Quietly, from 1799 to 1816, Robert Owen was conducting his "New Institute for the Formation of Character" at New Lanark. Wordsworth's lines seem to indicate his sympathy with these movements and with Lord Brougham's agitation to have the government assume the burden of educating the poor: an agitation which, after several years of unremitting energy, triumphed in moving Parliament to appoint a Select Committee to Investigate the Education of the Lower Classes of the Metropolis (1816). In 1818, after publishing his pamphlet "Letter to Sir Samuel Romilly . . . Upon the Abuse of Charities [Schools]" he saw his bill passed for a comprehensive Survey of Educational Charities. Brougham tirelessly worked to supply the unprivileged classes with practical information on a wide variety of topics through the tracts circulated by his Society for the Diffusion of Useful Knowledge, competing with the newly founded Bible Society, which distributed inexpensive editions of Holy Scripture among the literate poor. In 1835 Chambers founded his periodical, *Information for the People*. The establishment of a

---

[1] *The Excursion*, Book VIII.

training school for teachers at Battersea (1833) and the parliamentary grant of £20,000 for People's Schools marked the beginnings of organized, publicly supported, extension of education to the children of the lower classes.

Education of laborers proceeded in a similar hesitating manner. The first of the "Mechanics Institutions," established in 1800, was followed, after almost a quarter century (1823), by The London Mechanics Institute (which later became Birkbeck College). In 1825, Brougham published his pamphlet, "Practical Observations Upon the Education of the People, Addressed to the Working Class and Their Employers." In the same year Thomas Campbell wrote a letter to *The Times* proposing an English university, open to all regardless of creed or social status, modeled on the German university at Bonn. This led, two years later (1827), to the founding of London University. Because this new institution eliminated religious tests for admission, devout Anglicans feared it would spread infidelity and forthwith established King's College, London (1831), to offset its baneful influence. London University did not require residence for its degrees but provided opportunities for examination given in various parts of the kingdom.

Even these provisions did not adequately solve the problem of threatened disaster to the social fabric caused by economic strains and distresses which were dramatically manifested by the anti-Corn Law and Chartist agitations of the thirties and forties and reached their climax in the continental revolutions of 1848. In a passionate speech in the House of Commons on April 19, 1847, Macaulay displayed his anxieties over the severe strains on public security caused by farm hands and artisans in their riots, hay burnings, and ugly threats. "This, then, is my argument," he exhorted his hearers, "it is the duty of government to protect our persons and property from danger. The gross ignorance of the common people is a principal cause of danger to our persons and property. Therefore, it is the duty of government to take care that the common people shall not be grossly ignorant."

In this context, Kingsley's *Alton Locke* is a revealing social document. Perhaps Macaulay's notion of education, narrowly conceived for merely prudential reasons, may have moved Carlyle in his alarming sketch of the condition of England, "Chartism" (1848), to recommend a more humane motive: "Who would suppose," Carlyle wrote, "that Education were a thing which had to be advocated on the ground of local expediency, or indeed on any ground? As if it stood not on the basis of everlasting duty, as a prime necessity of man. It is a thing that should need no advocating; much as it does actually need. To impart the gift of thinking to those who cannot think, and yet who could in that case think; this, one would imagine, was the first function a government had to set about discharging."

From 1848 to 1862 William Ellis founded his Birkbeck Schools and in 1862, Robert Lowe, an Oxford don, gave considerable time to the work of improving elementary education by his Revised Code.

Matthew Arnold's appointment (1851) as one of three inspectors of schools reveals the importance the government placed upon elevating the quality of popular education. Though his biographers cannot dispense with this phase of his life, they have tended to slight it as prosaic and tedious; yet a more realistic view of his experience discloses that, in spite of the drudgery and fatigue the school inspections entailed, they provided opportunities for learning at first hand the conditions of a swiftly changing age, freeing him from the confined outlook resulting from his sheltered upbringing. His duties continued through thirty of the most important years of his life (1851 to 1882) and exacted much from him in the constant travel his duties demanded. But he was compensated by the opportunities offered him, in moving him to write essays which flooded the whole view of contemporary education of the English people with insights which only one with his background and quality of mind could render. The Newcastle Commission, appointed in 1859, delegated him to investigate schools in France, Holland, and Switzerland—an experience which enabled him to see in some perspective the defects and the needs of English publicly supported schools. His report, "The Popular Education of France with Notices of That in Holland and Switzerland" (1861), placed the subject on a plane higher than the solely prudential one which had moved Brougham and Macaulay. It appeared the year that the Taunton Commission was appointed: that commission sent him abroad a few years later to continue his investigations which he presented in another report, "Schools and Universities on the Continent" (1868). By comparing it with Herbert Spencer's *Education, Intellectual, Moral, and Physical* one may see how Arnold's concept of culture infused educational theory with an ideal missing from the great empiricist's proposals. In some measure, it was incorporated in the great Education Act of 1870 constructed by Arnold's brother-in-law, William Forster. Ten years later, in 1880, the Compulsory Education Act definitely legalized the improvements in popular education and made education generally mandatory throughout the realm. The appointment (1894) and the report (1896) of the Bryce Commission, with the enactment of the Education Acts of 1902 and 1903, corrected and adjusted provisions of the 1870 act.

Difficulties which Wordsworth had not foreseen in his *Excursion* passage, quoted above, had arisen through the six decades of Victoria's reign. Should popular education be financed and supervised by voluntary, or by governmental, agencies? Should religion and religious doctrine be an integral part of its program? Should education of the people be confined to the instruction of "skills" or should it primarily seek the development of moral character? "What was proposed in the Acts of 1902 and 1903," wrote Beatrice Webb, "applying to England and Wales only, was that all schools which provided elementary education up to a certain standard should come on the rates, and be controlled by the public authority; but that such of them as had been provided by a religious denomination should be permitted to choose leaders of their own creed, provided that they were efficient in secular subjects, and that, subject to a conscience clause, there should be religious teaching according to the creed of the denominational school." [2]

II

In some sense, not too clearly discernible, professional and higher education of English women in the nineteenth century accompanied the movement for popular education. The "moni-

---

[2] *Our Partnership* (copyright by Longmans, Green & Co., Inc.: New York, 1948), pp. 233–234. . . .

torial" system on which Bell and Lancaster relied, using older children to instruct younger, yielded to the need for adult teachers, properly trained in the skill of instruction. This opened new doors for women. Individual women, here and there, like Harriet Martineau and George Eliot, were sufficiently intrepid to venture into fields of higher learning generally then regarded as solely the sphere of men. But teacher training colleges offered an avenue of useful employment for women—apart from the traditional post as governesses in private families—in which they found scope for public service. From this beginning, they broadened their demands for opportunities in higher education and, stimulated by the growing strength of the woman's movement in the Victorian era, slowly succeeded in securing the establishment of women's colleges and the right to enter the universities, including Cambridge and Oxford.

The circumscribed educational field for women was a legacy of the previous century. Dr. Johnson had devised a triad of educational aims for women: cleverness in learning foreign languages, interest in science, and the general acquisition of quotable facts. These were to make her more attractive as maiden and more convenient and durable as wife and mother. This was a more sensible view than the sentimentalized notion then prevailing, celebrated in *Pamela* and *Clarissa Harlow,* which persisted well into the nineteenth century and was, indeed, illustrated in the good queen herself. It was also reflected in the tender verses of Laetitia Landon, Felicia Hemans, and Jean Ingelow. Mrs. Anne Jameson's *Heroines of Shakespeare,* in its unexcised, original version, frankly stressed the frailties of women who, by various arts of wit and suffering, held up a mirror for Victorian female virtues; it was a moral masterpiece, edifying for women in a world limited to pleasures of the parlor and the martyrdoms of marriage.

Mrs. Ellis's series of conduct-books, *The Women of England,* delineated the whole course of Victorian woman's behavior, from babyhood to the blessedness of the boudoir, gravely exhorting mothers to rear their daughters for careers of patient waiting until won by suitors (or, if not wooed, to endure mutely the long-suffering of inconspicuous spinsterhood); and thereafter as

Griseldas in the role of wife and mother. "The first thing of importance," Mrs. Ellis wrote in *Daughters of England*, "is to be inferior to men—inferior in mental power in the same proportion that you are inferior in bodily strength. . . . I confess I do not see the value of languages for a woman," she continued, questioning also the usefulness of the knowledge of science for women beyond making her an "intelligent listener" to men. As for the general acquisition of knowledge, she conceded that a knowledge of facts, however miscellaneous, might be handy "in connection with the proper exercise of a healthy mind," and "necessarily lead to a general illumination." Mrs. Ellis, like the many other women who shared her views, was moved to write in order to preserve and extend the ideal of the "proper female" in a generation whose literary tastes were appeased by the dainty gift books and annuals laden with verse, fiction, and scribblings which satisfied this ideal. It went further, saturating the minds of minor novelists, now forgotten, who conceived their women characters in this atmosphere of "namby-pambyism."

In this milieu and for this public, the young Alfred Tennyson alembicated some of the moods and themes of poets of the preceding romantic generation—of Wordsworth, Keats, Shelley, and even of the sentimental Byron of "Childe Harold"—electing himself the poetic voice of this dominant gynecocracy. Harmoniously in tune with current sentimentalizing of the proper female, he remained faithful to it throughout his life; not even Thackeray's revision of the concept in Becky Sharp, or contemporary women who demonstrated its inadequacy, restrained him in depicting it in *The Princess.* So long as Victoria was Queen, so long was he faithful to her view of woman's status. A glimpse of that view may be seen in the letter written by Mrs. Martin, the Queen's companion, in 1860: "The Queen is most anxious to enlist everyone who can speak or write to join in opposing this mad wicked folly of Women's Rights, with all its attendant horrors, on which her poor, feeble sex is bent, forgetting every sense of womanly feeling and propriety."

Woman's status began to be warmly discussed shortly after Victoria's accession. Critics attacked the notion that women preferred to be sheltered, anemic, deprived of careers. Women struggled for revision of ideas concerning education for their sex despite scepticism, ridicule, and stubborn resistance. By 1848 they succeeded in gaining recognition of their claims: in that year, the year Tennyson published his satiric "medley" *The Princess*, Queen's College, London, opened its doors for the liberal education of women, followed by the Bedford College for Women in the following year. Two graduates of Queen's College, Frances Mary Buss and Dorothy Beale, became notable pioneers in the movement. Others who participated in various ways were Sophia Jex-Blake, Anne Jemima Clough, Emily and Octavia Hill, Emma Cons, Barbara Leigh Smith, and Emily Davis who, in 1864, won a long fight to secure admission of girls to London University Local Examinations, and in 1869 founded the Women's College at Hitchin which, in 1875, moved to Cambridge and became Girton College. The National Union for Improving the Education of Women of all classes was organized in 1871 and was followed, the next year, by the Girls Public School Company. Seven years later, in 1879, London University opened its degree examinations to women; in 1881 women's colleges were founded at Oxford and, in 1884, Oxford permitted women to examinations in some of its Final Schools.

Public opinion grudgingly shifted during the decade of the eighties. Gilbert and Sullivan's *Princess Ida* was a timely parody of Tennyson's *Princess*. John Stuart Mill's *The Subjection of Women* had done its work in persuading many Liberals to adopt more sensible views. George Eliot had eminently demonstrated that a woman was as competent as any of the other sex in fundamental brainwork in philosophy or in fiction. In all fields of intellectual and social action Victorian women were becoming annually more conspicuous in contributing to knowledge and to ways of solving political and economic problems. By 1901, the year of the Queen's death, among the increasing number of notable women—whose achievements were destined not only to expose the inadequacies of Mrs. Ellis's views but were to reveal how a woman, no less "genteel," could attain happiness in marriage while engaged in the severest forms of research—was Beatrice Webb. Her autobiography, *My Apprenticeship* and *Our Partnership,* is a prime source-book for Victorian education in

some of its later phases. It discloses how an industrious, perse-
vering, intelligent woman continued the efforts, by scientific
methods, of Jeremy Bentham, John Stuart Mill, John Ruskin,
Robert Owen, and William Morris in assisting the mind of
England to confront and solve emerging industrial and economic
problems.

III

Education of artisans and mechanics developed concomitantly
with that of the children of the poorer classes and of women.
Instruction in technological skills undoubtedly made better
workmen without necessarily making them better citizens. Its
deficiencies moved high-minded Victorians to stress the importance of education as the cultivation of moral attitudes, enlarge-
ment of social vision, and the political responsibilities of
workingmen as citizens.

Except in individual instances, European consciousness of "a
proletariat" found slight acceptance in England, even during the
tumults of the forties—partly because of the traditional pride of
the Englishman of the lower classes, but more importantly because of the successive series of parliamentary compromises in
new legislation, and experimental efforts in creating new colleges
and universities to fit the needs of those who either could not
afford the expenses of Oxford and Cambridge, or would not con-
sent to the creedal impositions of the two old universities.
London University (1827), though not founded specifically for
workingmen—it provided university education for dissenters not
then admitted to Oxford and Cambridge—made no distinction
between the middle and lower classes in qualifications for study.
In its first period it was, according to Beatrice Webb, "merely
a corporation to confer university degrees. It had no professors;
it gave no teaching; it conducted no research; it awarded its
degrees to persons coming from all parts, on their passing examinations on papers set by examiners whom they had never
seen." [3]

In 1851, Owens College, the experiment which led to the

---

[3] *Our Partnership,* pp. 233–234.

establishment of the University of Manchester, opened in the heart of industrial England. Three years later (1854), the Workingman's College in Red Lion Square, London, was formally dedicated, crowning efforts made by Maurice, Furnival, J. M. Ludlow, Thomas Hughes, Charles Kingsley, and John Ruskin. Ruskin's "The Nature of Gothic," a chapter from his recently published *Stones of Venice*, was distributed to the large audience of workingmen as the rationale of this new venture. In it, Ruskin wrote:

It is verily this degradation of the operative into a machine which, more than any other evil of the times, is leading the masses of the nations everywhere into vain, incoherent, destructive struggling for a freedom of which they cannot explain the nature to themselves. Their universal outcry against wealth, and against nobility, is not forced from them either by the pressure of famine, or the sting of mortified pride. These do much, and have done much in all ages; but the foundations of society were never shaken as they are at this day. It is not that men are ill fed, but that they have no pleasure in the work by which they make their bread, and therefore look to wealth as the only means to pleasure.

. . . The great cry that rises from our manufacturing cities, louder than all their furnace blast, is all in very deed for this—that we manufacture everything there except men; we blanch cotton, and strengthen steel, and refine sugar, and shape pottery; but to brighten, to strengthen, to refine, or to form a single living spirit, never enters into our estimate of advantages. And all the evil to which that cry is urging our myriads can be met in only one way. . . . It can be met only by a right understanding, on the part of all classes, of what kinds of labor are good for men, raising them, and making them happy; by a determined sacrifice of such convenience, or beauty, or cheapness as to be got only by the degradation of the workman; and by equally determined demand for products of healthy and ennobling labour.

Ruskin's exhortation placed the idea of workingmen's education on a high plane, bringing it within a humanistic concept. In spite of strenuous efforts of Ruskin's disciples to make it prevail, it was regarded by practical people as iridescences on floating gossamers. A notable instance is Sir Josiah Mason, a self-made capitalist of Birmingham, who stringently excluded from his projected college (Mason's College, Birmingham, 1881), the study of theology, party politics, and "mere literary instruction." Yet even this college, like some other new institutions, invited men of active affairs—scientists, technologists, lawyers, clergymen, and literary critics—to address its working-class audiences, thus providing opportunities for men with vision to communicate their views.

Freed from inhibitions of statute, custom, and tradition, these colleges explored many avenues of knowledge neglected by Oxford and Cambridge. By adjusting theory and process to newer needs in a world rapidly changing its frames of reference, they enlarged the national mind. The movement was consolidated in the foundation of new urban universities: in Manchester (1880), Birmingham (1900), Liverpool (1903), Leeds (1904), Sheffield (1905), and Bristol (1906).

IV

Influences outside educational institutions also contributed to this extension. The most important were the advancement of natural sciences, the development of trade unions and the political activities of the Independent Labour Party, and the steady propaganda of the Fabian Society.

Annual meetings of the Royal Society constituted, in effect, a "university" of science in which the Baconian method of research, as well as the results of scientific experiments, were publicly announced and discussed. Significant books, like Lyell's *Principles of Geology* (1833) and Darwin's *Origin of Species* (1859), stimulated a shift of thinking which had impressive effects in fundamental thinking and in altering educational concepts in schools and colleges newly founded.

The intricate growth of labor organizations and their effects upon the public mind are recorded in the Webbs' *History of Trade Unionism* (1898). In disputes between labor and capital, and in internal disputes within unions themselves, aggressive personalities found a theater for airing their economic views, analyzing existing conditions, and proposing economic panaceas and policies of tactics. Inadequacies of idealistic proposals made evident the necessity for trustworthy data derived from exhaustive investigation by personal interviews, and by research in musty records of the past. In developing its corporate forms, British labor would have been rigidly materialistic in outlook and purpose had it not been infused by the humanism of Carlyle, Kingsley, Ruskin, and Morris. Indeed, altered by pressures of changing conditions and by shifts of stress, the conflict of humanism and utilitarianism, pointed out by John Stuart Mill in his essays, "Bentham" and "Coleridge," continued in other forms. As the political philosophy of labor evolved, the solution of basic problems (like ignorance, poverty, and crime) veered towards vaguely collectivist proposals; one derived from Robert Owen and his humanitarian experiment at New Lanark, another from John Ruskin's neo-medievalism in the Guild of St. George. Through the conjunction of the influences of John Stuart Mill, of Herbert Spencer, and of the scientific method, the Owen concept of utilitarian socialism and the Ruskin ideal of humanistic socialism fused in the speculative propaganda—buttressed by economic statistics and penetrating social analyses—of the Fabians, on public platforms and through their publications.

Carlyle's *Past and Present,* as well as his later vigorous manifestoes, steadily bombarded the Victorian public, awakening the conscience of the ruling middle class to the perils of the existing conditions which resulted from the less admirable features of capitalism. Superb as a diagnostician, Carlyle contributed a constructive clue to the solution of what he called "the condition-of-England" question: the imperative of retrieving the spiritual and moral dignity of impoverished classes. To achieve this, he urged strong will, emigration to solve overpopulation, and the responsibility of government to educate the masses. His zeal stimulated university idealists. Kingsley's *Yeast* and *Alton Locke,* Hughes' *Tom Brown at Oxford* are fictional footnotes of Carlyle; but the Christian Socialist movement of Frederick Denison Maurice, Charles Kingsley, and Thomas Hughes was industriously engaged in implementing Carlyle's remedies in *Latter-Day Pamphlets.* His chief disciple, however, the eminent Victorian who not only stressed his message but immensely expanded it, was that precocious "graduate of Oxford," John Ruskin, whose pilgrimage, beginning with a search for the central principles of art and beauty, culminated in an apocalyptic vision of a transformed England when labor would be dedicated to the making of beautiful things in a spirit of consecration and of Christian joy.

Carlyle, the Christian Socialists, and Ruskin supplied the vision; but translating the vision into a version was, and still is, a slow, devious, and painful process. Concrete situations, in the cumbersome efforts of laborers to unite in their unions and the subsequent deadlocks in relations of capital and labor, created expediencies in which labor became vocal in stating its concepts, articulate in outlining its demands and programs for their attainment. Discussions in Victorian periodicals (like *The Fortnightly Review, The Athenaeum, The Spectator,* and *The Nineteenth Century*), supplemented by books, brought the problems within the political sphere in the hope that legislation would provide the agency for the correction of economic abuses and distresses. The Second Reform Bill of 1867, by extending the franchise, was a gesture in this direction.

Diverse interests of reformed Parliament impeded action on bills submitted to lessen economic strains. Not content with political action alone, trade unions continued their struggle through their own techniques of economic action. Tradition— thanks to the great advances made by the scientific method in the study of history, which had been appropriated by the schools for the people—became evident in the 1880's, as British labor anticipated the centenary of the French Revolution. The Independent Labour Party, founded during the ugly times of severe economic stress, 1881 to 1885, organized the spirit of discontent by directing its attack on the capitalistic system through a program of revolutionary socialism. Urged by impetuous hotheads in labor unions, the atmosphere was charged with ominous threats of violence.

More realistic social analysts, acknowledging the imminence of catastrophe, turned towards a method of achieving economic and social advance more truly indigenous, more truly harmonious with the spirit of English tradition of social action: the method of "the inevitability of gradualness" through constitu-

tional socialism. The differences between revolutionary and constitutional socialism were pointed out by Sidney Webb in an
address delivered at the tenth anniversary of the foundation of
the Fabian Society, "Socialism, True and False":

"In 1884," said Sidney Webb, "the Fabian Society, like the
other socialist organizations, had its enthusiastic young members
—aye, and old ones, too—who placed all their hopes on a sudden tumultuous uprising of a united proletariat, before whose
mighty onrush, Kings, landlords and capitalists would go down
like ninepins, leaving society quietly to re-sort itself into a utopia.
The date for this social revolution was sometimes fixed for
1889, the centenary of the French Revolution. . . . It was
against all thinking and teaching of this catastrophic kind that
the [Fabian] Society came to set its face—not, as I believe,
because we were any less earnest in our warfare against existing
evils, or less extreme in our remedies, but because we were
sadly and sorrowfully driven to the conclusion that no sudden
or simultaneous transformation of society from an individualist
to a collectivist basis was possible or even thinkable. . . . In
short, we repudiated the common assumption that socialism
was necessarily bound up with insurrectionism, on the one
hand, or utopianism, on the other, and we set to work to discover
for ourselves and to teach others how practically to transform
England into a social democratic commonwealth." [4]

Fabians constituted an educational agency, analyzing economic and social conditions and institutions in England, and dis-
seminating a series of "tracts for the times" which proposed
correction of inadequacies in the interests of what they thought
was distributive economic justice. The title page of Fabian Tract
number 7 explained the name and method of the society: "For
the right moment you must wait, as Fabius did most patiently
when warring against Hannibal, though many censured his de-
lays; but when the time comes, you must strike hard, as Fabius
did, or your waiting will be in vain, and fruitless." According to
Beatrice Webb, "the Fabian Society studiously avoided any
quotations from Karl Marx, preferring indeed Robert Owen:
they translated economics and collectivism into the language of

---

[4] Quoted by Beatrice Webb, *Our Partnership*, pp. 105–106.

prosaic vestrymen and town councillors." [5] "The Fabians," wrote G. M. Trevelyan in *British History in the Nineteenth Century,* "were intelligence officers without an army—there was no Fabian Party in parliament—but they influenced the strategy and even the direction of the great hosts moving under other banners." "The Fabians," wrote Mrs. Webb, "in no way competed with the I. L. P. We were purely an educational body—we did not seek to become a political party. We should continue our policy of inoculation—of giving to each class, to each person, coming under our influence, the exact dose of collectivism that they were prepared to assimilate. . . . Of course, this slow imperceptible change in men's opinions and in the national institutions, is not favorable to the growth of a revolutionary party. There is some truth in Keir Hardie's remark that we were the worst enemies of the social revolution." [6]

Through the legacy of an eccentric Fabian, Henry Hutchinson, the London School of Economics was founded in 1895, modeled on L'Ecole Libre de Science Politique. Sidney Webb collaborated with R. B. Haldane (1856–1928) in drafting a bill for the reorganization of London University: "they were, in their several ways, both entirely free from the subtly pervading influence of the Oxford and Cambridge of those days, with their standards of expensive living and enjoyable leisure, and their assumption of belonging to an aristocracy or governing class." Haldane, graduate of Edinburgh and Göttingen, "among students living sparely in uncomfortable lodgings, undistracted by games, who looked forward to no existence other than strenuous brainwork, . . . believed intensely in the university, not only as a place for 'great teaching' but also as a source of inspiration of 'great minds,' producing in the choicer spirits, a systematic devotion to learning and research. . . . He, accordingly, designed a scheme of combining in a single university, of a new type, all three elements: namely, the external students influenced by a system of examinations which could be improved; an organized hierarchy of evening classes which, so far as London was concerned, the Technical Education Board was raising to the highest grade; and the group of autonomous colleges, in which a

---

[5] *Ibid.,* pp. 106–107.   [6] *Ibid.,* pp. 122–123.

professoriate in no way inferior to those of Germany and Scotland could be trusted to inspire self-elected groups of earnest students in every subject of study and research." [7]

The government in the summer of 1897 appointed a commission to devise a constitution and statutes for London University, but the London University Act of 1898 resulted merely in continuing the loose external examinations and in recognizing the teaching given in autonomous colleges. "The reorganized University," Mrs. Webb records, "started on what was little more than a formal existence in which the several parts wrangled over and largely counteracted each other's projects and proposals; some fresh convulsion, amounting perhaps to a new birth, was required to give the organism genuine life."

The possibilities for this great metropolitan seat of learning were outlined by Sidney Webb in an essay, "London University: A Policy and a Forecast" in *Nineteenth Century,* 1902. "It may at the outset," he wrote, "be granted that, for any university of the Oxford or Cambridge type, the metropolis is perhaps more unfit than any other spot that could be chosen. By no possible expenditure could we create . . . the tradition, the atmosphere, the charm or grace of collegiate life on the Isis or the Cam. Nor is it possible to secure, amid the heterogeneous crowds of London and its distractions, either the class selection or the careful supervision required by the parents of boys fresh from Eton or Harrow, with two or three hundred a year to spend in pocket money. . . . It may be that we must forgo in London University the culture born of classic scholarship and learned leisure. But, if we can show that there is no incompatibility between the widespread instruction of an undergraduate democracy and the most effective provision for the discovery of new truth; between the most practical training and genuine cultivation of the mind; between the plain living of hard-working students of limited means and high intellectual achievements, we shall not . . . appeal in vain. London University must take its own line. They are futile dreamers who seek to fit new circumstances to the old ideals: rather, must we strive, by developing to the utmost

---

[7] *Ibid.,* p. 403.

the opportunities that the present affords us, to create out of twentieth century conditions new kinds of perfection."

V

Popular education, the development of scientific, technological, and professional training, the creation of new colleges, and the admission of women to university degrees were phases of a noiseless revolution. They filled a need made conspicuous by developments of middle-class and aristocratic education since Elizabethan days.

Seen in the context of the whole Victorian frame, classical grammar schools and the two old universities formed a separate and exclusive system which tended to keep them immune from contemporary concerns. Winchester, Eton, Harrow, Rugby—to name only the best-known public schools—were, though separate corporations, organically connected in their educational policy with Oxford and Cambridge. The corporate independence of each of these institutions, their diversities of administration, in no way affected their consecration to a single inspiring idea, the idea of culture. In large measure, what Oxford and Cambridge thought and taught was reproduced in public schools because teachers of the latter were graduates of the former. Entrenched in custom and protected by tradition, these conservative institutions of learning preserved their standards. In the face of fierce attacks, they framed their "secret" in understandable words, becoming more conscious of the rightness of their procedures and the quality of their discipline. What their critics denounced as their "neglect" and "lethargy" was really their loyal devotion to their own continuities and to their concept of culture derived from a close and continuous study of the classics. They rallied against their opponents and boldly stated their philosophy of education; and, assuming the offensive, ventured to propose it to correct secularizing tendencies then increasingly prevalent.

Though Cambridge accepted Bacon as a supplement to its traditional reliance on Plato, Oxford rested on Aristotle as its guiding mind—the Aristotle of the *Poetics, Ethics, Politics,* and especially the *Logic.* Aristotle stimulated Oxford's tendency to analytical thinking, to the critical scrutiny of Graeco-Latin literature from which it derived and formulated the idea of culture. The play of mind which resulted from the continual criticism by Victorian Liberals caused Oxford humanists to reinterpret the idea of culture in a larger frame of reference. Hence, Matthew Arnold, engaging in the task of permeating middle-class thinking of Victorian England, defined it as "the disinterested endeavor to learn and to propagate the best that has been thought and said in the world," the "love of perfection" which motivates the five powers of life: the powers of manners, of morals, of literature, of science, and of religion.

"The great men of culture," Arnold indicated, "are those who have a passion for diffusing, for making prevail from one end of society to the other, the best knowledge, the best ideas of their time: who have labored to divest knowledge of all that was harsh, uncouth, difficult, abstract, professional, exclusive; to humanize it, to make it efficient outside the clique of the cultivated and learned, yet still remaining the *best* knowledge and thought of the time, and a true source, therefore, of sweetness and light."

From the beginning to the middle of the century, Liberal reformers urged changes which they believed would make these old institutions more truly national, more truly representative. Neither Oxford nor Cambridge considered scientific research its prime obligation and both universities had permitted their professoriate to fall into neglect. Both were loose confederations of colleges in which the tutorial system had developed, over the course of two centuries, at the expense of the university as a single, larger corporation. The successes of German universities —especially of Göttingen, Bonn, and Berlin—in extending the bounds of human knowledge, in Biblical criticism, in philosophy, and in the natural sciences, served reformers as models from which to point out the defects of Oxford and Cambridge. The *Edinburgh Review* maintained a continuous campaign for the reform of the two universities which, in 1808–1810 and 1832–1834, was unusually severe. Its acrimony, and indifference to the peculiar qualities of attitude and scholarly action which had silently developed in the universities, tended to irritate defenders of the *status quo* and, when the issue was taken up by the Liberal Party for parliamentary action, created in both institutions a resolute spirit of resistance.

This agitation for the adjustment of Oxford and Cambridge resulted from a notion that, as *national* universities, they were too exclusive in their conditions for admission, too rigid in insistence on religious conformity for tutors and professors, and too negligent in standards of academic scholarship.[8] Adam Smith in *The Wealth of Nations* (1776) and Edward Gibbon in his *Memoirs* (1795) had caustically criticized eighteenth-century Oxford: Gibbon invented the phrase which became a conventional description of the university: "a place of port and prejudice." Adam Smith had said that it "made no pretence at teaching." But, by 1800, one of the Oxford colleges—Oriel—had begun its own internal reform and, with the aid of influential scholars of other Oxford colleges, succeeded in instituting the "Final Schools," or what might today be called oral comprehensive examinations in the classics, conducted by the university to determine what undergraduates should receive the degree and in what order of merit. These "Final Schools" were the first indication of a willingness by the independent colleges of Oxford to concede the superior authority of the university, even though, for another half century, they continued as independent corporations, each with its own properties and endowments, its own customs and traditions, submitting to no external jurisdiction.

As a result of this administrative reform, slight though it was, a spirit of competitive scholarly rivalry developed among the colleges as their undergraduates strove for First Class Honors in the Final Schools. By 1837, when Victoria ascended the throne, the chief Oxford college was Oriel. It had, about the beginning of the century, abolished an abuse which prevailed in all Oxford colleges: the custom of electing its tutors for almost any reason except for scholarly merit and achievement. By a daring action, it substituted a scheme to appoint its fellows and tutors from

---

[8] *Creative Oxford: Its Influence in Victorian Literature* (Syracuse Univ. Press, 1925) by the present writer sketches specifically the criticisms of Oxford and Cambridge by the *Edinburgh Review* and efforts of Liberals in Parliament to legislate improvement.

among those students who had won distinction, First Class Honors, in the Final Schools. At the same time, it revised its method of studying Aristotle from memorizing passages of a paraphrase of the *Logic* to mastering its art and applying it in specific issues. Largely by initiating this shift, Oriel became conspicuous as Oxford's "blue-ribbon college." Its dons became gadflies, exercising an agile play of mind on fundamental questions, and were locally described as "The Noetics." One of the most prominent of the group, Edward Copleston, who later became provost of the college, vigorously replied to criticism of Oxford in a tract, *Reply to the Calumnies of the Edinburgh Review* (1810), which Newman had before him a half-century later when he wrote *The Idea of a University* (1852).

From this company of Oriel logicians came Thomas Arnold and John Henry Newman, men whose idea of the church and of the relation of Oxford to the church differed profoundly. Arnold relinquished his Oriel fellowship in 1820 (Newman was appointed to fill the vacancy). He was so successful preparing youth for the universities that he was appointed in 1828 as headmaster of Rugby where, during the following fourteen years (1828–1842), he radically changed the whole conception of education for pre-university students. By laying his stress on the formation of moral character and on the necessity for openmindedness in meeting new ideas, he sent to both old universities a succession of Rugbeians who quickly attained distinction in scholarship and were conspicuous for their liberal attitudes. Thomas Hughes' *Tom Brown at Rugby* and its sequel, *Tom Brown at Oxford,* delineate their moral earnestness, physical vigor, and novel openmindedness: attitudes which in life were displayed by Arthur Hugh Clough. While Arnold was at Rugby, Newman, associating with Oriel Noetics at Oxford, found a new intellectual life which he affectionately records in his *Apologia Pro Vita Sua.* He also records how he came to resist the innovating spirit in Oxford introduced by Arnoldian Liberals. In this struggle he became the "most eloquent" voice of the Tractarians. Employing dialectical instruments which Noetics revived, Tractarians strengthened Oxford as a citadel of the national church. Their agitations alarmed many who disagreed with their propaganda. Liberals intensified their demands for parliamentary reform of the two old universities which culminated in a tactical victory in 1851 when they succeeded in having a commission appointed to investigate Oxford and Cambridge.

By that time Newman was a Roman Catholic priest. While the committee investigated the universities, some of his fellow Catholics in Dublin invited him to deliver a series of lectures in that city to inaugurate a projected university. In those lectures on the nature of university education, Newman found an occasion to counteract the work of the investigating committee by anticipating their proposals for university reform, especially in their tendency to secularize higher education. His *Idea of a University* confessedly developed the idea of Oxford expounded four decades earlier by Copleston. Implicitly it rejected innovations like the lack of collegiate residence and the practice of granting degrees merely by passing examinations, both of which had been introduced by London University: it also resisted proposals to lay inordinate stress on laboratory experiment, a stress which disregarded the harmonious development of all human powers.

The ideal university, Newman asserted, was a place of learning in which a harmony of "sciences" prevailed. To him, "sciences" meant *all* studies, not merely the knowledge of physical phenomena. For the needs of teaching, knowledge was broken into separate subject matters; yet, he insisted, all of these "sciences" have "multiplied bearings one on another, and an internal sympathy, and admit, or rather demand, comparison and adjustment. They complete, correct, balance each other." Theology— the systematic study of God, nature, and man—regulated and organized other "sciences" in a reasonable relevancy, in a qualitative gradation of significant worth. In Newman's opinion, this harmony would be destroyed if theology were eliminated from the scheme of higher learning. Doubtless with London University in mind as something to avoid because it not only eliminated theology but also laid improper stress on examinations taken by students who remained at home in different parts of the kingdom, Newman emphasized the importance of collegiate residence.

"This," he said, "I conceive to be the advantage of a seat of universal learning, considered as a place of education. An assemblage of learned men, zealous for their own sciences, and rivals of each other, are brought by familiar intercourse and for the sake of intellectual peace, to adjust together the claims and relations of their respective subjects of investigation. They learn to respect, to consult, to aid each other. Thus is created a pure and clear atmosphere of thought, which the student also breathes, though in his case he only pursues a few sciences out of the multitude. He profits by an intellectual tradition, which is independent of particular teachers, which guides him in his choice of subjects, and duly interprets for him those which he chooses. He apprehends the great outlines of knowledge, the principles on which it rests, the scale of its parts, its lights and shades, its great points and its little, as he otherwise cannot apprehend them. Hence it is that his education is called 'Liberal.' A habit of mind is formed which lasts through life, of which the attributes are, freedom, equitableness, calmness, moderation, and wisdom. . . .

"To open the mind, to correct it, to refine it, to enable it to know, and to digest, master and rule, and use its knowledge, to give it power over its own faculties, application, flexibility, method, critical exactness, sagacity, resource, address, eloquent expression . . . is an object as intelligible as the cultivation of virtue, while, at the same time, it is absolutely distinct from it." [9]

Newman's lectures on the nature and scope of education were probably in the minds of many Parliament members during the debate on the bill for the reform of Oxford and Cambridge. When the 1854 act was passed, only administrative changes were legislated, without radically disturbing educational tradition: it lessened the autonomy of the colleges, it strengthened the professoriate, and abolished religious tests at matriculation.

A noteworthy minor change of the 1854 act permitted the professor of poetry to lecture in English instead of in the customary Latin. Hence, Matthew Arnold, the first incumbent after the reform, found his occasion to continue Newman's effort by em-

[9] *The Idea of a University*, Discourse v, Sect. 1.

ploying his powers to preserve Oxford's traditions in a time of uncertain transition. Himself stamped by Rugby and Balliol, and one of those whose spirit had been charmed by Newman, cherishing Oxford's beauty and memories, Matthew Arnold reminded his hearers of the magic of the place when encroaching Philistinism threatened extinction of its alluring traits. His *On Translating Homer, Essays in Criticism, First Series,* and *On Celtic Literature,* first delivered as Oxford lectures, were probably devised as "tracts for the times," illustrating Oxonian moods of urbanity and disinterestedness. His poems, "The Scholar Gypsy" and "Thyrsis," tenderly indicated his attachment to the dreaming spires and the happy leisure of his youth in the surrounding countryside. What he found worthy in literature, ancient and modern, were those qualities which had shaped his own mind and spirit in the Oxford of his youth: high seriousness, love of perfection, detachedness, reflectiveness. "She will forgive me, I know," he wrote, "if I have unwittingly drawn upon her a shaft aimed at her unworthy son. Queen of romance, there she lies, spreading her gardens in the moonlight, and whispering from her towers the last enchantments of the Middle Age."

His valedictory lecture (1868) became the first chapter of *Culture and Anarchy,* in which he communicated to English readers the saving grace of the Oxford spirit. The book was a penetrating survey of Philistine trends of the times, recommending attitudes and responses to offset too narrow effects of doing good. "There is a view," he wrote, "in which all the good of our neighbor, the impulses toward action, help, and beneficence, the desire for removing human error, clearing human confusion, and diminishing human misery, the noble aspiration to leave the world better and happier than we found it—motives eminently such as are called social—come as part of the grounds of culture, and the main and pre-eminent part. Culture is then properly described not as having its origin in curiosity but as having its origin in the love of perfection: it is a *study of perfection* . . . the aim of culture [is to set] ourselves to ascertain what perfection is and to make it prevail; but also, in determining generally in what perfection consists, religion comes to a conclusion identical with that which culture—culture seeking the determination of this question through *all* the voices of human experience which have been heard upon it, of art, science, poetry, philosophy, history, as well as of religion, in order to give a greater fullness and certainty to its solution—likewise reaches. Religion says: *The Kingdom of God is within you;* and culture, in like manner, places human perfection in an internal condition, in the growth and predominance of our humanity proper, as distinguished from our animality. . . . Not a having and a resting, but a growing and a becoming, is the character of perfection as culture conceives it; and here, too, it coincides with religion. . . . But, finally, perfection—as culture from a thorough, disinterested study of human nature and human experience learns to conceive it—is a harmonious expansion of *all* the powers which make the beauty and worth of human nature, and is not consistent with the over-development of any one power at the expense of the rest." [10]

Neither Newman nor Arnold excluded the study of natural phenomena from their ideal of rounded education, but they did resist attempts to make it central, to substitute it in place of the study of the dignity of man. The development of certain natural sciences—particularly of geology, biology, astronomy, mechanics, and heat—moved earnest educational improvers to demand inclusion of scientific studies in all educational levels from secondary schools to universities. Thomas Henry Huxley (1825-1895), the chief spokesman for scientific education, as principal speaker at the formal opening of Mason's College, Birmingham, overtly challenged Matthew Arnold's concept of culture in the address, "Science and Education." He asserted that "neither the discipline nor the subject matter of classical education is of such direct value to the student of physical science as to justify the expenditure of valuable time upon either"; and that "for the purpose of attaining real culture, an exclusively scientific education is at least as effectual as an exclusively literary education. . . . We cannot know all the best thoughts and sayings of the Greeks unless we know what they thought about natural phenomena. We cannot

---

[10] *Culture and Anarchy,* Chapter 1.

fully appreciate their criticism of life unless we understand the extent to which that criticism was affected by scientific conceptions. We falsely pretend to be the inheritors of that culture, unless we are penetrated, as the best minds among them were, with an unhesitating faith that the free employment of reason, in accordance with scientific method, is the sole method of reaching truth."

Yet Huxley conceded that scientific education was still "inchoate" and tentative and that he was "the last person to question the importance of genuine literary education or to suppose that intellectual culture can be completed without it. An exclusively scientific training will bring about a mental twist as surely as an exclusively literary training." Although apparently he debated the Arnoldian concept, he really was only extending it by a specific application in a particular situation. "Within these walls," he concluded, "the future employer and the future artisan may sojourn for a while, and carry, through all their lives, the stamp of influences then brought to bear on them. Hence, it is not beside the mark to remind you that the prosperity of industry depends not merely upon the improvement of manufacturing processes, not merely upon the ennobling of the individual character, but upon a third condition, namely, a clear understanding of the conditions of social life, on the part of both capitalist and the operative, and their agreement upon common principles of social action." Huxley's slighting reference to Arnold as one of the "Levites of Culture" prompted the latter's retort in one of his *Discourses in America*, "Literature and Science," in which, admitting some of Huxley's contentions, he insisted that Greek and Latin writers "have a fortifying, and elevating, and quickening, and suggestive power, capable of wonderfully helping us to relate the results of science to our need for conduct, our need for beauty. . . . And the more that men's minds are cleared, the more that the results of science are frankly accepted, the more that poetry and eloquence come to be received and studied as what in truth they really are—the criticism of life by gifted men, alive and active with extraordinary power at an unusual number of points—so much the more will the value of humane letters, and of art also, which is an utterance of life . . . be felt and acknowledged, and their place in education be secured."

This famous passage at arms had its background of action in the universities. During the decades of the seventies and eighties, both Oxford and Cambridge were fulfilling Newman's idea that "universities are the natural centers of intellectual movements." Oxford, in particular, continued as a theater of bold speculative discussion. Conflicting winds of doctrine met and modified each other: Rationalism, stimulated by John Stuart Mill's *Logic*,[11] Positivism, Hegelianism, Aestheticism, and Imperialism had each its champions. Fresh ideas freely circulated, creating an atmosphere in which classical authors were reinterpreted. The abolition of religious tests for fellows and tutors at Oxford, Cambridge, and Durham (1871), the beginning of Cambridge extramural teaching (1873), were preludes to the Universities Act of 1877. The founding of women's colleges in both old universities during the eighties, and generous scholarships awarded for academic merit, marked other signs of the influences of national thinking on Oxford and Cambridge.

Oxford's devotion to Aristotle as the chief organon of its intellectual discipline yielded to Benjamin Jowett's persistent crusade for the inclusion of Plato. This innovation, with the concomitant introduction of the study of Hegel, had immense effects upon the Oxford mind, tending towards greater pliancy, greater susceptibility to new causes. John Ruskin, brought back to Oxford as the first incumbent of the newly established Slade Professorship of Art (1870), vigorously exhorted his university audiences to their responsibilities in constructing a nobler England. For thirteen years (1871 to 1884) he expounded his ideals of beauty, of duty, and of comprehensive social and economic reconstruction. Scanning perilous horizons, he made his hearers keenly conscious of collisions of capital and labor, the rawness and threats of existing industrial England, and of the social coma of the masses. "Life without dignity is guilt," Ruskin urged, "and industry without art is brutality." During his Slade

---

[11] Frances W. Knickerbocker, *Free Minds: John Morley and His Friends* (Harvard University Press, 1943).

professorship, he tempered his burning denunciations with the comforting gospel of the holiness of work, when workmen, inspired by piety, loyalty, and noble aspiration, glorified God in their craftsmanship. He addressed himself to two audiences: to university students and (through a series of letters collected in *Fors Clavigera*) to workingmen throughout England. Back of all his books lies the mind of a teacher: as he became aware of imminent social disaster after his experience in 1848, his mind played increasingly on the urgency of the need of a right education. His thoughts on the subject were culled by William Jolly, an inspector of schools, who published them in *Ruskin on Education* (1894).

With William Morris, his chief disciple, Ruskin supplied Oxford and England with a new vision of society from which great national art would issue as the expression of inner, moral attitudes: of reverence, of humility, of joy in creative work. Though their social philosophy verged towards collectivism, its power lay in Christian motives. In practical efforts, they attempted to realize their ideas: Ruskin in his Guild of St. George, and Morris in his workshops. Ruskin's permanent memorial in Oxford is the workingman's college there which bears his name: it remains a symbol of the conjunction of two main lines of aspiration in the Victorian era, the instruction of working classes and the inculcation of culture.

VI

Victorian education thus became the arena of three rival forces: of anxiety concerning the unpredictable power of the restless lower classes which middle-class spokesmen believed might be alleviated by nationally diffused instruction; of the demand by workingmen themselves for higher education; and of militant resistance by old established institutions of learning to preserve their inherited concept of culture against encroachments by utilitarians, humanitarians, and economic adventurers. Within the area of controversy and movement, Victorians of all varieties matched their earnestness and energy, agreeing in the faith that education would accomplish a more adequate solution of economic and social tensions than reliance on any form of precipitate violence. In its more admirable forms, this faith expressed ideals of life in a society traditionally committed to the will for good in compulsions of necessity, when necessity was clearly demonstrated by exercise of reason in a condition of freedom. Crises like Chartism and the Reform Bills intensified the discussion, providing occasions for legislative action in solidifying advances in educational vision and practice. Impact of these forces not only raised the intellectual level of the populace but vastly widened the range of literary interest and diversified taste.

Humanists believed that education was incomplete if limited to the accumulation of miscellaneous facts, to appease curiosity, or to master a skill which earned one's daily bread. What gave true worth to education, they thought, was a spiritually directed idea which inspired a search for perfection in all phases of human need: an attitude to which they gave the name "culture." Truly defined, in the light of long experience, education is the process in which culture motivates and shapes the unceasing adjusting of the whole state of individuals and of society. It was aptly summarized by John Morley, statesman son of Oxford, who, addressing an audience of laborers at a mechanics institute, stated: "The great need in modern culture, which is scientific in method, rationalistic in spirit, and utilitarian in purpose, is to find some effective agency for cherishing within us the ideal. Literature alone will not make us good citizens; it will not make us a good man. History affords too many proofs that scholarship and learning by no means purge men of acrimony, of vanity, of arrogance, of a murderous tenacity about trifles. Nor would I pretend for a moment that literature can be any substitute for life and action. . . . It is life that is the great educator. But the parcel of books, if they are well chosen, reconcile us to this discipline, they interpret this virtue and this justice; they awaken within us the diviner mind, and rouse us to a consciousness of what is best in others and ourselves." [12]

In an effort to attain a satisfying mode of action for the democratic process, Victorians found education to be a clue to

---

[12] Morley, *Miscellanies,* Vol. I, "Books."

stabilizing divergent, and frequently conflicting, political and economic claims. It became, indeed, a medium of the era's main effort: to accommodate a conservative national mind to new conditions forced by new tensions in England, and by catastrophic events abroad, during a period in which she experienced a spectacular rise in international power through her commercial and industrial supremacy. But, by maintaining its lines of communication with its past, by restraining those who veered towards a complete abandonment to materialism, Victorian education developed the humanizing power of man in society through inculcating the idea of culture.

The Role of the Artist

E. D. H. JOHNSON

In 1940, when Hitler's armored divisions were overrunning Europe, the distinguished poet Archibald MacLeish issued a stern reprimand to American intellectuals for their failure to act in the crisis confronting western culture. His declaration, entitled *The Irresponsibles,* attributed this lack of serious commitment to the fact that scholars and imaginative writers had become divided into separate professions, each of which, engrossed in perfecting its special skills, had lost all concern for the general welfare of humanity. In contrast to the irresponsible attitude of his contemporaries, MacLeish evoked the concept of the artist's role which had prevailed during the nineteenth century:

A century ago the professions of the writer and the scholar were united in the single profession of the man of letters and the man of letters was responsible in everything that touched the mind. He was a man of wholeness of purpose, of singleness of intention—a single intellectual champion, admittedly responsible for the defense of the inherited tradition, avowedly partisan of its practice. . . . Whatever threatened learning or the ends of learning challenged the man of letters. Whatever struck at truth or closed off question or defiled an art or violated decency of thinking struck at him. And he struck back with every weapon masters of the word could find to strike with.[1]

---

[1] Archibald MacLeish, *The Irresponsibles: A Declaration* (New York, 1940), pp. 21–23.

From E. D. H. Johnson, ed., *The World of the Victorians* (New York: Charles Scribner's Sons, 1964), pp. 253–262.

There is hardly a major author of the early and mid-Victorian periods who does not qualify under MacLeish's definition of the man of letters. No Victorian writer influenced the thinking of his time more than Carlyle,[2] and none took a more exalted view of his profession. In 1840 when he was at the height of his fame, he delivered six popular lectures *On Heroes, Hero-Worship, and the Heroic in History*. Embodied in the title is the speaker's philosophy of history. "For, as I take it," he asserts,

Universal History . . . is at bottom the History of the Great Men who have worked here. They were the leaders of men, these great ones, the modellers, patterns, and in a wide sense creators, of whatsoever the general mass of men contrived to do or to attain; all things that we see standing accomplished in the world are properly the outer material result, the practical realisation and embodiment, of Thoughts that dwelt in the Great Men sent into the world: the soul of the whole world's history, it may justly be considered, were the history of these.

Among the different categories of heroes whom Carlyle discussed, including great religious and military leaders, lectures were devoted to "The Hero as Poet" (Dante and Shakespeare) and to "The Hero as Man of Letters" (Samuel Johnson, Rousseau, and Robert Burns).

For Carlyle, poet and prophet are equivalent terms. "The true Poet is ever, as of old," he declares, "the Seer; whose eye has been gifted to discern the godlike Mystery of God's Universe, and decipher some new lines of its celestial writing; we can still call him a *Vates* and Seer; for he *sees* into this greatest of secrets 'The open secret;' hidden things become clear; how the Future (both resting on Eternity) is but another phasis of the Present: thereby are his words in very truth prophetic; what he has spoken

---

[2] Of Carlyle's lifelong involvement in the problems of his age, John Morley, another eminent Victorian man of letters, wrote: "One of Mr. Carlyle's chief and just glories is, that for more than forty years he has clearly seen, and kept constantly and conspicuously in his own sight and that of his readers, the profoundly important crisis in the midst of which we are living. The moral and social dissolution in progress about us, and the enormous peril of sailing blindfold and haphazard, without rudder or compass or chart, have always been fully visible to him, and it is no fault of his that they have not become equally plain to his contemporaries. The policy of drifting has had no countenance from him."

shall be done." The attributes of the great writer are no different from those which denote the Carlylean hero in other fields of activity. In the first place, his powers of imagination give him inspired insight into ultimate truths. And this grasp of reality carries with it phenomenal intensity of moral commitment. The prophetic vision which he sees, he is in turn impelled to transmit to his age. As a recent study has demonstrated,[3] Carlyle was by no means the only Victorian writer who donned the prophet's mantle in addressing his audience. Nor was that audience reluctant to have its literary spokesmen assume this role. The historian W. E. H. Lecky remarked that men of letters had taken the place of "the clergy in the direction of the thought of England." "It is our lay writers," he says, "who are moulding the characters and forming the opinions of the age."

The life of almost any eminent Victorian could be cited to illustrate how seriously the artists of the period regarded their public responsibilities. Tennyson's early poems, for example, are the expression of a profoundly melancholy and introspective temperament, most at home in the private world of the imagination. While a student at Cambridge, however, Tennyson joined the "Apostles," an association of brilliant young scholars ardently interested in contemporary problems, much like the group, including Auden, Isherwood, and Spender, which appeared at Oxford exactly a century later. The dawning sense of mission which Tennyson took away from Cambridge can be traced through the lyrics of *In Memoriam*, which beginning as a personal lament grew into a manifesto of faith for Victorian England. Writing in 1894, two years after the laureate's death, James Anthony Froude, the historian and biographer of Carlyle, would say that Tennyson ranked alone beside Shakespeare, "with this relative superiority even to Shakespeare, that he speaks the thoughts and speaks *to* the perplexities and misgivings of his own age." A similar progression is observable in the fiction of Dickens, from *Pickwick*

---

[3] John Holloway, *The Victorian Sage: Studies in Argument* (London, 1953). The author analyzes the stylistic means through which certain representative "sages," including Carlyle, Newman, Disraeli, Matthew Arnold, and George Eliot, sought to communicate their messages to Victorian England.

Papers, conceived as pure entertainment, to the burning indignation against institutionalized morality which darkens the pages of the great later novels, such as *Bleak House* and *Little Dorrit.* Of Dickens' achievement in awakening the conscience of his times a Nonconformist preacher made the somber pronouncement: "There have been at work among us three great social agencies: the London City Mission; the novels of Mr. Dickens; the cholera."

But the ways in which the cultural crises of the nineteenth century determined the role of the artist in society can perhaps be best illustrated by a brief résumé of the careers of two of the most influential critics of the period: Ruskin and Arnold. Ruskin, the pampered son of wealthy parents, should by all rights have been a dilettante. When he began at the age of twenty-three to write art criticism, his immediate purpose was to defend the daringly impressionistic later style of the great English landscapist J. M. W. Turner. From this germ grew the five volumes of *Modern Painters* (1843–60), in which the author established the moral aesthetic to which his contemporaries so largely subscribed. In essence, Ruskin argued that the greatness of any work of art depends on its ethical significance, the extent to which it provides "noble grounds for noble emotions." Surface realism is not enough in itself, though it is important; in faithfully transcribing his perceptions, the artist must at the same time educe the ideal truth and beauty which inhere in all phenomena. Ruskin was calling for a fusion of realism and symbolism, such as he thought he recognized in the primitivistic school of Pre-Raphaelite painters, which emerged at the mid-century. A member of this group, George Frederick Watts, spoke of his aims in terms which Ruskin would have fully endorsed: "My intention had been not so much to paint pictures that charm the eye as to suggest great thoughts that will appeal to the imagination and the heart, and kindle all that is noblest and best in humanity."

With this approach to art, it was inevitable that Ruskin should in time turn from painting to architecture. As a moral discipline painting is of limited validity. A picture is the product of a single highly trained talent; and in a period when art galleries were scarce and before modern techniques of reproduction had been

developed, there was little opportunity for the populace to benefit from the work of painters and sculptors. Structures such as
churches, railroad stations, and post offices, on the other hand,
unite many workmen in a communal endeavor; they also serve
public purposes and must be erected with these uses in mind.
Again, however, just as in his response to painting, Ruskin examined architectural styles primarily for the moral values they exhibited. "Every form of noble architecture," he wrote (and he
was among the first to perceive this), "is in some way an embodiment of the Polity, Life, History, and Religious Faith of nations."
The principles of social cohesion and corporate responsibility
which Ruskin missed in Victorian society, he found most perfectly exemplified in the hierarchic structure of the mediaeval
world, where it was symbolically configured in Gothic church-
building; and through *The Seven Lamps of Architecture* (1849)
and *The Stones of Venice* (1851–53), he lent his vast personal
prestige to fostering the revival of that style. That the principal
architect of Victorian Gothic, Augustus Welby Pugin, shared
Ruskin's vision is apparent from his statement: "The mechanical
part of Gothic architecture is pretty well understood, but it is the
principles which influenced ancient composition and the soul
which appears in all former works, which is so lamentably deficient, nor . . . can anything be regained but by a restoration
of the ancient feelings and sentiments."

Despite the frequent incisiveness of his critical judgments,
Ruskin had all along, of course, been putting the cart before the
horse in recommending art as an agent of social regeneration.
The cultural climate of the Middle Ages produced Gothic architecture, not the reverse. The newly rich middle classes might
purchase the paintings and erect the kind of buildings that
Ruskin praised, but beneath the veneer of culture their commercial attitudes remained unaltered. In time Ruskin came to realize
this; here is his saddened admission on the eve of a change in
residence:

I have had an indirect influence on nearly every cheap villa-builder
between this and Bromley; and there is scarcely a public house near
the Crystal Palace but sells its gin and bitters under pseudo-Venetian
capitals copied from the Church of the Madonna of Health or of

Miracles. And one of my principal notions for leaving my present house is that it is surrounded everywhere by the accursed Frankenstein monsters of, indirectly, my own making.

With the publication of *Unto This Last* in 1862, therefore, Ruskin took up the work of social reform which at incalculable cost to his reputation was henceforth to enlist his best energies. "You will never love art well," he now proclaimed to his age, "till you love what she mirrors better," and

The beginning of all ideal art must be for us in the realistic art of bestowing health and happiness. The first schools of beauty must be the streets of your cities, and the chief of fair designs must be to keep the living creatures round us clean, and in human comfort.

Just as Ruskin's career as man of letters expanded through three successive phases, Arnold's literary life presents no fewer than four aspects, exclusive of his vocation as inspector of government schools. Along with Tennyson and Browning, he forms the triumvirate of great Victorian poets; but he suffered under the sense of a hostile *Zeitgeist*, convinced that the spirit of the times was unpropitious for artistic creativity. As a result, he had virtually abandoned imaginative writing when he became Professor of Poetry at Oxford in 1857; and in the following years he devoted himself to the literary studies in which are revealed the finest critical intelligence of the age. In essay after essay, many to be gathered in the two series of *Essays in Criticism* (1865 and 1888), he passed authoritative judgment on an astonishing range of authors from all periods and in many languages. As a critic, Arnold shared Ruskin's moral preoccupations. Literature must offer a "criticism of life"; not until modern writers, drawing on the best that had been thought and said in the world, were again prepared to make "noble and profound application of ideas to life" would they be worthy of their high calling. "Modern poetry," he wrote in a letter to his friend, the poet Arthur Hugh Clough, "can only subsist by its *contents:* by becoming a complete *magister vitae* [guide to life] as the poetry of the ancients did: by including as theirs did, religion with poetry, instead of existing as poetry only. . . ."

Like Ruskin, however, Arnold moved on to social criticism

out of the conviction that the loss of artistic vitality in his period was indicative of more deep-seated maladjustments, and that in confining his attention to literature he had been treating symptoms rather than the malady itself. In *Culture and Anarcy* (1869) he subjected Victorian society to an extraordinarily subtle analysis, showing how loss of contact with the great sustaining traditions of western civilization had materialized and vulgarized English habits of mind and ways of life. As a panacea for the anarchy into which the period was drifting, he proposed the ideal of culture. The terms of Arnold's definition of what he means by culture in the Preface to his work clearly suggest the relationship between his social theories and the literary criticism of which they were the logical outgrowth:

The whole scope of the essay is to recommend culture as the great help out of our present difficulties; culture being a pursuit of our total perfection by means of getting to know, on all the matters which most concern us, the best which has been thought and said in the world; and through this knowledge, turning a stream of fresh and free thought upon our stock notions and habits, which we now follow staunchly but mechanically, vainly imagining that there is a virtue in following them staunchly which makes up for the mischief of following them mechanically.

Under existing conditions only a privileged minority could aspire to the intellectual enlightenment which for Arnold was the hallmark of culture; and as he came to realize, its guardians would at best form a small, though influential, elite. His concern for the cultural well-being of society at large led him in due course to propose a more accessible ideal, summarized in the statement: "Religion must provide for the many the guidance literature provides for the few." In the religious writings which now followed, of which *Literature and Dogma* (1873) is the most memorable, Arnold's consistent purpose was to recommend that the Bible, when read as literature rather than as a work of divine revelation, is still the one sure sanction for man's moral nature and the source from which he can best derive satisfaction of his spiritual needs.

The alert student of Victorian life and letters cannot fail to perceive after the mid-century a change in literary climate, symptomatic of a radical shift in aesthetic sensibility. The later writings of nearly all the authors hitherto discussed are gloomy in tendency; their tone is shriller and more petulant; the reader's impression is of deepening disillusionment with the signs of the times. The Victorian prophets, he concludes, had discovered that they were without honor in their country, that they were voices crying in the wilderness of a soulless age that refused to heed their message. At the same time there appears on the scene a new type of artist, altogether different from the typical Victorian man of letters. The poet and painter Dante Gabriel Rossetti may stand for this type. He had early disassociated himself from the original Pre-Raphaelite Brotherhood, whose artistic goals Ruskin sponsored, and gathered around himself a group of younger men who were unfeignedly estranged from the society of their day. To Rossetti it was simply inconceivable that the professional artist should feel any sense of social responsibility. His resistance to such commitment was in the cause of a higher obligation, what Henry James called "the terrible law of the artist—the law of acceptance of *all* experience, of *all* life, of *all* suggestion and sensation and illumination."

Rossetti, however, no controversialist, asked only to be allowed to go his own way, seeking full and uninhibited self-expression in his dreamlike poems and paintings. The role of champion for what became known as "art for art's sake" devolved upon another poet, Algernon Charles Swinburne. Fiery and aggresive by temperament, Swinburne took up the cudgels over the hostile reception of his *Poems and Ballads* (1866), a collection of poems, exquisitely wrought, but outspokenly licentious and blasphemous in theme. In conducting his own defense with consummate boldness and skill, he followed the lead of the great French poet Charles Baudelaire, whose aesthetic theories were an expansion of ideas first expressed by Edgar Allen Poe in "The Poetic Principle" (1848). The modern artist, according to Baudelaire, is menaced by the "heresy of didacticism": "if the poet has set himself a moral goal, he has diminished his poetic force; and it's not a bad bet that his work will be bad. Poetry cannot, under pain of death and failure, associate itself with knowledge or morality; its object is not truth, its object is itself." This was to be the position of Swinburne and of the generation of artistic rebels for whom he spoke. "Art for art's sake first of all," he wrote in his pioneer study of William Blake (1868), "and afterwards we may suppose the rest shall be added (or if not she need hardly be overmuch concerned), but from the man who falls to artistic work with a moral purpose shall be taken away even that which he has— whatever capacity for doing well in either way he may have had at starting."

It remained for a shy Oxford don, Walter Pater, to formulate the theoretical principles of art for art's sake and to assume leadership of the so-called Aesthetic Movement. Distrustful of all absolutes in an age which was discrediting one traditionally received truth after another, Pater based his philosophy on the belief that the mind like all else is in a perpetual state of flux and can know nothing beyond the fleeting impressions which constantly stream through the human consciousness. The fine art of living is to respond to each passing moment with the greatest possible intensity. For Pater the supreme value of art is that through its means this fullness of response is made possible:

For our one chance lies in expanding that interval, in getting as many pulsations as possible into the given time. Great passions may give us this quickened sense of life, ecstasy and sorrow of love, the various forms of enthusiastic activity, disinterested or otherwise, which come naturally to many of us. Only be sure it is passion—that it does yield you this fruit of a quickened, multiplied consciousness. Of such wisdom the poetic passion, the desire of beauty, the love of art for its own sake, has most. For art comes to you proposing frankly to give nothing but the highest quality to your moments as they pass, and simply for those moments' sake.

The artist can know only his own response to any given experience; but the effort to impose form on that experience is his way of arresting the flux, of capturing and perpetuating in ideal aspect one of its manifestations. As Rossetti had written in the introductory poem to his sonnet cycle, *The House of Life:*

> A sonnet is a moment's monument,
> Memorial from the Soul's eternity
> To one dead deathless hour . . . .

In Pater's own words, the artist strives "to realize the unity in variety, to discover *cosmos*—an order that shall satisfy one's reasonable soul—below and within *chaos*." Here is the true meaning of the creative impulse, as it seeks to express itself in works of art that shall be autonomous, a law unto themselves, and enlisting to that end the creator's single-minded allegiance.

From the first Pater had had misgivings lest his young disciples pervert the doctrine to which his own devotion was so austere and pure; lest, for example, his sense of the importance of making refined discriminations between sensations be construed as an invitation to indiscriminate sensationalism. There was the very real danger that some would be attracted by his teachings for the wrong reasons, and that these would be all too inclined to turn, as he phrased it, to "art, or science, to the experience of life itself, not as to portions of human nature's daily food, but as to something that must be, by the circumstances of the case, exceptional; almost as men turn in despair to gambling or narcotics, and in a little while the narcotic, the game of chance or skill, is valued for its own sake. The vocation of the artist, of the student of life or books, will be realized with something—say! of fanaticism, as an end in itself, unrelated, unassociated." And, indeed, certain morbid tendencies within the Aesthetic Movement did come to the surface, so that in its later phase it became known as the Decadent Movement. During his brief heyday Oscar Wilde was the center of a later generation of aesthetes who, like the protagonist of his novel *The Picture of Dorian Gray* (1891), professed "a new Hedonism"

that was to recreate life, and to save it from that harsh, uncomely Puritanism that is having, in our own day, its curious revival. It was to have its service of the intellect, certainly; yet, it was never to accept any theory or system that would involve the sacrifice of any mode of passionate experience. Its aim, indeed, was to be experience itself, and not the fruits of experience, sweet or bitter as they might be. Of the asceticism that deadens the senses, as of the vulgar profligacy that dulls them, it was to know nothing. But it was to teach each man to concentrate himself upon the moments of a life that is itself but a moment.

The worst excesses of aestheticism came to an end with the Wilde trial in 1895, by which time writers like Henry James,

Joseph Conrad, and William Butler Yeats had assimilated the elements of enduring value in the doctrine of art for art's sake. Meanwhile, of course, the opposing doctrine of art for society's sake had never really been in eclipse, but had continued to find its advocates, whether among socialists such as William Morris and Bernard Shaw, or among popular story-tellers and poets like Rudyard Kipling, who helped to fan the imperialist spirit in late Victorian England. . . .

The Development
of the Historical Mind

RICHARD A. E. BROOKS

A vivid measure of the popularity of history in Victorian England can be found in the check for £20,000 written by Longmans to Macaulay for royalties on the third and fourth volumes of his *History of England* eleven weeks after their publication.[1] A less vivid but perhaps more significant measure is found in the development of the schools of modern history at Oxford and Cambridge from their humble status in 1800 to being the most popular schools today, for Macaulay was a statesman and man of letters and the present schools are the training grounds for professional historians.

But these schools may perhaps also represent other values accorded to history. A. L. Rowse, Fellow of All Souls College, Oxford, states that "history is of the utmost importance at the universities, as a preparation for the teaching profession, the Civil Service, our political leadership in its highest sense, leaders of the press and public opinion, no less than for politicians. A knowledge of history is indispensable to the higher direction of

---

[1] Sir Charles Firth, *A Commentary on Macaulay's History of England* (London, 1933), p. 13. Sir Charles does not make clear that the sum did not wholly represent accrued royalties. I am reliably informed that it was partially advanced royalties.

From Joseph E. Baker, ed., *The Reinterpretation of Victorian Literature* (Princeton: Princeton University Press, 1950), pp. 130–152.

society; that is why it is especially important in higher education, and the higher up the more important." [2] He goes on to say that "The truth is that without the sense of human history life as we know it would be unthinkable; history is as fundamental to our lives as that. It is only through a knowledge of history that our own brief lives—such a short span of experience—become one with the record of the human race; it is only through history that we can know anything of the record and can share it. The life of the individual breaks its barriers and becomes coterminous with humanity. Bound as our lives are to the tyranny of time, it is through what we know of history that we are delivered from our bonds and escape—into time." [3]

While it might be remarked that in earlier times literature and the scriptures helped to hand on the story of the past and to make man a trifle less lonely in the present, it is obvious that today history, like many other human activities, has become a specialized study and that it holds an important place in modern consciousness. As M. R. Cohen has said, "the extension of the scope of history throughout the nineteenth century was one of the major events in the intellectual life of Europe." [4]

There had been great historians even before the eighteenth century; and that century itself had its great historians, saw history become interesting to a wider public, and handed on to its successor more skillful methods of historical study than it had inherited. But the more rigorous methods of examining historical documents which the nineteenth century developed and the wider variety of objects and fields of human activity which came within the province of the historian as evidence of man's past, gave a remarkable stimulus to the writing of history and to the public's interest in it. At the same time, too, there were other factors which played—as cause, as effect, and as interacting cause-and-effect—on the study and use of history to produce important results in many phases of European life; and not the least interesting are those on English literature, criticism, and scholarship.

---

[2] *The Use of History* (New York, 1948), p. 18.
[3] *Ibid.*, p. 30.
[4] *The Meaning of Human History* (La Salle, Illinois, 1947), p. 14.

Thus, though England did not enjoy that hegemony in historiography in the nineteenth century which she did in industry and politics, one might consider some of the interrelationships between history and English literature while being mainly concerned with the latter. At the beginning of our century, it would have required temerity for a student of literature to make such an attempt; but contemporary criticism of the theories of history—which, gaining momentum in Germany toward the end of the last century, has recently engaged the attention of English and American philosophers and historians—rather emboldens one to try. Let us briefly narrate part of the sequence of events in the writing of history in the nineteenth century, especially as this relates to the contention between the professional historians and men of letters who wrote histories; stating some of the happenings in the area common to historiography and literature, especially as this area became increasingly accessible to an ever larger public in the middle and lower classes, with no invidious connotation attached to "middle class" and "lower class"; pointing out possible studies which might gain from such a consideration; and evaluating some of the gains and losses in the study of English caused or occasioned by the spread of historical awareness and by the nineteenth century's concept and development of the historical method. If my own ignorances had not limited me to English literature and historiography, the profuse, rich, and complex growth of European historiography and literature would have done so. Lastly, it ought to be said that this is written from a point of view (maybe it would be more correct to say bias) that is tentative and can perhaps be described as that of a humanist who is interested in science.

II

G. P. Gooch's *History and Historians in the Nineteenth Century* makes unnecessary here an extensive retelling of the development of Victorian historiography. And while later historical thinking has given different significances to this development, none can deny the growth of English historical scholarship, even while admitting that the universities were tardy in recognizing the significance of contemporary German historical scholarship.

Without belittling the great influence of Gibbon, Hume, and
Robertson, it can rightly be said that the Romantic movement
gave a strong impetus to interest in history in England and on
the continent in the first half of the century and that the most
important figure in this respect is Sir Walter Scott. If Thomas
Carlyle disparaged the historical value of the Waverley novels,
and if Carlyle's contemporary, Leopold von Ranke, said that the
differences between Commines and *Quentin Durward* led him
to become a historian, Scott most deeply affected the mind of
the French historian, Augustin Thierry, who as a boy had had
his imagination fired by Chateaubriand.[5] (Gooch says that in
France in 1802 Chateaubriand's *La Génie du Christianisme* was
"an event in politics and religion, in historiography and literature." [6]) The antiquarianism associated with the Romantic movement in England and Germany paved the way to the reading
public. The Romantic movement produced romantic historiography in England—that is, history written usually by men of
letters who, though they did much research in preparation for
their work, were unacquainted with the newer methods of scru-
tinizing historical evidence and who wrote histories with dramatic narratives, which bore a strong impress of the author's
philosophy, and which espoused causes. Carlyle, Macaulay, and
Froude are the outstanding historians of this type, historians
whom Gooch calls amateurs and Trevelyan literary historians;
and J. R. Green's *A Short History of the English People* can be
termed the finest single volume. Of this book Gooch writes:
"The publication of the 'Short History' in 1874 forms an epoch
in historiography. The English-speaking world received the
first coherent and intelligible account of its own past. The hero
of the book was the people. . . . Dynasties come and go, battles are won and lost, but the people remain. . . . His work possesses the living interest of a biography and the dramatic unity

---

[5] Gooch, *History and Historians in the Nineteenth Century* (London,
Toronto, and New York, 1935), pp. 170–171. The gist of the book, which
was first published in 1913, is to be found in Gooch's "The Growth of
Historical Science," *Cambridge Modern History* (Cambridge, 1910), xii,
816–850.

[6] *Ibid.*, p. 162.

of an epic. . . . Hundreds of thousands of all ages became for the first time intelligently interested in the history of their own country." [7] Green, however, might be called a beneficiary of the scientific school of historiography if he is not considered a happy fusion of both schools. He has been described as a "picturesque historian"; and though he was not a professional historian—he was a clergyman and, after his health failed, librarian at Lambeth—he was intimate with the professional historians at Oxford, where Stubbs was his great admirer.

The scientific method of studying history developed and flourished in Germany in the first half of the nineteenth century. Its pioneer was the philologist Niebuhr, who "raised history from a subordinate position to the dignity of an independent science." [8] The examination of historical evidence became progressively more rigorous, and the historian aimed at complete objectivity in the treatment of his material. (Ranke's phrase, *wie es eigentlich gewesen ist*—"as it actually happened," is a convenient and often quoted summary of this aim.) Philology provided the key to many locked rooms of man's recorded past, and it made brighter many rooms heretofore dimly lighted. Political history, which in its turn had been an advance over the compiling of annals, was augmented by legal, institutional, social, and cultural history; and through systematic study evidence of man's past was wrested from language, myth, archives, coins, inscriptions, and archaeological excavations. Germany produced a succession of brilliant historians, of whom the century considered Ranke and Mommsen the giants and to whom went to school the historians of France, the United States, and, somewhat belatedly in the latter half of the century, England. Giving powerful support to this historical method and its authority with the public was the work of the geologists—who vastly altered western man's temporal horizons—and of the biologists. (Darwin's work only set the keystone in the evolutionary thinking of his predecessors, and through Huxley it reached a greater audience than the scientists and philosophers had.) As the consciousness of history became more widespread and the historical method became more gener-

---

[7] *Ibid.*, pp. 354–355.   [8] *Ibid.*, p. 14.

ally used, the study of history became a more popular but more specialized study at the universities, and the writers of histories began to be almost exclusively university professors. The indisputable achievement of greater objectivity did not, however, free the professional historians from bias: nationalism, for instance, appears in English, French, and German histories. Finally, as the century drew to a close, the professional historian was the recognized superior of the amateur, but his writings were less and less read by the general reader. Trevelyan comments on the situation thus: "What was wrong with the historical reaction at the end of Victoria's reign, was not the positive stress it laid on the need for scientific method in weighing evidence, but its negative repudiation of the literary art, which was declared to have nothing whatever to do with the historian's task." [9] And Rowse, perhaps with his eye more on contemporary developments of the same situation, says, "Of course, all this [the insistence that history is a science] made history much more difficult to write—at any rate, well—and much less interesting to read. On the other hand, since this point of view attached little importance to literary quality, it meant a great increase in the amount of history books turned out by people who did not know how to write. Never was there such a quantity of raw hunks of historical research, malformed, undigested, indigestible, as poured forth from the presses." [10]

For a variety of reasons the "literary" historians held sway longer in England than they did on the continent, but they did more to stimulate interest in history than did their European confreres. (Gooch says, that, except for Macaulay, no one during the first half of the century had "given such an impetus to historical study as Carlyle." [11]) Unquestionably, one reason for this is that they wrote well, yet the professional historian's slow rise to preeminence was due in the main to the state of the study of modern history at Oxford and Cambridge. The Regius chairs of modern history at these universities were established in 1724;

---

[9] G. M. Trevelyan, *History and the Reader* (London, 1945), p. 11.

[10] *Op. cit.*, pp. 87–88.

[11] *Op. cit.*, p. 323.

but "at Oxford in 1850, out of 1500 or 1600 students, the average attendance at the modern history course was eight." [12] Cambridge, which by the end of the century became the center of modern historical study in England, fared somewhat better. John Symonds was the first occupant of the Cambridge chair to discharge his duties (1778); and Seely, appointed in 1868, produced "the first important historical work written by a holder of the Cambridge Chair" and was "the first scholar of front rank to hold the post, and the first to realize the immense significance of German scholarship." [13] Besides, "the union of Church and State in England and the establishment of the Regius professorships to be filled by appointees of the Crown . . . [gave] rise to a very real cause of dissatisfaction among" the historians.[14] A novelist, poet, and clergyman, Kingsley could be professor of modern history at Cambridge; Stubbs, whose chief interests before being appointed Regius professor of modern history at Oxford had been medieval history and who had earlier been passed over for that chair because of his religious views, left his chair to become Bishop of Chester; and, lastly, each university preferred to appoint one of its own men. The English distrust of specialization has its weaknesses as well as its strengths. The appointment of Acton to the chair of modern history at Cambridge in 1895 marked the accomplishment of a change, for he was not only a distinguished historian but a Roman Catholic.

The star of the "literary" historian apparently set with the bitter controversy over Froude's *History of England from 1529 to the Death of Elizabeth,* in which the professional historian Freeman led the attack. Though Stubbs, who had found fault with some of Froude's work as a historian, had praised its strong

---

[12] J. W. Adamson, "Education," *Cambridge History of English Literature* (Cambridge and New York, 1917), xiv, 464.

[13] Gooch, *Studies in Modern History* (London, Toronto, and New York, 1931), p. 313 *et passim.*

[14] L. M. Salmon, *Why Is History Rewritten?* (New York, 1929), p. 118. Pages 118–123, from which the data of the next sentence were taken, give a full account of these difficulties. Miss Salmon's chapter on historiography in England is worth attention.

points in 1876, and though Trevelyan had taken up the cudgels for Carlyle in 1899,[15] the educated public came to think that the field was indisputably the scientific historian's. A succeeding generation of historians has begun to revise this view; and it is interesting to note that R. G. Collingwood, A. L. Rowse, and M. R. Cohen, who do not share the same philosophy of history, all three speak well of Macaulay, Carlyle, and Froude. This does not mean, however, that students of literature are barred from further work on these "literary" historians. For example, though Carlyle has fared better than most of them, it has recently been pointed out by a critic that he needs even closer scrutiny than the latest scholarship has given to his writing of history.[16] Froude and Macaulay await further treatment; Lytton Strachey's chapters on Froude and Macaulay in *Portraits in Miniature* and Professor Bald's article on Froude in *The Nineteenth Century and After* do not seem to me to have exhausted the field. Lytton Strachey, however, illustrates some of the pitfalls for one who would undertake new estimates. A beneficiary of the Cambridge school of scientific history, he had a strong Edwardian bias against the Victorians. And there is truth, I think, in Leonard Bacon's observation that "Strachey was really a novelist *manqué* and belongs in Thackeray's street—by no means in Gibbon's." [17]

III

Besides the work of the "literary" and the professional historians in spreading an awareness of the past in Victorian England there were the historical societies, the historical study of literature, the museums, historical painting, and historical novels. The value of these as factors in the writing of social history has been amply proved by contemporary historians' use of them; what concerns us here is their bearing on literary scholarship and appreciation.

---

[15] Salmon, *op. cit.*, p. 110, n. 1, gives Stubbs's words. Trevelyan's defense of Carlyle is his "Carlyle as an Historian," *Nineteenth Century,* XLVI (1899), 493–503.

[16] René Wellek, "Carlyle and the Philosophy of History," *Philological Quarterly,* XXIII (1944), 55–76.

[17] "An Eminent Post-Victorian," *Yale Review,* XXX (1941–42), 324.

Since Elizabethan times there had been antiquarian and learned societies in England, but the second quarter of the nineteenth century witnessed an unparalleled flowering of historical societies which was characteristic of the Victorian period. The revival of interest in the medieval which the Romantics helped to create made Englishmen even more conscious than eighteenth-century scholars had been that much of Anglo-Saxon and Middle English literature was still unavailable; and it also produced a wave of bibliomania. These two forces joined with the renewed interest in history to bring into existence what R. H. Steeves [18] has called book clubs and general publishing societies, whose aims and scope testify to the widening concept of the historical. From the Roxburghe Club, an exclusive society for the publication of very limited editions of old English literature, evolved such societies as the Camden, Chetham, English Historical, Hakluyt, Parker, and Surtees which were less exclusive and dilettante than their prototype. Concerned with publishing pre-seventeenth century material bearing on civil and ecclesiastical as well as literary history, they made available a substantial body of Old and Middle English literature—among which were the *Towneley Mysteries,* Bishop Bale's *King John,* and the *Ancren Riwle.* At the same time arose philological and text societies particularly concerned with English literature considered from a scholarly and historical point of view. Though most of these sprang up in the forties, there is evident in them after Furnival established the Early English Text Society in 1864 a wholly new scholarly tradition which was largely derived from Germany. They became indispensable to contemporary scholarship, and with them were associated most of the famous Victorian scholars of English.

These societies, however, reflect the growth of the historical mind among the educated. Other developments show a diffusion of a sense of the past among the middle and lower-middle classes, and they enable one to measure it. The most conspicuous element in this connection is the amazing increase of literacy in

[18] *Learned Societies and English Literary Scholarship* (New York, 1913), p. 98. For the material of this paragraph I am greatly indebted to pages 98–203 of Steeves's book.

England during the century. The product of many complex forces, this increase was affected by mechanical developments. As an Irish literary historian noted in 1878:"The influence of the great change—the substitution of the steam *printing-press* for the hand-worked *printing-press*—has been felt in every corner of the land, where a cheap book or penny newspaper has found its way." [19] Cheap books began appearing in 1823 when "several London booksellers . . . commenced the publication of cheap weekly sheets, either containing portions of some standard book; or a series of miscellaneous literary articles, chiefly extracted from other works." [20] This led not only to Brougham's Society for the Diffusion of Useful Knowledge but also (through the practice of competition, which was as common among publishers as among mill owners) to the *Penny Magazine*, whose circulation of over 50,000 opened up the field of magazine publishing.[21] Among the cheap books were selections from English literature of which perhaps the best known was Robert Chambers' *Cyclopædia of English Literature*, which first appeared in 1844. On a far higher artistic level and even more famous is Palgrave's *Golden Treasury*, which "exercised a decisive influence from its publication" in 1861.

Histories of literature began appearing in ever greater numbers for increasingly wide and diverse audiences, which ranged from university students to those in mechanics' institutions. Professor Wellek's *The Rise of English Literary History* treats that subject up to the end of the eighteenth century. Of Thomas Warton, who is the culminating figure of the study, Wellek writes on page 201, "All the major problems of nineteenth-century literary history were formulated by Warton, even if his

---

[19] W. F. Collier, *A History of English Literature* (London, 1878), p. 440. Collier is quoting J. Hamilton Fyfe's *Triumphs of Invention and Discovery* (from a passage which describes the printing of *The Times* in 1872).

[20] Robert Chambers, *History of the English Language and Literature* (Edinburgh, 1837; 4th ed.), pp. 269–270. First published in 1836, this is the first history to deal with all types of English literature and to be concerned solely with them.

[21] Chambers, pp. 269–270, has an account of the history of cheap books from 1823 to 1835. He says (p. 270) that *Constable's Miscellany*, which started publication in 1826, was "the first work actually to be published in which original literature was made to depend for remuneration on a multitude of purchasers attracted by cheapness."

superstructure of ideas did not always properly control his materials." In a critique of literary history [22] Wellek has briefly com-
mented on some of the major nineteenth-century writers of
literary history; and he has pointed out, quite correctly, that
some of these writers treated "literature as mere document for
the illustration of national and social history" and that others,
though recognizing that literature is first and foremost an art,
"seem to be unable to write history." [23] Though, with the excep-
tion of J. A. Symonds, their use of the evolutionary concept was
of dubious value, by the seventies they had—thanks to the labors
of their predecessors—treated the full range of English literature.
Certainly Arber was exaggerating when, in the preface to the
first volume of *An English Garner* (1877), he wrote that "few of
us adequately realize the immense literature which has de-
scended from our ancestors." The histories aimed at large publics
stress the pictorial aspects of the past; the more scholarly are
organized around one or more ideas (Taine's history is a good
example); and there is a development, parallel with that in historiography, from the romantic to the scientific.[24] One does not
hear again the note struck in 1835 by Chateaubriand in the
preface to his *Sketches of English Literature:*

In this Review of English Literature I have treated at considerable
length of Milton, because it was written expressly on account of the
Paradise Lost. I analyse his different works, I show that revolutions
have approximated Milton to us; that he is become a man of our
times. . . .
I ought to premise that in this Historical View I have not stuck
close to my subject. I have treated of everything—the present, the
past, the future; I digress hither and thither. When I meet with the
middle ages, I talk of them; when I run foul of the reformation, I
dwell upon it; when I come to the English revolution, it reminds me
of our own, and I advert to the actors and events of the latter. If an

[22] René Wellek, "Literary History" in *Literary Scholarship: Its Aims and
Methods* (Chapel Hill, 1941), pp. 91–130. It is a pleasure to express my
gratitude for Professor Wellek's help and generosity, which is all the more
appreciated since he is working on a further study of Victorian literary
history that will bring his study down through Hallam.
[23] *Ibid.*, p. 116.
[24] Cf. Norman Foerster, "The Study of Letters," *Literary Scholarship: Its
Aims and Methods,* p. 9.

English royalist is thrown into jail, I think of the cell which I occupied at the prefecture of police. The English poets lead me to the French poets; Lord Byron brings to my recollection my exile in England, my walks at Harrow on the Hill, and my travels to Venice—and so the rest of the book.

Only rarely does one encounter such blatant moralizing as one finds in Chambers' *Cyclopædia of English Literature* (aimed at a middle-class audience) in this comment on Theodore Hook: "He obtained the distinction he coveted, in the notice and favour of the great and fashionable world; for this he sacrificed the fruits of his industry and the independence of genius; he lived in a round of distraction and gaiety, illuminated by his wit and talents, and he died a premature death, the victim of disappointment, debt, and misery. This personal account is the true 'handwriting on the wall,' to warn genius and integrity in the middle classes against hunting after or copying the vices of fashionable dissipation and splendour." [25]

Related to the increase of literacy and literary history is the teaching of English, which became more and more historical in approach. English became an important subject in the curriculum of nonconformist academies in the eighteenth century,[26] and after 1858 was increasingly important in the growing secondary schools.[27] From the early days of Oxford and Cambridge, rhetoric had treated literature, albeit mainly the classics; Sir Henry Spelman established the first lectureship in Anglo-Saxon at Cambridge in 1623; [28] and poetry and Anglo-Saxon were given chairs at Oxford in the eighteenth century; [29] but English did not become a pass subject at Oxford until 1873 and an honours one

[25] Chambers, *Cyclopædia* (Edinburgh, 1844), II, 534.

[26] Stephen Potter, *The Muse in Chains* (London, 1937), p. 108.

[27] The Cambridge Local Examinations, instituted in 1858, made English a major subject to "provide an adequate test and stimulus for schools which lie between the great Public Schools and the National schools, and to raise their standard of instruction" (J. B. Mullinger, *A History of the University of Cambridge*, London, 1888, p. 214).

[28] Wellek, *The Rise of English Literary History*, p. 22. The lectureship lapsed on the death of the first incumbent, Abraham Wheelock, in 1653. (*D. N. B.*, xx, 1354.)

[29] The Chair of Poetry was established in 1708 (*D. N. B.*, article on Henry Birkhead). The Rawlinson Chair of Anglo-Saxon was established in 1795 (C. E. Mallet, *A History of the University of Oxford*, London, 1927,

until 1893.[30] The universities and colleges in Scotland and Ireland and London University were ahead of Oxford and Cambridge in this respect.[31] The influence of the scientific approach in scholarship associated with Germany became evident in the increased study of philology.[32] Whether the increased teaching of English tended, as the decades passed, to create a finer or more general appreciation of English literature in England is, however, questionable.[33]

Museums and picture galleries played a larger part in diffusing a sense of the past among the urban middle and lower-middle classes than is generally realized. Outside of London, these classes usually had little to stimulate their consciousness of the past visually. There was not the royal and municipal pageantry which is the delight of Londoners; the collections of art which the aristocracy and the wealthy had acquired mostly in the eighteenth century were, even in London, rarely open to the public

---

III, 127). It is worth noting here that Matthew Arnold was the first holder of the Chair of Poetry at Oxford to deliver his lectures in English, and that he held the chair from 1857 to 1867.

[30] Mallet, III, 453–454. At Cambridge the first examination for the Medieval and Modern Language Tripos was held in 1886 (Mullinger, *op. cit.*, p. 209). Cf. also Sir John Firth, *Modern Language at Oxford* (London, 1929).

[31] Chairs of history and English literature were established at the three Queen's Colleges in Ireland (at Belfast, Cork, and Galway) from their founding in 1845. The Chair of English at Trinity College, Dublin, was created in 1867; that of English Language and Literature at Glasgow, in 1861. The Merton Professorship of English Language and Literature at Oxford was established in 1885. Even at London, where English "occupied from the first [1836?] an important place in the examination, . . . except for the Quain Chair there was until recently [1920] a comparatively small provision of teaching posts in English." *The Teaching of English in England* (London, 1921), pp. 243–45.

[32] Potter, p. 172. Cf. also Raymond W. Chambers, *Concerning Certain Great Teachers of the English Language* (London, 1923) and *Man's Unconquerable Mind* (London, Toronto, and New York, 1939), pp. 342–408.

[33] Potter maintains that the teaching of English decreased the appreciation of literature. *The Teaching of English in England,* pp. 252 and 256, comments on the indifference to literature prevalent among middle- and working-class people. Writing in the nineteenth century (and, of course, not thinking of England particularly), Jacob Burckhardt says in *Force and Freedom: Reflections on History* (New York, 1943; ed. J. H. Nichols), p. 152: "The greatest innovation in the world is the demand for education as a right of man; it is a disguised demand for comfort."

in the first half of the century; [34] and the Nonconformist chapels everywhere were, on principle, bare of paintings and statues. The Gothic Revival—itself an effect and a subsequent cause of historical awareness—was, I think, less influential in this respect than paintings because it was primarily architectural. (Old buildings, of course, induce a feeling of the past, but the beholder must have some knowledge of iconography or at least of the history of art to get the same sort of awareness of the past he can get from pictures—especially from the anecdotal historical painting of the nineteenth century.) Except for the British Museum, public museums were a nineteenth-century innovation in England; and their use as educational instruments, an American—and largely twentieth-century—practice. [35] London led the way here, but Manchester established a city art gallery even when its labor and housing conditions were beginning to cause concern among thoughtful people. [36] Most cities, however, did not acquire art galleries until the late eighties. [37] The lack of such

---

[34] Even a casual reading of Dr. Waagen's *Treasuries of Art in Great Britain* (London, 1854) and *Galleries and Cabinets of Art in Great Britain* (London, 1857) will quickly show that the average middle-class Englishman had small chance of seeing these private collections. Waagen was director of the Royal Galleries of Pictures in Berlin, knew Eastlake (president of the Royal Academy) and others prominent in art circles in England, and was thus able to get quick *entrée* to these private galleries. Cf. also Peter Cunningham, *London as It Is* (London, 1865), p. 11, for a list of the private galleries in London which were either closed entirely to the public or which required the owner's written permission for admission.

[35] Most museums then could have been described in the words of a little boy I once knew: "You go in and you see 'em." For those interested in a segment of the sociology of art Ruskin's writings on museums might well merit a monograph. Cf. "On the Present State of Modern Art, with Reference to the Advisable Arrangement of a National Gallery" (1867), "The Opening of the Crystal Palace" (1854), and "A Museum or Picture Gallery: Its Function and Formation" (1880). But see also R. H. Wilenski, *John Ruskin* (New York, 1938), pp. 369–383.

[36] The National Art Gallery was founded in 1824, the Manchester Corporation Gallery in 1829. The Soane Museum came to the city of London in 1835. The Dulwich Gallery, opened in 1814, was the chief public gallery in England in the early years of the century; it had no historical paintings. (Cf. *Catalogue of the Pictures of the Dulwich Gallery*, 1926.) Browning's connection with this gallery is well known; Ruskin used it; and Kingsley praised it in *Alton Locke* (ch. 6).

[37] The Bristol Museum and Art Gallery was founded in 1835; the Walker Art Gallery in Liverpool, in 1877. The galleries in Birmingham, Leeds,

galleries in the provinces is inferred in *Alton Locke* (chapter 25)
when one of the laudable acts of Lord Ellerton was throwing
"open his picture gallery, not only to the inhabitants of the neigh-
boring town, but what (strange to say) seemed to strike the party
[at Dean Winnstay's home] as still more remarkable, to the laborers of his own village."

In these museums and galleries were paintings which certainly reflect both the growing awareness of the past and the
growing nationalism. By 1900 the National Gallery possessed
twenty-three paintings by Englishmen of scenes from English
history.[38] Fortunately the aesthetic quality of English nineteenth-
century historical painting does not concern us here; its efficacy
in helping people visualize the past does. This was a result of
Benjamin West's innovation, painting historical scenes natural-
istically rather than in conventionalized classic décor. The following, from a popular Victorian book about English painters,
graphically illustrates the interest in this type of painting early in
the century: "It [Eastlake's painting of Napoleon on the deck of
the "Bellerophon," made while she was in Plymouth on her way
to St. Helena] was nothing remarkable in the way of art, but it
was a good likeness of the caged lion, with his uniform and
decorations, also painted from the life, for they had been sent
on shore for the painter's service. Five Plymouth gentlemen com-
missioned a large repetition of it, which was exhibited in London
and all over the provinces, and brought the painter not only
fame but £1000 in solid cash." [39] Lithography made possible the
reproduction of historical paintings in color in secondary school
history textbooks.

Whether paintings and galleries—especially through the con-

Sheffield, and York were founded after 1885. (This latter is based on a
comparison of Patterson's *Guide Book to the United Kingdom*, 1885, and
Baedeker's *Great Britain*, 1890 and 1901.)

[38] Cf. Sir Edward J. Poynter, ed., *The National Gallery* (London, 1900),
III. Paintings of legendary subjects, like Millais' "The Knight Errant," or
of scenes from historical fiction, like Yeames's "Amy Robsart," are not
included in this figure. Scott and Bulwer Lytton supplied painters with
subjects of this last named type.

[39] Allan Cunningham, *The Lives of the Most Eminent British Painters*
(London, 1890), III, 314.

stantly improved methods of reproducing pictures—affected literature by bringing about a decrease in the type of description so dear to Scott and his readers (and not so dear to the contemporary reader) is uncertain; [40] but there are interrelations between the two arts. The effect of the Elgin Marbles on Keats is well known; and though we are aware of the influence on Browning of the Dulwich Gallery, and of pictures elsewhere, it could stand further investigation. There is a field of study for students who have actual experience in both the arts, for I believe that there may be a close connection in method in the case of an artist who both writes and paints or plays a musical instrument. Thackeray, Ruskin, Rossetti, Morris, and Samuel Butler were painters; Hardy was an architect; and Browning and Hopkins were at least talented amateurs in music.

Most important, however, of all these media in spreading a sense of the past was the historical novel, which sometimes did not share the opprobrium of the novel among the more strictly religious. Despite the admittedly great influence of the "literary" historians, I think more people got their knowledge of the past from historical novels than from histories. Certainly, English schoolboys often absorbed more history from Scott, Lytton, Marryat, and even Henty than they learned from their textbooks, though they had a guilty feeling that this was not "real" history. Gooch and Trevelyan have essays on the historical novel, but most historians have passed it by. In 1940, however, Sir John Marriot, a historian who admits to having had a prejudice against historical novels though he read novels as a diversion, published *English History in English Fiction;* and in his opinion the historical novelists come off rather well in their treatment of history. Where, in the seventies, Sir Leslie Stephen, a man of letters, could say "Sir F. Palgrave says somewhere that 'historical novels are mortal enemies to history,' and we should venture to add that they are mortal enemies to fiction," [41] Sir John Marriot,

---

[40] I am inclined to think that the camera is a factor in the rise of abstract painting in our time and that the movie camera may have had an analogous effect—qualitative if not quantitative—on description in the work of serious writers.

[41] *Hours in a Library* (First Series) (London, 1887; 2nd ed.), p. 240. To the second half of Sir Leslie's statement the contemporary historical novel would make one say, "Marry, and amen."

a professional historian, says: "To the Temple of Clio are many different avenues. Constitutional and legal history obviously provides no appropriate material for the historical novelist. Would any novelist dream of making his story revolve around the origins of the English Parliament, or the evolution of the cabinet system? Shakespeare in *King John,* while making much play with the relations of the King and the Pope, never mentions Magna Carta. . . . The historical novel may on the other hand be an invaluable adjunct to the study of political, social, or even economic history. What historian would, for instance, write the Social History of the nineteenth century without reading Disraeli's *Sybil,* Mrs. Gaskell's *Mary Barton,* Kingsley's *Yeast,* or even Anthony Trollope's *Barchester Towers,* or John Galsworthy's *Forsyte Saga?*" [42]

As A. T. Sheppard notes, "the Golden Age of the historical novel began with 'Waverley' and ended within a quarter of a century of Scott's death," and though an occasional novel of worth appeared, the historical novel fell into disfavor until the seventies, when it became fashionable for a time.[43] Other than Scott, no nineteenth-century English writer of major status confined himself to the historical novel, but studies of the lesser figures might be profitable. Professor Carl J. Weber has found "the shadow . . . of Ainsworth on many of the pages of the Wessex novels." [44] What might be even more profitable than a study of the historical novel in England during this century would be one that, not confining itself to a genre, examined many writers' use of the historical, especially in the light of more recent concepts of history. Almost every Victorian writer of note— Browning, Dickens, Thackeray, Eliot, Tennyson, and Hardy— made his *devoirs* at least to the current interest in history. Now, it is obvious that Scott and the romantic historiography of the first half of the century should find their reflections in Browning's

[42] *English History in English Fiction* (London, 1940), p. 1. Sir John does not limit himself to novelists who portrayed an age earlier than their own (a definition of a historical novel which seems valid to me), as is indicated from the novels mentioned in the quotation.

[43] *The Art and Practice of the Historical Novel* (London, 1930), p. 65. Sheppard carries further H. Butterfield's *The Historical Novel* (Cambridge, 1924).

[44] "Ainsworth and Hardy," *RES,* XVII (1941), 193–200.

historical dramas, Macaulay's *Lays of Ancient Rome,* Bulwer Lytton's historical novels, and even *A Tale of Two Cities, Henry Esmond,* and *The Virginians,* and also in the historical paintings of Turner, Stanfield, Maclise, Wilkie, Eastlake, and Huggins. But, without putting undue stress on mere correlation,[45] one might examine the possible relationships between the resurgence of historical painting in the eighties and nineties (Lady Butler, Gow, Orchardson, Pettie, Schetky, Waller, and Whitcombe), the popularity of the historical novel in the seventies which Sheppard notes, and Tennyson's historical dramas, Browning's "Hervé Riel," and "Clive," and Hardy's *The Trumpet Major* and *The Dynasts* (all of which were published between 1871 and 1904)—and this at a time when the romantic historian was discredited. Had the Franco-Prussian War anything to do with a resurgence of nationalism in England at this time? Was it in some way related to Victorian satisfaction over England's imperial greatness? One might also examine whether there is any significance in various authors' choice of historical material. The impact of Napoleon is noticeable everywhere: even Meredith has a poem on him. Carlyle made many references to Napoleon or his battles in *Frederick the Great,* quite forgetting that at least half his readers did not share his boyhood memories; and *The Dynasts* shows how long the impact was felt. The use of the Arthurian material and of the Civil War might also bear examination in this connection as well as the influence of changing concepts of history from the romantic to the more scientific (measured from *Waverley* to *The Dynasts*).

Nationalism was unquestionably an element in the progressive interest in the historical which is evident in the arts and agencies treated here. Artists, readers, beholders, and critics could hardly be expected to be exempt from an influence to which even some of the most severely objective historians succumbed. But nationalism is a broad term which extends from patriotism to all that is evil in chauvinism. And patriotism, as Virginia Woolf observed in *Three Guineas,* begins with a love

---

[45] Cf. M. R. Cohen, *op. cit.,* p. 101, for a brief discussion of the limitations of repeated succession as a principle of causation.

of a particular spot of land. Might it, therefore, be possible that among relatively rootless city folk in Victorian England the national past as they saw and read it became a kind of substitute for the *lares* and *penates* of the countryman and the dweller in a small town?

IV

Our indebtedness to historical scholarship is so great that it is difficult to know where to begin an acknowledgment. Perhaps all that is necessary to indicate the gains is to point to the *New English Dictionary* and repeat the epitaph on Christopher Wren's tomb in St. Paul's. Our editorial procedures, monographs dealing with limited aspects of a subject, and cooperative scholarship are further evidences of our obligations to the historians. The less happy effects would appear to arise from the almost inevitable slowness of one branch of scholarship in keeping abreast with even a cognate branch and from an unwise use of historical methods by literary scholars. Any consideration of these less happy effects, however, is proof of the secure place which history now holds in western thought.

The degree to which history is, or is capable of being, a science is as much a matter of debate today as it was in the nineteenth century, but the debate has taken on, quite naturally, aspects other than those it had earlier. So far as the procedures for examining evidence of the past, critically, are concerned, it is generally conceded that history is scientific—that is, subject to verification which is, so far as is humanly possible, free from the biases of the investigator. Here the value of the legacy of the nineteenth century to historical and literary scholars is not in question. The accumulation of fact by researchers of less skill than the great practitioners in both fields has justly drawn down on itself sharp criticism which is scarcely mitigated by the realization that it is a natural result of emulation (if not imitation) of procedures which were spectacularly successful in the natural sciences in the nineteenth century. There has, however, been a modification of the view of the method of scientific induction which Mill held. Modern thought no longer believes that the scientific investigator collects and examines data with an almost blank mind, and in circles outside those of the pure sciences there is increasing awareness of the use of hypotheses made by the scientists.[46] It appears to be generally agreed among historians that in the writing of history a historian, by having to select from among the facts which he has investigated and by having to give them some interpretation, uses procedures similar to those employed by artist and scientist—though in the interpretation the historian resembles the artist more than the scientist. Some have held that a historian is objective if he is aware of the principle on which he selects and interprets his material. (The question of the responsibility of the historian for making and keeping his reader conscious of his principle is a moral one; and the related question of the reader's ability or willingness to keep in mind even a faithful discharge of this responsibility by the historian takes one into the subject of communication.) In practice, if not in theory, means are apt to combine with ends and to lead one into an area in which history, literature, science, and philosophy overlap. How far objectivity can or should keep clear of moral judgments, or even of moral presuppositions, is currently of interest to scientist and historian alike. The extent to which history can become part of a scientific study of man as some sociologists envisage such a study, is a question for historians, sociologists, and philosophers of history to venture into.[47] However these questions are viewed, it is obvious today that the "literary," or non-academic, historian is expected to have a more systematic and self-conscious grasp of his methods than his Victorian forebear.

The contemporary interest in examining the nature and limits of many kinds of specialized knowledge which the last two

[46] Cf. *Theory and Practice in Historical Study: A report of the Committee on Historiography* (New York, 1946), pp. 31–32, and M. R. Cohen, *op. cit.*, pp. 76–82. The subject is more fully treated in Cohen's *Reason and Nature* (New York, 1931), pp. 115–125.

[47] Cf. F. J. Teggart, *Theory of History* (New Haven, 1925), and also *Theory and Practice in Historical Study.* This latter, a bulletin of the Social Science Research Council, has an excellent bibliography.

Here it is a pleasure to acknowledge my gratitude to my colleagues, Professors Mildred L. Campbell and Evalyn A. Clark of the Department of History at Vassar College, for many valuable suggestions about books on the theory of history.

centuries have made possible, has brought about a vigorous examination of the theories of history. The vigor of the criticism is matched by the diversity of views, and the practising historian finds himself perhaps only less embarrassed by this activity than the literary scholar who strays into the arena. It would appear that the determinism which underlay eighteenth- and nineteenth-century scientific thinking rather naturally led some historians to accept a similar concept for their interpretations. And it led people who, like Spencer, wanted to remake society into an uncritical faith in materialistic determinism, a faith the best of the historians could not share. The importance of economic determinism in our day tends, however, to overshadow idealistic determinism (of which Hegel's is a good example). Monistic explanations are alluring, and the desire for them seems deeply imbedded in human nature. But beyond making one aware that no man can ever attain the complete objectivity he can conceive and in large measure apply in the natural sciences, the contemporary criticism of monistic theories of history by thinkers as different as Croce, M. R. Cohen, and Sidney Hook—to mention those I am acquainted with—is both an outgrowth of the nineteenth century's development of history and a liberation from dogmatism. Except among those who adhere to an uncritical economic determinism, there has come into existence a tempered and flexible use of determinism by historians, particularly when they are dealing with periods where there is ample documentation.[48]

How far some of the contemporary criticisms of the theory of history might serve to change or illuminate literary scholarship, I am not competent to judge; but I am inclined to think that it might repay us to become aware of some of the criticisms of the nineteenth-century concepts of progress and causation in terms of analogy with geology and biology. R. G. Collingwood's concept of the historical imagination [49] seems to me even more useful to the literary scholar than to the historian as a description of the process of arriving at a synthesis. M. R. Cohen's concept of "po-

---

[48] Cf. Sidney Hook, *The Hero in History* (New York, 1943), for a study of uncritical uses of determinism in history.

[49] R. G. Collingwood, *The Idea of History* (Oxford, 1946), pp. 231–248.

larity and oscillation between opposite poles" [50] seems to me at least an effective corrective to the prevalent idea of evolution as it is applied to human events.

Useful and illuminating as any philosophy of history can be and is (whether in a limited study or in one that takes in a wide sweep of events), the historian must wrestle with what individuals or groups of individuals did. The expanded province of his field sends the historian to ever more complex and remote regions for explanations. His disciplines enable him to make interpretations which are as impersonal as the problems of his times permit. But since human beings are rather more complex than the entities which even the most abstruse contemporary science deals with, the historian confronts the age-old problems that have always confronted the poet and the philosopher—fate, free will, and the nature of man. Though here, unlike the poet, he cannot arrange the sequence of events to suit his pattern, he must, like the poet, rely on sympathy, imagination, and insight. And the literary scholar can do no less.

---

[50] M. R. Cohen, *The Meaning of Human History*, p. 273.

The Social Background
[to the Growth of a Mass Reading Public]

RICHARD D. ALTICK

I

The mass reading public developed in nineteenth-century England against a background of profound social change. From 1760 to 1801 the population of England and Wales had increased from roughly seven million to almost nine million; but this was only a moderate growth compared with what was to come.[1] In the first half of the nineteenth century the population doubled (from 8.9 million to 17.9 million), and by 1901 it was more than three and a half times as great (32.5 million) as it had been a hundred years earlier. In no decade was the rate of increase less than 11.7 per cent, and in one (1811–21) it was over 18 per cent. Meanwhile the population of Scotland, which formed an important market for English books and periodicals, grew from 2.09 million in 1821 to 4.5 million in 1901.[2]

The reservoir from which the reading public was drawn therefore became larger and larger.[3] At the same time, the class struc-

---

[1] Basil Williams, *The Whig Supremacy* (Oxford, 1939), p. 119.

[2] Porter, *The Progress of the Nation* (1912 ed., used throughout unless otherwise noted), pp. 3–4.

[3] Gross population figures are not, of course, an accurate indication of the size of either the practicing or the potential reading audience. From the totals must be deducted over a third who were under fifteen years of age and who therefore would not ordinarily have been interested in adult reading matter. In addition, there is the all-important factor of literacy . . .

From Richard D. Altick, *The English Common Reader* (Chicago: The University of Chicago Press, 1957), pp. 81–98.

ture and the occupational and geographical distribution of the people underwent alterations which affected the availability of reading matter, educational opportunities, the conditions under which reading could be done, and the popular attitude toward print. The development of the mass reading public, in fact, was completely dependent upon the progress of the social revolution.

At once, therefore, we must acquire a general notion of the social structure. Unfortunately no uniform system of nomenclature or of census classification prevailed throughout the century, so that a consistent statistical summary is not possible. The greatest disagreement was on the difference between the lower-middle and the lower classes, and especially on the social level to which skilled artisans belonged. As the economist Leone Levi pointed out in 1884, mechanics and skilled artisans were "as far removed from common labourers and miners as clerks and curates are from those who have reached the highest places in the liberal professions or wealthy merchants and bankers, all of whom pass under the category of the middle classes." [4] Some authorities ranked them in the lower class; others gave them the relative dignity of place at the bottom of the middle class. In any case, the rule of thumb favored during most of the century was that the "working class," taking the lower-middle and lower classes together, constituted at least three-quarters of the total population. In 1814 Patrick Colquhoun estimated that out of about 17 million people in the United Kingdom (hence including Ireland), 1.5 million belonged to the upper and "respectable" middle classes, while 2.8 million were of the shopkeeper-small farmer class, and 11.9 million were mechanics, artisans, menial servants, paupers, and vagrants. (In that period, just before Waterloo, slightly less than a million additional men and their dependents were credited to "Army and Navy.") [5] In 1867 the economist Dudley Baxter, classifying 9.8 million actual recipients of income in England

---

[4] Levi, *Wages and Earnings of the Working Classes*, p. 25.

[5] Patrick Colquhoun, *A Treatise on the Wealth, Power, and Resources of the British Empire* (1814), pp. 106–107. For two different detailed charts based on Colquhoun's estimates, attributed to 1801 and 1814, respectively, see Cole and Postgate, *The Common People*, 1938 ed., p. 70, and 1947 ed., p. 63.

and Wales (and omitting, therefore, some 11 million dependents), numbered the upper and middle classes at 200,000, the
lower-middle class at 1.85 million, and the working class (including 1.1 million skilled laborers) at 7.78 million.[6]

Whatever classification was used, one fact was undeniable.
There was a great increase in the amorphous stratum between
the old-established middle class (merchants and bankers, large
employers of labor, superior members of professions) and the
working class proper—the ranks of unskilled labor. This increase,
brought about by the changing economic basis of English life,
has special significance in the history of the reading public. It was
principally from among skilled workers, small shopkeepers, clerks,
and the better grade of domestic servants that the new mass
audience for printed matter was recruited during the first half
of the century. These were the people who chiefly benefited
from the spread of elementary education and whose occupations
required not only that they be literate but that they keep their
reading faculty in repair. And because these people shared
more in the century's prosperity than did the unskilled laborers,
they were in a somewhat better position to buy cheap books and
periodicals as these became available.

The growth of two occupational groups is particularly noteworthy. By 1861 the total of domestic servants of both sexes was
more than a million—a few thousands more than the total employed in the textile industry.[7] Whatever newspapers and other
periodicals a household took in would, in the normal course of
events, filter down to the servants' quarters. In estimating the
number of hands through which a given copy of a middle-class
paper, or even a cheap book, might pass, one must not forget that
the Victorian household contained not only a sizable family but
also one or more servants with whom the paper wound up its
travels.

The segment of the middle class proper which grew with unusual speed was that of physicians, teachers, civil servants, and
other professional or white-collar workers. In 1851, the census

---

[6] Cole and Postgate (1938 ed., used hereafter unless otherwise noted), p.
347.

[7] Porter, pp. 31, 42.

placed 357,000 persons in that class; ten years later there were 482,000, and in 1881 the total was 647,000—an increase of 80 per cent in only thirty years.[8] These people, because of the special requirements of their daily work as well as the general cultural tradition of the professional class, constituted an important audience for reading matter.

As the century began, most of the English people, despite the spread of the enclosure system and the growth of factory industry, still were engaged in farming or in cottage crafts. But the peasant, the yeoman, and the handicraftsman steadily were being transformed into the factory-hand, and the process gathered momentum with the years. Of the total employed population of England and Wales in 1841 (6.7 million), 39.05 per cent were engaged in commerce, trade, and manufacture, and less than half as many— 18.80 per cent—in agriculture. Fifty years later, the percentages in commerce and industry and in agriculture were 68 and 10, respectively.[9]

The industrial revolution caused a vast migration of the people, from village and farm to the sprawling new factory towns of the Midlands and the North. Manchester and Salford more than quadrupled their joint population between 1801 and 1861; Leeds grew from 53,000 to 172,000 in the same period; and Bradford from 13,000 to 104,000.[10] By the 1880's, approximately two-thirds of the English were town-dwellers.[11] The occupational and geographical relocation of the people—the total disruption of their old way of life; their conversion into machine-slaves, living a hand-to-mouth existence at the mercy of their employers and of uncertain economic circumstances; their concentration in cities totally unprepared to accommodate them, not least in respect to education; the resultant moral and physical degradation—these, as we shall see, had significant consequences in the history of the reading public.

In the first half of the century English society was shaken as it

[8] Robert Giffen, "Further Notes on the Progress of the Working Classes in the Last Half Century," *Journal of the Statistical Society,* XLIX (1886), 90.

[9] Porter, p. 38; Lynd, *England in the Eighteen-Eighties,* p. 28.

[10] Cole and Postgate, p. 300.

[11] Clapham, *Economic History of Modern Britain,* II, 489.

had not been since the end of the Middle Ages. The ancient class structure, which generally, in past centuries, had well served the cause of domestic peace, began to crumble. The working class, losing its old sense of place under the stress of hunger, bewilderment, and the exhortations of radical politicians, began to demand social, economic, and political rights unthought of only a generation or two earlier. The widening of economic opportunity afforded by the development of industrial capitalism permitted many thousands to climb in the social scale. They quickly acquired the social prejudices characteristic of the class in which they found themselves, among which was a powerful desire to protect their substance and privileges against the encroachments of the class they had lately left. Those above them, in turn, felt all the more strongly the need for defending their own position against the newly arrived.

Hence the nineteenth century witnessed on every hand a sharpening of class consciousness. To the upper class and especially the older portion of the middle class, everything depended upon preserving the hallowed structure, though cautiously modified here and there to suit new conditions; to the lower class, or at least its more sensitive part, the supreme need was for sweeping social reconstruction in the direction of democracy. These conflicting aims inevitably bred social tensions which deeply affected the fortunes of the mass reading audience. For, as literacy and interest in reading spread, the "superior orders of society"—a term much in favor in the period—reacted to the phenomenon in terms of their special interests. Once they conceded it was impossible to prevent the lower ranks from reading, they embarked on a long campaign to insure that through the press the masses of people would be induced to help preserve the status quo and bulwark the security and prosperity of the particular sort of national life that they, its upper- and middle-class rulers, cherished. . . .

II

What, now, of the conditions of life that encouraged the spread of reading, or, on the other hand, inhibited it?

Obviously, one cannot read without some leisure in which to

do so. Leisure has never been equitably distributed in any civilized society, but in nineteenth-century England it was allotted with particular unevenness. In the middle class, even to some extent in its lower reaches, growing prosperity and the cheapness of labor enabled men and women to hire others for tasks they had hitherto done for themselves. The greater availability of cheap manufactured and processed goods—soap and candles, for instance, and food—gradually led people to give up producing such commodities for their own use, a practice that in any event was impossible for city-dwellers. Households in which repair work had formerly been done by father and sons now called in carpenters and masons. And most important of all, the menial chores which were traditionally the lot of wife and daughters could be transferred, at small expense, to domestic servants, one of whose regular duties, as often as not, was to exchange books at the circulating library or buy the new issue of *Eliza Cook's Journal* from the corner news agent. Hence to scores of thousands of families touched by the prosperity of the new age, relief from household duties provided a degree of leisure undreamed of in earlier generations.

But while leisure increased in the middle class, the ways it could be used were drastically limited, since this was the class most affected by the spread of evangelical principles. "For multitudes of the respectable population, outside entertainments, such as the theatre or the music-hall provided, were practically non-existent. Dancing was a snare of the devil. Even concerts, though Catalani might be singing and Paganini playing, were not encouraged by the unworldly; and it was not till the undeniable 'goodness' of Jenny Lind conquered the prejudice, that anything but oratorio was considered safe.[12] Nonconformists and Claphamites, therefore, on evenings not set aside for missionary meetings, shunned outside dangers, and spent the time in 'profitable' instruction and 'harmless' entertainment. Cards, of course, were forbidden, and, while a game of bagatelle might be allowed,

---

[12] And there were plenty of people, among them George Eliot during her brief but fervent flirtation with Evangelical principles, who regarded even oratorio as dangerously sensuous.

billiards, even in the home, were never mentioned." [13] In so scrupulous an atmosphere, the reading habit flourished. The place of the evening reading circle in Victorian middle-class family life is so well known that it need be merely mentioned here. How widespread the institution was, and how deeply it influenced the tastes of the children who grew up in such homes, is attested in countless memoirs.

However, only the relatively well-to-do minority of the middle class, the merchants, bankers, professional men, manufacturers, and so on, could spend full evenings with their families and their books. In the lower levels of that class, most men spent long days at their work, small employers and overseers keeping as long hours as their workmen.[14] Retail tradespeople, a million and a quarter of them by the 1880's, were in their shops from seven or eight in the morning until ten at night, and on Saturdays until midnight. For skilled and unskilled laborers, the working day was so long during the first half of the century as to be a national scandal. Hundreds of thousands of miners and factory- and mill-hands crept to their employment before dawn and emerged after sunset. The fourteen-hour day was commonplace, and the sixteen-hour day was not rare. Only gradually were the hours reduced. London handicraft workers won a ten-hour day before the 1830's, and in 1847 a bitterly fought act of Parliament introduced it into the textile industry. Actually, however, the working day was longer than the bare figure suggests, for artisans and handicraftsmen frequently worked overtime, and in textile mills "ten hours" really meant 6:00 A.M. to 6:00 P.M. By the seventies, London artisans, after long agitation, achieved a fifty-four-hour week, while the textile trades worked two and a half hours longer. In the nineties the average workweek for such trades as shipbuilding, iron founding, cooperage, and building ranged from fifty to sixty hours, depending on the locality and, in outdoor trades, the season of the year. In the warehouses of

---

[13] Kellett, "The Press," p. 49.

[14] The ensuing discussion of working hours is based on Sidney Webb and Harold Cox, *The Eight Hours Day* (1891), *passim;* Gregg, *Social and Economic History of Britain,* pp. 134–36. On the "Early Closing" movement, see E. S. Turner, *Roads to Ruin* (1950), chap. iii.

the so-called "Manchester trade" the fourteen-hour day was still common.

On weekdays, therefore, few workers had time to read. Those in even the most favored trades came home no earlier than six or seven o'clock, and after the evening meal only an hour or two remained until fatigue and the prospect of rising before dawn the next day drove them to bed. Not until the sixties was the Saturday half-holiday generally introduced; and this involved only a modest curtailment of the working day—in the case of London building artisans, for instance, from eleven to seven hours. For shop assistants there was no relief at all. Saturday remained their longest day, a matter of sixteen hours behind the counter. Under such circumstances it was only natural that the workman confined most of his reading to Sundays. Hence the great popularity of the Sunday newspaper, and, beginning in the late forties, the weekly miscellany-*cum*-sensational-fiction paper which was issued on Saturday.

During the decades which witnessed the worst oppression of the wage-earning masses, the townsman with time to kill on Saturday night and Sunday had little choice of diversion. He could get drunk at a public house, or, to the accompaniment of song, at a concert room or a dancing saloon; he could visit a brothel, he could get into a fist fight or attend a bear-baiting, he could loaf in the streets—and not much else. The teeming cities had virtually no provision for decent public recreation: few theaters or music halls, no parks for strolling and picnicking, no museums or art galleries, no free libraries. In 1844 Preston was the only town in all of Lancashire with a public park. But shortly thereafter, local authorities were for the first time allowed to use public funds for recreational facilities, and parks and other places of resort appeared in most cities.[15] There remained, however, the somber pall of the English Sunday. While the working class as a whole was indifferent to Sabbatarianism, it nevertheless shared the consequences of the ban on Sunday recreation. In 1856 proposals to open the British Museum and the National

---

[15] Hammond, *The Age of the Chartists,* pp. 29–30. The Hammonds' two chapters on "The Loss of Playgrounds" are a good summary of this topic.

Gallery after church services on Sunday and to hold Sunday band concerts in the London parks were shouted down from the pulpit, and not until forty more years had elapsed were London museums and art galleries opened on Sunday afternoons. Only in the seventies did the Midland workman have access to such institutions on his one day of relaxation.[16] Until well past mid-century, therefore, the man who was not content with aimless loafing or with grosser amusements had little alternative but to spend his Sunday leisure with a book or paper.

When the workweek was shortened and strict Sabbatarianism began to fade, the English worker found many ways of passing his leisure apart from reading. Railways ran special cheap trains to the country and the seaside; theaters and music halls multiplied; cricket, football, and other spectator sports became increasingly popular. Among the middle class, the partial emancipation of women encouraged the whole family to move outdoors for its pleasure, so that the domestic reading circle declined as an institution. The new fashion for participant sports—cycling, rowing, tennis, walking, croquet—offered powerful competition to the reading habit. Thus the spread of leisure both favored and discouraged the development of the reading public. There was more time to read, but eventually there were also many more things to do with one's spare time.

One major innovation, at least, resulted in an unquestionable increase in reading: the coming of railway travel. Cheap, swift, and more or less comfortable transportation was available to the ever greater number of men whose business required travel, as well as to those who wished to visit relatives or have a holiday in the Cotswolds or by the sea. A railway trip meant an hour or a day of enforced leisure; and to escape the boredom of staring out the window or listening to one's chance companions, one read. It was by no means accidental that from the 1850's onward a whole class of cheap books was known as "railway literature," and that a large portion of the retail book and periodical trade of England was conducted at railway terminals. Every passenger train of the hundreds that roared down the rails in the course of a single day

---

[16] Gregg, p. 349.

carried a cargo of readers, their eyes fixed on *Lady Audley's Secret* or the *Times*. Perhaps no other single element in the evolving pattern of Victorian life was so responsible for the spread of reading. The effect was increased still further when, with the rise of dormitory suburbs around the great cities, commuting between home and business became a daily occupation of many thousands.

In the country, meanwhile, conditions of life among the masses offered little incentive or opportunity for reading. Education was hard to come by, and most children, if they went to school at all, did so for only a year or two and then were put to work in the fields, at crow-scaring if they were not yet strong enough for manual labor. Working hours for all laborers were long. Paul Tregarva, the studious gamekeeper in Kingsley's *Yeast*, observed: "As for reading, sir, it's all very well for me, who have been a keeper and dawdled about like a gentleman with a gun over my arm; but did you ever do a good day's farm-work in your life? If you had, man or boy, you wouldn't have been game for much reading when you got home; you'd do just what these poor fellows do,—tumble into bed at eight o'clock, hardly waiting to take your clothes off, knowing that you must turn up again at five o'clock the next morning to get a breakfast of bread, and, perhaps, a dab of the squire's dripping, and then back to work again; and so on, day after day, sir, week after week, year after year. . . ." [17]

While printed matter became more easily accessible in the towns and cities, with their coffeehouses and news vendors and free libraries, the humble countryman met few books or papers in his way through life. Hawkers came to his door occasionally with broadsides, tracts, and number-publications; but, with agricultural wages consistently the lowest in the nation, there was little money to buy them. In a certain Kentish farming parish in the 1830's, only four out of fifty-one families possessed any books besides the Bible, Testament, and prayer and hymn books, and only seven parents "ever opened a book after the labours of the day were closed." [18] Nor was this parish unusual. Again and again

---

[17] *Yeast*, chap. xiii.
[18] *Central Society of Education Publications*, III (1839), 108.

in the records of the time we find evidence of how little printed matter—perhaps no more than a copy or two of a cheap magazine—regularly came to a country village. Not until the cheap periodical press made efficient use of railway transportation and local distributors, and rural education received much-needed aid under the Forster Act of 1870, did the majority of country-dwellers acquire much interest in reading.

III

Victorian writers and speakers never tired of reminding their audiences that the taste for reading has an almost unique advantage in that it can be indulged at any time and in any place. One must go from home to satisfy a love of nature or sports or the fine arts, and he must do so at certain hours or seasons; but one can read any time at one's own fireside—a great point in an age that venerated domesticity. Such a notion was not, however, very realistic. The typical nineteenth-century home was not a place where a man could read quietly and uninterruptedly during whatever free hours he had. For every household in which it was possible there were a hundred where it was out of the question.

This is not the place to rehearse the appalling story of housing conditions in the new industrial England, or, for that matter, in the countryside, where the sentimentally celebrated English cottage was, oftener than not, a ruinous hovel. It is enough to recall that town workers lived in bestial squalor, packed together in dark, stinking warrens in which privacy, quiet, and the most rudimentary comforts were alike unknown. To such people, as to the gamekeeper Tregarva, praise of books as a means of contenting one's self during a peaceful evening or a Sunday must have seemed a bitter jest. How, with a distraught, sickly wife complaining and a brood of ill-fed squalling children filling the room, and drunken neighbors brawling next door, could a reader, no matter how earnest, concentrate upon a book? It was even worse if, as was true of many working-class dwellings, some sort of handicraft was carried on on the premises. In 1849 a missionary to the handweavers of Spitalfields—once aristocrats of labor, with neat gardens beside their homes, and mutual-improvement societies—told a committee of Parliament, "I frequently find as many as seven or eight persons living all in one room; in that

room, perhaps, there will be two looms at work, so that the noise
and discomfort render it almost impossible that a working man,
if he were ever so well inclined to read, could sit down and read
quietly." [19] John Passmore Edwards, the son of a Cornish carpen-
ter, recalled how as a child he read by the light of a single candle
in the midst of a talkative and active family. "Hundreds and
hundreds of times I pressed my thumbs firmly on my ears until
they ached, in order to read with as little distraction as possible." [20]

To try to read in the midst of the domestic hurly-burly meant,
too, that one would be subject to the ridicule, or at best the well-
meant disapproval, of those who failed to share one's inclination.
Thomas Burt, the future trade-union leader and M.P., grew up in
a cottage that was virtually a neighborhood crossroads. "At it
again, Thomas!" a constant visitor, who was a Methodist coal
miner, would exclaim. "What can thoo be aiming at? Thou won't
join the church; thou won't preach or address temperance meetings. What's the meaning of all this poring over books, this plod-
ding search for knowledge that thou won't use? Thou'll destroy
thy health, and nobody will be the better for thy labours." [21] This
was not the least of the difficulties which the pursuer of knowledge had to face.

It was not to be marveled at, then, that most workingmen, no
matter how much they may have wished to read, sought relaxation outside the home. The street, the public house, the cheap
theater if one was nearby, and later the park and the sports field
were to be preferred to a fireside which was anything but
peaceful. Nor was overcrowding confined to working-class tenements and cottages. It was found, to a scarcely smaller degree, in
the homes of the lower-middle class. At no time in the century
did residential building keep pace with the growth of the population, and in any case incomes were insufficient to rent quarters

---

[19] Public Libraries Committee, Q. 2751.
[20] A Few Footprints (1905), p. 6. It was Edwards' recollection of this
maddening experience which led him, as the millionaire proprietor of the
London Echo, to found free libraries where people could read in comparative
tranquillity.
[21] Burt, Autobiography, pp. 122–23.

that were adequate according to the most modest standards of our own day. Taking the nation as a whole, the average number of persons to a living unit fell in the course of the century only from 5.67 to 5.2, and as late as the 1880's one-fifth of the entire population of London lived more than two to a room.[22]

Nor was this all. In the ordinary home, decent lighting was not to be found until late in the century. In the period 1808–23 the window tax, a relic dating from 1696, reached its highest level. Houses with six windows or less were taxed 6s.6d. to 8s. annually; seven-window houses, a pound; nine-window houses, two guineas, and so on up. Even an aperture only a foot square was considered a window. Although in 1823 the tax was halved, and in 1825 houses with less than eight windows were exempted, builders still were discouraged from putting any more openings in a house than were absolutely necessary, with the result that only one-seventh of all the houses in Britain fell under the tax.[23] Not without reason did Dickens remark that the window tax (abolished, finally, in 1851) was an even more formidable obstacle to the people's reading than the so-called "taxes on knowledge"—the duties on newspapers, advertisements, and paper.[24]

The average early nineteenth-century home was dark enough during the day; at night it was no brighter. In most houses at the beginning of the century tallow dips (rush lights) or candles were the only sources of illumination apart from the fireplace. During the thirties and forties colza-oil and whale-oil lamps were introduced into the households of the well-to-do, followed by paraffin lamps in the fifties and eventually by gas. It may well be that these improvements were hastened as much by the increased amount of reading being done in such homes as by the contrast between the brilliancy of gas lighting in streets and public places and the feeble illumination afforded by candles. In the dwellings of the working class, however, candles and rush lights remained the usual sources of light. They were not cheap. In the first half of the century a pound of candles (two dozen) cost about 7d. and in humble homes was made to last a week or longer. Each

[22] Clapham, II, 490; Porter, p. 91.
[23] Hammond, pp. 84–85 n.; Cole and Postgate, p. 300.
[24] Dickens, *Letters* (Nonesuch ed.), II, 205.

candle provided from two to three hours' light. When only one or two were used at a time, continuous reading was a trying experience. Rush lights, being cheaper, were used in the poorest households, but they gave an even feebler light. To the devoted reader, however, even they were precious; Kingsley's Alton Locke, for instance, recorded how, after putting out his candle for the night, he continued his studies by the glimmer of a rush light he had earned by bringing bits of work home from the tailor's sweatshop.[25]

Reading in such light could not help taxing the eyes. This was a powerful deterrent to the spread of the reading habit, especially in an age when print was villainously small (largely because the high paper duties requiring crowding as much as possible on a page). The eyestrain involved in many manufacturing operations, such as loom-tending, was great, and mills and factories were often wretchedly lighted. Furthermore, since the diet of the masses was not only scanty but ill balanced, poor nutrition must have affected the sight of countless thousands.

Spectacles were used, of course, but by no means everbody who needed them had them; in the country and slums especially they were something of a luxury. It was a remarkable event in the life of young Carlyle when he was able to send presents of two pairs of glasses to his parents from Edinburgh in 1821.[26] Not until the middle of the twentieth century, indeed, were spectacles freely available to all Englishmen. Without them, during the nineteenth century, a multitude of would-be readers, their eyes weakened by faulty diet or taxing occupation or simply by age, were barred irrevocably from the pleasures of print.

There was, finally, the element of sheer fatigue. A man's eyes might be perfect, but after working all day at some monotonous or strenuous task he was so tired that unless his will to read was very strong he was likely to fall asleep over his book or paper. Far preferable in his state of exhaustion was a refreshing visit to a

---

[25] This material on household illumination is derived from Porter (1851 ed.), p. 582; Marjorie and C. H. B. Quennell, *A History of Everyday Things in England, 1733–1851* (1933), p. 181; *Early Victorian England*, ed. G. M. Young (1934), I, 81, 127, 129; Kingsley, *Alton Locke*, chap. iii.

[26] *Early Letters of Thomas Carlyle*, ed. C. E. Norton (1886), II, 2–4.

public house (where, to be sure, he could glance over a paper if he were so disposed) or simply an hour or two spent loafing before his door. It would take a type of literature especially suited to men and women with dulled minds and tired bodies to turn manual workers into habitual readers.

IV

It is hard, perhaps impossible, to recreate the spirit of so large and inarticulate a community as the English working classes in the nineteenth century. If we attempt to do so by examining only the immense body of sociological data assembled by parliamentary committees and statistical societies, we must believe that men and women were so brutalized out of any semblance to normal mortals that they were physical organisms and economic units alone, without any of the emotional life and the intellectual and spiritual aspirations which mark the man from the animal. But this is an incomplete view, springing from the limited nature of the age's humanitarianism. Reformers like Chadwick, Kay-Shuttleworth, and Shaftesbury were concerned simply with ameliorating the common man's physical existence, and parliamentary inquiries never showed the slightest curiosity, except where it was a question of religious observance or ordinary morality, about the inner lives of the workers—a subject which in any case hardly lends itself to investigative treatment.

One-sided though it is, the impression we receive of the worker and his family from the classic sources of early nineteenth-century social history is not wholly false. If there was ever a time when the English masses approached a state of downright bestiality, it was then. The great migration from village to city produced a crisis in popular culture. Though they were already deteriorating, there had still survived in the eighteenth century the rural institutions of holiday-making, pageantry, and fairs. There was still the lore of the countryside and the songs and stories that had been handed down in the cottage from generation to generation. Illiterate though the common countryman may have been, his participation in the popular cultural tradition saved him from being a stolid brute.

When the villager was transformed into the slum-dwelling factory laborer, however, this tradition was lost to him. In addition, whatever contact he had earlier had with printed matter became more tenuous. Many cottages had had their little shelf of worn and precious books, family possessions passed down through a century or more—the Bible, *Robinson Crusoe, Pilgrim's Progress,* ballads, and chapbooks bought at a fair long ago or from a peddler at the door. But when the children moved to the cities, the books were left behind or soon were lost in the course of their owners' restless migration from one tenement to another, and there was little chance to replace them. The custom of reading by the fireside vanished, along with other homely habits, and books no longer were prized as symbols of a family's continuity.

Tragically, it was at this very time that the worker most needed the spiritual and emotional strength which reading might provide. He desperately needed some relief from the deadly monotony of factory work, which was, Friedrich Engels observed, "properly speaking, not work, but tedium, the most deadening, wearing process conceivable. The operative is condemned to let his physical and mental powers decay in this utter monotony, it is his mission to be bored every day and all day long from his eighth year." [27] It was no cause for surprise, as Engels went on to say, that drunkenness and sexual promiscuity—the only two solaces the worker had regularly available—reached such alarming proportions in the manufacturing towns.

Even more dreadful was the loss of personal individuality. Workers' lives were regulated by the ringing of the factory bell and regimented by a system of rules and penalties. They had no personal pride in their work, for the product of their labor was not theirs alone but that of many other workers. They had no sense of personal destiny, for their lives were totally at the mercy of conditions beyond their control, the fluctuations of trade, the whim of the employer, the invention of new labor-saving machinery.

And perhaps worst of all was the overwhelming loneliness the individual man and woman felt in the midst of the crowd. "The sons of farmers and agricultural laborers who congregated in

---

[27] *Condition of the Working Class in 1844,* p. 177.

newly created slums were natives of all four corners of England and Wales. They were foreign to each other, they even spoke different dialects and they were completely lost in that human flotsam and jetsam. The new rows of tenements had no parish church, no local vicar with his school, no cultural background or local tradition. In their native villages they were human personalities, although subordinate; here they became ciphers, an economic commodity which was bought and sold according to the market price of labour." [28] The only strong bond that held the victims of the industrial revolution together was a common misery of body and soul.

Torn away from the old cultural tradition, battered and adrift in a feelingless world, the millions of common people needed decent recreation more urgently than any generation before them. As Sir John Herschel, who was gifted with rare insight in this matter, observed in 1833, "The pleasant field-walk and the village-green are becoming rarer and rarer every year. Music and dancing (the more's the pity) have become so closely associated with ideas of riot and debauchery, among the less cultivated classes, that a taste for them for their own sakes can hardly be said to exist. . . . While hardly a foot of ground is left uncultivated, and unappropriated, there is positively not space left for many of the cheerful amusements of rural life. . . . It is physically impossible that the amusements of a condensed population should continue to be those of a scattered one."

Books, said Herschel, were the answer to the pressing problem of the workingman's amusement. Reading "calls for no bodily exertion, of which he has had enough, or too much. It relieves his home of its dulness and sameness, which, in nine cases out of ten, is what drives him out to the ale-house, to his own ruin and his family's. It transports him into a livelier, and gayer, and more diversified and interesting scene, and while he enjoys himself there, he may forget the evils of the present moment, fully as much as if he were ever so drunk." And most important of all, Herschel remarked, "Nothing unites people like companionship

---

[28] Nicholas Hans, *New Trends in English Education in the Eighteenth Century* (1951), p. 211.

in intellectual enjoyment." With books, the dreary clouds of despair and loneliness could be driven away.[29]

With a few noteworthy exceptions like Herschel and Dickens, contemporary social critics and reformers failed to understand, or at least to sympathize with, this imperative need for escape on the part of the physically and spiritually imprisoned. The great majority of the missionaries of reading, who came bearing social soporifics put up by the church or by Brougham's Society for the Diffusion of Useful Knowledge, simply could not countenance this motive. The result was that their zeal to spread the taste for reading was seriously, almost fatally, misapplied. They preached true doctrine—the rewards that lie in the printed page—but for the wrong reasons. Had they recognized the deep-seated desire for imaginative and emotional release which disposes ordinary people to read, and not insisted upon their own well-meant but unrealistic program, their efforts would have borne far healthier fruit. Any man, observed Wilkie Collins, "can preach to them [the common people], lecture to them, and form them into classes; but where is the man who can get them to amuse themselves? Anybody may cram their poor heads; but who will lighten their grave faces?" [30]

The obstacles in the way of the spread of reading among the masses were varied and numerous. . . . But while the impediments were great, the need was greater. The hunger for diversion was only one of the incentives that sooner or later drew men to the printed page. Others were almost as powerful: the desire to keep up with the events of the fast-changing world; the spirit of self-improvement which permeated down to the masses from the prevalent individualistic philosophy of the age; and the seething social unrest which found expression and focus in the radical propaganda of the period from 1815 to 1850. The size of the audience that devoured the writings of Cobbett and the Chartists is perhaps the best proof that the working class had not been reduced to a completely bestial condition. "The very vileness of the life in the herded towns and the very misery and discontent,"

---

[29] "Address," pp. 8–10.
[30] *A Rogue's Life,* chap. vi.

says A. S. Collins, "became creative forces. . . . For the harsh discipline of the factories and the ugly wretchedness of the houses that were often no better than hovels, led men naturally to a sphere where they might find some self-expression, and to dreams and theories which might feed hope in their starved spirits. . . . Those gloomy tenements were the forcing houses of intellectual discontent, and from them shot up a new class of uneducated readers." [31]

Whatever they read—escapist fiction, or recipes for improving their economic position through increased knowledge and application to their trade, or virulent diatribes against political and social injustice—the English common people of the nineteenth century were, like human beings in all ages, dreamers of dreams. However drab, weary, and monotonous their lives, somewhere in their oppressed souls persisted an unquenchable desire for a happier gift from life than unremitting toil and poverty. Of these millions of Englishmen, H. G. Wells's late Victorian Mr. Polly is as good a symbol as any. Deep in his being, despite the deadening influence of the elementary school and life as a draper's assistant, "deep in that darkness, like a creature which has been beaten about the head and left for dead but still lives, crawled a persuasion that over and above the things that are jolly and 'bits of all right,' there was beauty, there was delight, that somewhere—magically inaccessible perhaps, but still somewhere, were pure and easy and joyous states of body and mind." [32]

There were uncounted numbers of Mr. Pollys in nineteenth-century England. Few read as widely or as constantly as he did; but a great many found in the printed word at least something of the same excitement and imaginative release. Among them, whose forebears had lived on the outermost fringes of the literary tradition, if, indeed, they had touched it at all, the frustration produced by the birth-throes of a new society bred a wholly novel veneration for the printed word.

---

[31] *The Profession of Letters,* pp. 42–43.
[32] *Mr. Polly,* chap. i.

IV

Economics and Politics

ÉLIE HALÉVY
[*Malthus, Bentham, and Utilitarianism*]

W. W. ROSTOW
*Economic Factors and Politics: Britain in the
Nineteenth Century*

CRANE BRINTON
[*Victorian Political Thought: Conclusions*]

[*Malthus, Bentham, and Utilitarianism*]

ÉLIE HALÉVY

Malthus's famous work, the *Essay on the Principle of Population,* had appeared in 1798. The father of Thomas Malthus was
a Jacobin, an executor of Rousseau's will, and a disciple of the
leveller and anarchist William Godwin. But the son did not share
his father's humanitarian optimism, and refused to subscribe the
creed of Priestley, Condorcet, and Godwin, the belief in unlimited
progress. He held that mankind had grown up in a hostile environment, and is doomed to a never-ending warfare against it—
that a life of plenty is not for man. For population tends to increase more rapidly than the means of subsistence. When he
came to put in writing his objections to his father's faith, Malthus
believed he could enforce his theory by giving it a mathematical
form. 'Population has,' he maintained, 'a constant tendency to
increase beyond the means of subsistence. . . . Population,
when unchecked, increases in a geometrical ratio. . . . The
means of subsistence could not possibly be made to increase
faster than in an arithmetical ratio.' And 'the necessary effects
of these two different rates of increase, when brought together,
will be very striking'.

It was a gloomy book. Its conclusions were purely negative.
But it appeared during the height of the anti-Jacobin reaction,
and the moment was propitious for a refutation of the French
Utopias. This amply accounts for the immediate success of the

From Elie Halévy, *England in 1815,* 2nd ed. Vol. I of A *History of the
English People in the Nineteenth Century* (London: Ernest Benn Limited,
1949), pp. 572–587. Footnotes have been renumbered.

first edition—a small book hastily put together, a mere pamphlet of the moment. But is it a sufficient explanation of the permanent success of the book, of the astounding popularity of the Malthusian doctrine?

To account for it we must first of all remember that the economists of the British school differed from the physiocrats by regarding labour, not the bounty of nature, as the sole source of wealth, from the Continental economists by finding the standard of value in labour, not in utility. But to maintain that labour is the sole source of wealth and the sole standard of value is to maintain that every pleasure is purchased at the cost of an equivalent or almost equivalent pain, that man is not born to plenty, that a parsimonious nature doles out to him in scanty measure the means of subsistence, and that population exercises on its resources an unremitting pressure. Malthus's doctrine was contained implicitly in the doctrine of all the preceding British economists. It can even be found explicitly, if incidentally, enunciated by Hume, Adam Smith, and Stewart. Malthusianism, therefore, confirmed prejudices already dominant in economic science, fitted into the established tradition. This explains a permanent success which survived the accidental popularity enjoyed by the first edition of the *Essay*.

And we must also bear in mind that at the close of the eighteenth century the Poor Law was a source of perpetual anxiety to the English legislator. His object was to obtain from the paupers relieved by the public a due return of labour. But during a period of grave distress he felt himself obliged to permit serious relaxations of principle. A host of pamphlets were published, whose authors, in conformity with the principles of Adam Smith and his followers, maintained that the system of poor relief, as it was administered in Great Britain, was opposed to the laws of nature, put a premium on idleness and incompetence, and encouraged the population to outgrow the means of subsistence. Among these pamphlets was Malthus's work.[1] In 1798, at a moment

---

[1] To realize how closely the work of Malthus is attached to this entire class of literature, see especially the little treatise of John Townshend, *A Dissertation on the Poor Laws by a Well-wisher to Mankind*, 1786. Townshend is a forerunner of Malthus and even, through Malthus, of

when the guardians were distributing relief with a reckless extravagance, Malthus endowed the economists with arguments of a novel and striking character to denounce the waste and to pass a wholesale condemnation upon the system of poor relief.

It would, therefore, be a grave error to treat Malthus, as the student might be led to treat him by a consideration of the circumstances in which his work was first published, as a mere pamphleteer of the counter-revolution. Certainly the harsh attitude which it implied towards the proletariat recommended Malthusianism to the middle class. But the English middle class, though it remained sternly opposed to revolution and sentimentality, was increasingly open to the ideas of the Liberal reformers, as the anti-Jacobin panic faded from the public memory. The Tory organ, the *Quarterly Review*, was anti-Malthusian; the *Edinburgh Review*, the organ of the Radical Opposition, erected Malthusianism into a dogma.

No doubt in its author's pseudo-mathematical statement the Malthusian thesis is not easy to maintain; it would be difficult even to give it an intelligible meaning. Nevertheless, Malthus's combination of extreme simplicity and apparent scientific accuracy may well have recommended his book to a middle-class public which, though without any very solid education, prided itself on its scientific temper. It was hard to resist the suggestion made, and refuse to credit the existence of a law stated with such assurance, defined so precisely. In the matter of scientific truth the self-taught man is easily satisfied. Nor is his public more exacting. The historian Hallam would even declare the mathematical formulation of Malthus's principle of population to be as indubitable as the multiplication table.[2] And the day was at hand when Ricardo, more Malthusian than Malthus

---

Darwin himself. We may also consider the following significant passage (*First Report of the Philanthropic Society*, 1789, p. 15): 'So deeply perverted is the whole system of parish government, so defective in execution, as well as wrong in principle, that it falsifies the most substantial maxim in police, that population is the strength and riches of a State. By the creed of an overseer, the number of births is the standard of a nation's decay, and the command to increase and multiply was given as a scourge to mankind.'

[2] Quoted by Harriet Martineau, *Autobiography*, 1877 ed., vol. i, p. 210.

himself, was going to base on that principle the entire theory of the distribution of wealth, indeed wellnigh the whole of political economy.

The son of a Jewish stockbroker, Ricardo had never received a classical education. In fact his education had scarcely exceeded the standard of what we should now term primary education. Hardly fourteen years of age, he had entered business. In his scanty hours of leisure, and without a teacher, he completed his education as best he could. He studied chemistry and mineralogy, installed a laboratory in his home, was one of the first members of the Geological Society. But his favorite study was political economy. For it was related to the matters which were the subject of his professional work. We have already noticed his share in the controversy occasioned by the depreciation of the banknote, when a series of newspaper articles had revealed his capacity as a thinker. He was already a celebrity, if not yet the head of a school. That position would be his only when another economic question had attracted public attention, and Malthus had distinguished himself by a further discovery.

Since 1805 Malthus had been teaching history and political economy in the college established by the East India Company for the education of its servants. Little by little he had reached an original theory of rent which he regarded as the direct consequence of the *Principle* which he had formulated in 1798.[3] Since population tends to increase more rapidly than the means of subsistence, man is continually obliged to bring under cultivation soils of an inferior quality. Hence of necessity a constant increase in the cost of foodstuffs, which would increase also the reward of labour and of capital spent upon the lands first cultivated, did not both wages and profits tend to the normal level in the manner explained by Adam Smith. In consequence a surplus accrues from the more fertile areas which is the landlord's income—his rent. Thus the increase, nay the very existence of rent, is an effect, not a cause, of the increase in the cost of living. In England economic conditions favoured the acceptance of this

---

[3] For the modifications introduced into the passages which deal with rent in the successive editions of the *Principle of Population,* see Bonar, *Malthus and his Works,* p. 222.

theory. On the other hand, the census returns showed a rapid increase of population, and the soil of the United Kingdom was no longer sufficient to feed its inhabitants. On the other hand, rents were continuously rising. Plainly the two phenomena must be related as cause and effect. When the restoration of peace was followed by an agricultural crisis, a parliamentary commission was appointed to investigate its causes. A large proportion of the witnesses before this Commission maintained, almost unconsciously, the theory of Malthus.[4] Buchanan, in his edition of the *Wealth of Nations* published in 1814,[5] and the economist West in an essay published in 1815,[6] maintained theories very similar to his. Malthus decided that, if he were not to lose his property in the theory, he must no longer delay its publication. He therefore published his essay on 'The Nature and Progress of Rent'.[7]

This was the signal for Ricardo to intervene. In a short essay 'On the Influence of a low Price of Corn on the Profits of Stock',[8] he accepted the two laws which Malthus had formulated and of which the latter depended upon the former, his law of population, and his law of rent. But he rejected the protectionist consequences which Malthus deduced from his laws in his essay of 1815. And to prove his own doctrine of Free Trade he built upon both an original system of laws regulating the distribution of wealth.

The law of wages is the first consequence of the law of population. According to this law, the amount of wages received by the labourer, the natural price of his labour, is the amount necessary to enable him to subsist and to perpetuate his species 'without increase or diminution'. For wages cannot decrease without starving the labourer, nor increase without an increase of the

[4] Cannan, *A History of the Theories of Production and Distribution in English Political Economy from 1776 to 1848*, pp. 147 sqq.

[5] *Observations on the Subjects treated of in Dr. Smith's Inquiry into the Nature and Causes of the Wealth of Nations*, vol. iv, pp. 33 sqq.

[6] *An Essay on the Application of Capital to Land by a Fellow of University College*, Oxford, 1815.

[7] *An Inquiry into the Nature and Progress of Rent and the Principles by which it is regulated*, 1815.

[8] *An Essay on the Influence of a low Price of Corn on the Profits of Stock, showing the Inexpediency of Restrictions on Importation*, 1815.

population which will re-establish the equilibrium with the means of subsistence.

The law of profits followed. If the amount of wages, as calculated in terms of foodstuffs, remains fixed, that amount, as calculated in terms of money, must constantly increase, since the cost of extracting from the soil an equal amount of nourishment increases constantly, as the growth of population compels the cultivation of inferior soil. But this alteration of wages cannot affect rent which is a fixed quantity. It must therefore affect profits. In this way the law of differential rent and, by implication, the principle of population explain a phenomenon universally verifiable—the progressive decrease of profits. With the natural progress of society the labourer remains at an equal level of bare subsistence, and the capitalist receives a constantly decreasing income. The landowner alone grows continually more wealthy, and this increase of wealth represents neither labour nor risk. Such was the outline of the system which Ricardo now set himself to develop in all its details and applications. Not till 1817 would he publish, as the fruit of two years' labour, his classic, the celebrated *Principles of Political Economy and Taxation*.

This famous work is abstract in its treatment, its style arid. But because Ricardo is a difficult author to read, it does not follow that his work is academic, out of touch with practical life. What indeed was the origin of the principle of population on which the entire edifice is constructed? A pamphlet inspired by the circumstances of the moment, the whim of a publicist, indignant at the maladministration of the Poor Law. What, again, were the books with which in 1809 and in 1815 Ricardo had paved the way for his Political Economy? The reflections of a business man upon a controversy which was occupying Parliament and the Press. The first principles from which Ricardo sets out in his attempt to construct an entire system of economics, were taken practically unaltered from the phenomena of contemporary life. His new theory of the distribution of wealth was an abstract defence of the passions which were exciting the London mob to riot, and were effecting a coalition of Labour and Capital against the landlord. This explains its immediate adoption as their political creed by an entire party, and the ease and rapidity with which it was popularized. In her *Conversations on Political Economy* which appeared in 1816, and whose aim, as the sub-title informs us, was 'to explain in familiar language the elements of that science', Mrs. Marcet explained successfully the entire doctrine of Ricardo without misrepresenting a single point of importance.[9] 'I know not why,' said the hero of a Bulwer Lytton novel, published a few years later, 'this study' (Political Economy) 'has been termed uninteresting. No sooner had I entered upon its consideration, than I could scarcely tear myself from it.'[10]

Thus by 1815 the theories of Malthus had been incorporated by Ricardo into the classical tradition of political economy. But contemporaneously Ricardo's teaching was itself incorporated into an entire system of philosophy whose action upon British public opinion would be profound and lasting, the philosophy of Bentham and his school.

Unlike Malthus and Ricardo, Bentham did not achieve an immediate success. His *Introduction to the Principles of Morals and Legislation* had been written about 1775, contemporaneously with the publication of Adam Smith's *Wealth of Nations,* and had been published in 1788 without attracting any attention. The countless manuscripts in which he expounded the plan of an entire system of jurisprudence, wholly different from the established system, emancipated from the domination of metaphysical fictions and founded on the rational and lucid principle of 'general utility' or 'the greatest happiness of the greatest number', had been written before the *Introduction* was published. But it was not until 1802 that Dumont published in France the *Traités de Legislation Civile et Penale.* And even after their publication England continued to ignore Bentham, or, if he was known at all, it was not as a writer but as a philanthropist and, moreover, as an unsuccessful philanthropist. He had invented a novel type of prison, a circular prison equipped with a system of central supervision, the Panopticon or house where everything is visible. He had done his best to persuade the British Government to

---

[9] *Conversations on Political Economy, in which the Elements of that Science are familiarly explained,* 1816.

[10] Bulwer Lytton, *Pelham,* Book I, chap. xxxvi, 1st ed., 1828, vol. i, p. 336.

adopt it, had offered to undertake the financial responsibility and administer himself the institution he proposed. He had even purchased a site for the future prison out of his private means. But the passage through Parliament of an Act in favour of the scheme had borne no fruit. Neither Pitt nor his successors had given Bentham the support he had been promised. Already sixty years of age, unknown as a philosopher, impotent as a philanthropist, his fortune devoured by the Panopticon scheme, he believed his career at an end, and his life a failure, when in 1808 he made the acquaintance of James Mill, who had just come up to London from Edinburgh University, and was laboriously earning a livelihood by hard work with his pen. Bentham converted Mill to his philosophy. Mill in return restored Bentham's self-confidence, propagated his ideas, and gathered around him a school of disciples. In the history of social science in Britain during the early nineteenth century the formation of this Benthamite school was an event of the first importance. The Benthamites were in the strictest sense of the term a sect and their influence is comparable in its extent to the influence of the Clapham sect. Possessed by an equal enthusiasm, their inspiration was widely different. Their thoroughgoing rationalism was in striking contrast with the emotionalism of the Evangelicals.

Only seven years had passed since the junction between Bentham and James Mill, only five since Mill had taken a house at Westminster, next door to Bentham's, and already the influence of Benthamism was spreading in every direction. James Mill was expounding its creed in the *Edinburgh Review* and in the *Philanthropist,* the magazine of the Quaker William Allen. In the House of Commons Bentham's lifelong friend, the barrister Romilly, was urging year by year in conformity with his friend's principles a mitigation of the penal code, a reduction in the number of 'capital felonies'. James Mill introduced Bentham to Robert Owen and Lancaster, indeed, to all who were seeking the reform of society in a system of popular education . . . James Mill became the friend of Ricardo and introduced him to his master: without Mill the *Principles of Political Economy and Taxation* would perhaps never have been written. And finally, it was through Mill that Bentham made the acquaintance of

Francis Place, the famous electoral agent of the Westminster constituency. We have remarked the formation at Westminster about the person of Bentham of the youthful party of 'Radicals'. Fame had come to Bentham and with fame wealth. In 1813 Parliament had voted him an ample indemnity as compensation for the losses incurred in his Panopticon propaganda. A kindly and eccentric old man, owner of a house in town and a country seat, he commanded an army of disciples. The philosophic and social ideas of the eighteenth century had awoken from a slumber of twenty-five years. What was the common philosophic principle on which the Utilitarians built their jurisprudence, their political economy, and their politics? Man seeks pleasure and avoids pain. This, according to Bentham and his disciples, is the fundamental law of human action. The *summum bonum* is pleasure—not indeed the passing pleasure of the individual, which would render impossible a scientific treatment either of happiness or morality—but 'general utility', 'the greatest happiness of the greatest number'. Hence a rational art of conduct presupposes the knowledge of the conditions which produce pleasure and pain—that the former may be sought, the latter avoided. And this knowledge is in turn to be obtained only by constructing a psychology modelled on the natural sciences already in existence. But these fall into two classes, the sciences which collect facts, and the sciences which explain and construct a system of laws. It was after the pattern of the latter class, the sciences whose objects are elementary and simple phenomena, that the Utilitarians conceived their new science of human nature.

Such was the spirit of their age and country. It is a current belief that the English are cautious observers, with a keen eye for detail, careful to respect the complexity of nature, as opposed to the French, who delight in intellectual constructions and in generalization. This belief, however, is far from the truth. In reality simplification has been the distinctive character of British thought during the nineteenth century. British men of science . . . united the inexperience and the boldness, a boldness often successful, of the self-taught man. They were reasoners who sought and discovered simple laws, men of intuition, who claimed to perceive beneath the manifold of natural phenomena, the outlines of a machine, whose parts are few and whose motions are all sensible.[11] It was because it was at once the simplest hypothesis, and the most easily visualized that Dalton adopted the atomic theory: it rendered the fundamental composition of bodies visible. And the method of Bentham and his school was Dalton's method applied to the moral sciences. In both departments there was the same simplification, the same 'atomism'.

The human soul is a compound of psychical atoms, elementary feelings, agreeable and disagreeable, which differ in intensity, duration, number, and the manner of their mutual combination.[12] And the laws which govern their association are few and simple, the law of association by likeness, and the law of association by contiguity. Possibly even these two laws could be reduced to one, the law of association by likeness being a special case of the law of association by contiguity.[13] Bentham had translated a work of the Swedish chemist Bergmann. James Mill was the intimate friend of Thomas Thomson, a champion of Dalton's atomic theory. Both were conscious imitators of the methods of the new chemistry. Their ideal moralist, educator, and legislator must practise a mental chemistry and learn from the chemist the art of constructing complex psychoses by combining simple elements.

The art of education would thus consist in effecting in the

---

[11] This explains the small progress made by English scientists of this period in higher mathematics. The algorithm of algebra repelled them. They had no liking for this blindfold search of truth. Thomas Young, who cared the most for pure mathematics, avoided symbolic forms of proof, and used as far as possible the language of everyday life, thus making his works more difficult of understanding, by his very attempt to render them more popular (Peacock, *Life of Thomas Young*, pp. 116-7, 183). Similarly, when Berzelius, having accepted the atomic theory, attempted to describe the composition of bodies by formulæ in which the atoms were represented by letters to which were appended co-efficients showing the number of atoms in a particular combination, Dalton denounced this new algebra, and described Berzelius's symbols as 'horrible'. The student of chemistry, he maintained, could as easily learn Hebrew (W. C. Henry, *Memoirs of John Dalton*, p. 124).

[12] Bentham, *Principles of Morals and Legislation*, chap. iv (*Works*, vol. i, pp. 15 sqq.).

[13] James Mill, *Analysis of the Human Mind*, chap. xi (ed. 1878, vol. i, pp. 376-7).

minds of children such an association of ideas that the child could no longer separate his personal happiness from the happiness of his fellows. The art of legislation would consist in producing a similar effect in the mind of the adult. By associating the idea of certain actions with the idea of certain penalties the legislator would intimidate the potential criminal and prevent crime. The scientific analysis both of the crime and its penalty into their constituent elements, their atoms, and the establishment of an accurate proportion between both sets of factors, constituted, for the Utilitarian, the entire science of penology. Evidently a science of calculation and reasoning and nothing beyond. The Utilitarians neglected as useless learned research, knowledge of the historical growth of law. Their method was, as they fully realized, in radical opposition to the historical method which the professors of Germany were bringing into fashion. 'One might,' wrote Bentham in scorn, 'open an historical school *à la mode d'Allemagne.* Der Herr Savigny in Germany could furnish admirable masters. . . . To the army and the navy of a country substitute, for example, a history of the wars waged by that same country . . . to an order on a cook for dinner substitute a fair copy of the housekeeper's book as kept during the appropriate series of years.' [14] These words express the hatred of the reformer for the traditionalist, of the self-educated man for the university scholar.

We may now adopt a slightly different point of view and consider not, as hitherto, the mutual combinations of simple psychoses in the individual consciousness, but the association of individuals to form a society. Bentham and his followers saw in society only an agglomeration of individuals, by nature existing in isolation, and united solely by deliberate acts of choice. A certain proportion of individuals were happy, a certain proportion unhappy. Which side of the account showed a surplus? This was the balance which you must strike whenever you would appraise a law or a custom. Such simple operations of addition and subtraction composed the entire intellectual task of the

---

[14] *Bentham, to his fellow Citizens of France, on Houses of Peers and Senates,* 1830 (*Works,* ed. Bowring, vol. iv, p. 425).

Utilitarian reformer. And this individualism may be regarded as a kind of sociological 'atomism.' It explains the line of reasoning which led the Utilitarians to political radicalism. And it was the foundation-stone of the entire edifice of the new political economy.

Suppose all the individuals, the atoms, out of which the social body is composed, perfectly selfish, inaccessible to any motive except a self-regarding prudence. Suppose them also perfectly rational, free from any liability to be blinded by passion. And finally, suppose them perfectly free, admitting no external constraint in the pursuit of their economic end. We thus construct a society as unlike any actual human society, as the simplified world of the sciences is unlike the world of sensible experience, but capable of rendering equal service in the explanation of phenomena. In fact, the hypothesis, precisely because of its simplicity, rendered possible an almost mathematically exact description of several economic phenomena such as the circulation of currency, exchange, and banking. It even provided a sufficiently accurate account of the exchange of manufactured goods. And Ricardo believed that, when taken in conjunction with the Malthusian law of population, it made it possible to explain with equal accuracy the distribution of the profits of labour between the landlord, the capitalist, and the labourer. No attempt was made to discover empirical laws by observation. Nor was economic theory controlled by statistics. Political economy, as understood by Ricardo and James Mill, was built up by the series of hypothetical constructions whose character we have explained above. And this individualist theory was applied by individualist practice. The Utilitarians regarded the State as in principle incapable of controlling economics. It must stand aside and leave individuals free to regulate their economic interests, whether as between class and class, or nation and nation.

Thus was erected the finished edifice of Utilitarianism. It was frankly irreligious. Neither as the explanation of history, nor as the foundation of ethics or law did it invoke the supernatural, or any principle transcending sensible experience. Nor is it sufficient to call Utilitarianism irreligious. It was aggressively anti-religious, and regarded religion as a whole and Christianity in particular as the bane of civilization. For religion was of its very nature a form of asceticism, a perversion of feeling which made men desire pain and shun pleasure. And asceticism had produced a taste of slavery of every description, political, legal, and economic. Above all, it was responsible for the notion of punishment as an 'expiation', which had induced men to regard the infliction of punishment as a good thing in itself, and had thus led to that useless severity of the criminal code against which from the commencement of his literary activity Bentham had never ceased to protest. It would be impossible, without unduly anticipating the future, to relate the campaign of anti-Christian propaganda—no longer Deist as in the days of Tom Paine, but frankly Atheist—to which the Utilitarians would lend their aid. It dates from the years which followed the conclusion of peace. But even before 1815 the body of doctrines which composed philosophic Radicalism exercised in every direction a subversive influence. Thus with Bentham and his friends we are at the opposite pole alike to the Toryism of the Government, and to Evangelical pietism. How then are we to explain the success of the Utilitarian propaganda in face of the hostility of Government, and the influence, felt universally, of the Protestant revival?

When the Tories wished to discredit Utilitarianism, they denounced it as an unpatriotic philosophy, inspired by foreign ideas, and especially by French ideas. Were not the political principles of the Benthamites the democratic principles of the Jacobins? Did they not derive their ethics and their jurisprudence from Helvétius and Beccaria, their psychology from Condillac, their philosophy of history and their political economy from Condorcet and Jean-Baptiste Say? Were they not irreligious Voltairians? Had not Bentham composed in French and published at Paris his *Traités de Legislation*? [15] But the Utilitarians could reply with truth that all these so-called French ideas, of whose importation they were accused, were in reality English ideas which had found a temporary home abroad.

---

[15] For these French influences, see Halévy, *Formation du Radicalisme Philosophique*, vol. i, pp. 23 sqq.; vol. ii, pp. 219 sqq., 232 sqq.; vol. iii, pp. 231 sqq. and *passim*.

Before its appearance in France democracy had been the political theory of the Anglo-Saxon rebels in America, and the Americans had themselves taken the principles which inspired their rebellion from Locke and the English republicans of the seventeenth century. Condillac's psychology had been the psychology of Hartley and Hume before Condillac ever set pen to paper. It was in England that Voltaire had learned to be a Freethinker. Throughout the anti-Jacobin reaction there had been thinkers—Erasmus Darwin, Thomas Day, Edgeworth, the political agitator Horne Tooke, Unitarians of the school of Priestley—who defended what they believed to be the national tradition against the innovations of the Tories. Among the ideas which composed the Utilitarian system, their economic theories tended more and more to take the first place. And, however great the influence of the French physiocratic school, Hume and Adam Smith were undoubtedly the founders of the new political economy, and the action of the latter was influential in circles impervious to the complete Utilitarian system. The English are a nation of traders and can be governed only by men who possess the commercial mentality. Pitt, the leader of the anti-Jacobins, was a disciple of Adam Smith. Burke, at once the orator and the philosopher of the counter-revolution, was as zealous in the defence of economic individualism, as in the denunciation of political. When the Tories became a party of landlords and country squires, they signed their own death warrant. In this way its economic principles obtained for Utilitarianism an entrance into the governing classes.

Twenty-five years of Tory reaction, a reaction, when all is said, only skin deep, had proved insufficient to destroy intellectual traditions so deeply rooted. And moreover, what official body was in existence on which the party in office could rely to combat the ideas of the Benthamites? The Scottish universities? We have seen the empirical spirit which inspired the philosophers of the Scottish school. If they shrank from the conclusions of Hartley and his followers, their hesitation was due only to the extreme simplicity of Hartley's generalizations. For they were men of university training, not self-educated men. But at bottom

they differed from the radical empiricists only by their greater
caution. Was Cambridge less exposed to the infection of Utilitarianism? We have seen that Cambridge had always professed
Whig ideas in political philosophy and in philosophy generally.
Locke, Paley, and Hartley were the philosophers studied. A few
years hence Benthamism will be the fashion among the Cambridge undergraduates.[16] There remained the impregnable citadel of Oxford. But Oxford was asleep and no one could
possibly regard the remnants of Aristotelian scholasticism taught
in her schools as a living intellectual tradition.

To be sure, for the past twenty years there had existed on the
Continent a new system of philosophy professed by men of
genius, capable of attracting the rising generation and counter-
acting Utilitarianism. But it was not English. And how many
Englishmen were able to read Kant, Fichte, and Schelling in the
original? The Scottish professors attempted to make acquaintance with the new systems through the channel of French interpreters, Madame de Staël and De Gerando; [17] and what they
understood, they disliked. Alone in England the poet Coleridge
had been deeply influenced by German thought. He had abandoned verse for prose, and exchanged the naturalistic pantheism
of his youth for a transcendental theology inspired by Schelling.
But Coleridge, far more than Bentham, was an eccentric and
lonely thinker. He belonged to no teaching body, to no national
tradition. In 1815 his influence still counted for nothing.

England is a free country in which government pressure plays
no part in the formation of public opinion. It is not therefore
surprising that the Utilitarian propaganda overcame the opposition of official Conservatism. It is more difficult to understand the
influence exercised by Utilitarianism in an environment so impregnated with Evangelical religion as was the England of the
early nineteenth century. Was the action of the two forces successive? And was Utilitarianism in 1815 a growing force, Evangelicalism on the verge of decline? Such an explanation would do

---

[16] John Stuart Mill, *Autobiography*, pp. 76–7.
[17] Dugald Stewart, *Dissertations* (*Works*, 2nd ed., 1877, vol. i, pp. 394,
413, 416).

very central

violence to the complexity of the situation. The fundamental paradox of English society . . . is precisely the partial junction and combination of these two forces theoretically so hostile.

We have already spoken of the philanthropic activity common to both parties. Utilitarianism was a philosophy wholly practical. Bentham and his friends were ardent advocates of the Panopticon model prison, whose very idea had been conceived by their leader, of Lancaster's model school, and Robert Owen's model factory. They regarded these institutions as 'moral' inventions, akin to the important technical inventions which were transforming industry, as 'moral' machines ingeniously constructed for the automatic production of virtue and happiness. The Christian philanthropists, whatever their repugnance to such a mechanical conception of psychology and ethics, could not be deaf to the appeal of inventions so beneficent as these. Between the Utilitarians and the 'old Dissenters' there existed little short of a permanent alliance. And even the Methodists and Evangelicals sympathized with the Utilitarian philanthropy. As their contribution to the common task the Christians brought their zeal, their missionary spirit, their love for a self-imposed discipline. Nor did the Utilitarians fail to appreciate these qualities. 'Townshend,' wrote Bentham, 'was once what I had liked to have been, a Methodist, and what I should have been, had I not been what I am.' [18] And the Utilitarians contributed their practical sense, their conviction of the possibility of a social technique, an art of employing the right means to obtain the desired end. Many Christian philanthropists, educated in the school of industrialism, shared their convictions on this point. But we may go further and discover closer affinities between Benthamite Utilitarianism and Protestant pietism.

It would be a mistake to establish an irreconcilable opposition between the Utilitarian ethic and the Christian on the ground that the former is founded on pleasure, the latter on sacrifice. For Utilitarian morality cannot be described without qualification as hedonism. It was based simultaneously on two principles. One of

---

[18] *Works,* ed. Bowring, vol. x, p. 92. Cf. ibid., p. 508: 'If to be an antislavist is to be a saint, saintship for me. I am a saint!'

these, it is true, was the identification of the good with pleasure; but the other, of equal importance with the former, was the duty incumbent upon man, in virtue of the natural conditions to which his life is subject, to sacrifice present pleasure to the hope of future, and purchase happiness at the cost of labour and suffering. This law of work, implicit in Bentham's moral arithmetic, was the principle explicitly proclaimed by the entire system of the classical political economy, and introduced into Utilitarianism an undeniable element of asceticism.[19] How can we explain the popularity of the Malthusian thesis at the very period when public opinion was apparently attached more closely than ever to the Christian tradition? Undoubtedly it contradicted one of the fundamental doctrines of the Bible. But it also refuted the atheistic humanitarianism of the eighteenth century, and taught that man is destined by his very nature to an unending struggle for existence, to a perpetual condition of hardship. And this appealed to the ascetic and Christian preconceptions of the public. It was in vain that the Benthamites attempted to reconcile the principle of population with the creed of unlimited progress, the pessimism of Malthus with the optimism of Condorcet. Their efforts could not abolish the distinction between the standpoint of the French Utilitarians and that of their English teachers. Benthamism, as its principles were popularized about 1815 by James Mill the Scotsman, was the French philosophy of the eighteenth century adapted to the needs of a nation moulded by a dogmatic and austere religion.

And moreover, the Utilitarians were individualists. The object of their entire ethical teaching was to bring home to the individual that society existed only through him and for his sake, and that it is his personal duty to maintain his rights and pursue his interest. To be sure, this individualism was not that theological individualism of the Protestant, whose character has been described above. And moreover, the new type of Protestantism,

---

[19] For the kinship between economic asceticism and Protestant asceticism, see the subtle, often indeed the excessively subtle, observations of Max Weber, *Die Protestantische Ethik und der Geist des Kapitalismus* (*Archiv für Sozial Wissenschaft und Sozial Politik*), 1905, vol. xx, pp. 1 sqq.; vol. xxi, pp. 1 sqq.

which had sprung from Wesley's preaching in the previous century, was in this respect an enfeebled type. The organization of the Methodist sects was more hierarchic than that of the old seventeenth-century sects; and the Evangelicals were Methodists who had refused to break with the Anglican Church. But no Protestant revival could fail to be, in some measure at least, a revival of religious individualism. Between the secular individualism of Bentham and the authoritarian Christianity of the High Churchman, the liberal Protestantism of the Unitarians, Scottish Calvinism, the Methodist sects, the Evangelicalism of the Low Church party, constituted a series of imperceptible transitions. Nor was the individualism of the Utilitarianism radically antisocial. It did not exclude in principle all state intervention. For the Utilitarians looked to the legislature to establish a harmony of interests in the community by imposing obligations sanctioned by penalties. And even where they rejected government interference, they encouraged the formation of voluntary associations whose members would pursue a common end by the free surrender of a portion of their independence. Secular philanthropy and Protestant Dissent stood in equal need of such associations. They were thus among the typical expressions of private initiative in nineteenth-century England. British individualism is a moderate individualism, a mixture whose constituents are often mingled beyond the possibility of analysis, a compound of Evangelicalism and Utilitarianism.

Economic Factors and Politics: Britain in the Nineteenth Century

W. W. ROSTOW

I

Virtually all who work within the terrain of history or the social sciences must seek to relate economic forces to social and political events. Many have resolved the problem to their satisfaction within the context of particular investigations. There has been, however, relatively little generalized and formal treatment of the issue in recent years. All would now agree that economic factors, in some sense, are important for politics; virtually all would agree that, in some sense, economic factors are not sufficient to explain political events. From that point, however, the subject tends to disappear into the realm of *ad hoc* formulations and private faith. This chapter constitutes an effort to expose some of the complexities inherent in the relationships among the levels of activity which constitute the structure of society. It is an exploratory discussion, and presents no new self-contained system of analysis; it is, rather, an effort to make explicit some of the assumptions which appear to underlie a great deal of contemporary thought and writing, academic and otherwise.

A reviewer has recently criticized a study in which a rather rigid and whole-heartedly economic interpretation was applied

From W. W. Rostow, *British Economy of the Nineteenth Century* (Oxford: Clarendon Press, 1948), pp. 126–144. Footnotes have been renumbered.

to a complex set of political and social events. The reviewer concluded: [1]

> Now, such an extreme position is neither science nor history. It is merely a new theology—not even good theology, because it is uninspired. It has faith in nothing but a verbal formula. It would rule Christ out of the Christian Church, Lincoln and the idea of national unity out of the Civil War, Roosevelt and the concept of human dignity out of the battle against the Nazis . . . even a great scholar knows only a very little and may not understand the little he knows. Facts are easily acquired by industry and diligence. The meaning of the facts, all their meaning, is beyond the ken of any scholar—perhaps beyond the ken of mortal man.

It would be widely accepted that any satisfactory explanation of political events must leave a place for the role of ideas and for the individual; and the ultimate meaning of facts, indeed, belongs to philosophy, if not to religion, rather than with history or the social sciences.

The rejection of a rigid and monolithic economic interpretation of politics, however, is not in itself a satisfactory answer to the problem. The study of history moves towards general history, where a conscious effort is made to relate economic, social, and political phenomena; while social scientists seek increasingly to bring their various techniques to bear in a co-ordinate way on common bodies of data. Such communal effort within the social sciences demands, if it is to be fruitful, a minimum explicit agreement concerning the manner in which the various strands into which human society forms itself relate to one another.

A more refined view of society as a whole and of the interrelations among its parts is not merely an appropriate academic objective. Its achievement may prove prerequisite to successful resolution of major problems of policy at home and abroad which characterize the post-war period. A much expanded range of functions has now fallen into the hands of governments in both their domestic and foreign responsibilities. They are not likely to

---

[1] F. Tannenbaum, 'A Note on the Economic Interpretation of History', *Political Science Quarterly*, June 1946.

diminish substantially over the foreseeable future. Their exercise demands at bottom no less than the conscious manipulation of whole societies. Decisions of priority and of technique which have confronted governments in the tasks of domestic reconstruction have been made, explicitly or implicitly, on theories concerning the way society as a whole operates: the ends it will accept, and the stimuli required to produce the actions which will achieve them. Problems of policy in the occupation of Germany and Japan involve assumptions of equal breadth and inclusiveness, as do other aspects of contemporary foreign policy. The relationship between economic factors and politics is thus a matter of wide and not wholly academic concern.

II

A useful refinement can be achieved by distinguishing the economic forces which impinge on politics, directly or indirectly, with respect to the time-periods over which they persist. The number of categories one might derive by application of this criterion is obviously very considerable. As a first approximation, however, we shall distinguish and illustrate three types of economic impulse, operating over long,[2] medium, and short periods.

Long-period impulses are, for these purposes, those which proceed from the way people earn their living. Whether a man owns a large estate or is an agricultural labourer; whether he works in a cotton mill or a mine; whether he manages industry, engages in commerce, or goes each day to an office in a bank, obviously affects his outlook on society and on the political system; and it is one factor which enters into his judgement concerning particular policies and political events.

This long-run economic influence has much to do with the way people dress, the sort of houses they build, the standards of

---

[2] It is evident that society is also shaped by forces operating over much longer periods than those distinguished as 'long' here: geography, climate, and the mysterious heritage of communal life persisting over centuries. These very long-run forces which form a large part of the subject-matter of anthropology, as well as history, are not considered here except briefly. . . .

behaviour which govern their relations to one another, the literature and art and science which they generate. The nature of social life in, let us say, rural England, of the early nineteenth century cannot be deduced from the simple fact that it was an agricultural society proportioned in a certain way among large and small landowners and farm labourers. But its analysis would not be meaningful if it were not placed within such a framework. This is the sort of economic influence which is associated with the conventional analysis of the Industrial Revolution. The long process of industrialization shifted drastically the proportions of the population working at different occupations. The economic balance of society altered, and with that change came, gradually, shifts in the social life and the political structure of the country. In the study of the nineteenth century, volumes on literature as well as politics can begin, quite properly, by paying their respects to the Industrial Revolution.

The long-run economic impulse, among other factors, affects the judgement of individuals on particular political issues; but it may operate at several removes indirectly. And its influence may take various forms. When, for example, the Ten-hour Bill was under discussion in the 1840s, representatives of the landowning interests took various positions. Some, representing the strand of responsible public service embedded in the social tradition of their class, pressed for the Bill on paternal humanitarian grounds; others supported the Bill as a tactic of embarrassment to the manufacturers who were striving concurrently to repeal the Corn Laws; others joined the manufacturers in opposing the Bill as a general threat to men of property. In each case a part of the political position of the agriculturalists on this issue can be traced to the long-run impulse imparted by their general economic background; but the form of its expression, and even the net position taken, varied widely. There is no simple one-to-one relationship necessary between the long-run impulse and a given political judgement.

Perhaps the most important political influence of this type of economic impulse is in setting the political structure of a society: the nature of the electorate, and the distribution of power among the branches of government. The two great Reform Bills of

1832 and 1867 incorporate the effects of this long-run influence.[3] The link between the increase in relative economic importance of the industrial and commercial middle classes and the Reform Bill of 1832, the link between the rise of the industrial working classes and the Reform Bill of 1867 are, of course, familiar. The timing of the passage of these acts, the role in their evolution of the concepts of modern democracy, and the complex political battles which preceded their acceptance cannot be deduced from a knowledge of the changing composition of the British working force; one can deduce, however, a strong pressure to alter the balance of political power in definable directions.

James Madison, in the discussions which led to the adoption of the American Constitution, expressed clearly the predominant influence he assigned to economic factors in politics; and since the issue of a national Constitution was structural, long-run economic factors in these terms would be relevant.[4] Madison defined the function of government as the peaceful resolution of differences of opinion and interest within the community, or the regulation of factions, and he wrote:[5]

. . . the most common and durable source of factions has been the various and unequal distribution of property. Those who hold and those who are without property have ever formed distinct interests in society. Those who are creditors, and those who are debtors, fall under a like discrimination. A landed interest, a manufacturing interest, a mercantile interest, a moneyed interest, with many lesser interests, grow up of necessity in civilized nations, and divide them into different classes, actuated by different sentiments and views. The regulation of these various and interfering interests forms the principal task of modern legislation. . . .

---

[3] The passage of the Third Reform Bill of 1884, which enfranchised agricultural workers and some of the remaining industrial workers, notably miners, was not, of course, due to a growth in relative importance of the agricultural working classes. It was due, primarily, to the desire of certain groups of Liberals to strengthen the left wing of the party, as well as to a widening acceptance of the concept of universal suffrage. See G. M. Trevelyan, *British History in the Nineteenth Century*, pp. 389–91 and J. L. Garvin, *Life of Joseph Chamberlain*, vol. i, chap. xxi, pp. 459 ff.

[4] The timing of the Constitutional Convention and the urgency which characterized its proceedings were, of course, related to the troubled course of economic and political events over the period 1783–7.

[5] *Federalist*, No. 10.

It is the long-run impulses from the economic system which change the balance of power among factions.

A second type of impulse imparted to the social and political systems by the economy can be described as operating over the medium-run or over trend periods. The British economy in the period 1790–1914 operated in a manner such that trend movements of (say) longer than a decade existed which placed particular pressures on one part of the community or the other. In the period of the French wars, for example, agriculture prospered; but the working classes suffered from chronically high food-prices. In general these years were pervaded by a contented spirit among agriculturalists and by a working class unrest out of which the conceptions and aspirations of the modern British working-class movement took their initial shape. The Speenhamland System and the Combination Acts reflect two of the diverse responses of politics to the pressures exerted by the working classes, generated in turn by very specific economic trends. From 1815 to the mid-century, on the whole, agricultural prices fell, and important segments of the farming community were discontented and defensive, with consequences which infected the whole sequence of political life. After 1873, for a quarter century, industrial prices tended to fall, and industrial profit margins as well. It is no accident that, in these years, the assumptions of mid-century *laissez-faire* were questioned not only by socialists, but also by the advocates of fair trade and by those who formed the international steel-rail cartel. In many ways the new imperialism of these years was a Great Depression phenomena; and it is a just, if fortuitous, irony that Joseph Chamberlain's battle for power was lost in 1906 because several basic trends of the Great Depression had, by that time, changed their direction: capital exports were very much on the rise, in part due to policies Chamberlain had previously sponsored in the Colonial Office; British exports were expanding; prices and profit margins were on the increase; tariff reform no longer appealed.[6]

---

[6] See E. Halevy, *A History of the English People, 1905–1915,* p. 14. The election of 1906 was affected not only by the turn in the trends from their

The trend movements of the economic system generate new attitudes of mind among the classes and interests affected, and they lead often to the formulation of major legislative proposals which form, over considerable periods, the focus of political life, the concrete issues over which ministries fall and reputations are made and broken. The attrition against measures of protection from 1815 to the final repeal of the Corn Laws is a political sequence strongly affected by the trends within the economic system over the three decades preceding 1846. Another important example was the trend movement of real wages from 1900 to 1914. There were many deep and long-run influences which made likely the development, in these years, of a political party representing the British working classes, and the formulation in British society of a concrete programme designed to increase working-class security. But that development was given a special urgency and impetus because the economic system in its normal relatively free workings, yielded a more rapid rise in retail prices than in money wages. Much of the political pressure which was mobilized for the Liberal reforms in the pre-1914 decade derived its immediate strength from the desire of the working classes, conscious or otherwise, to redress by legislative action the balance of income distribution decreed by the economic system.[7]

A third type of impulse imparted to politics by the economy is the short-period impulse, associated with the fluctuations of the trade-cycle and of the harvests. In the nineteenth century severe unemployment or a passage of high food-prices did not usually determine the nature of the major political issues nor the basic relative strength of the forces which arrayed themselves on either side; but they tended to detonate the underlying forces, by accentuating unrest, and to achieve some slight but occasionally significant shift in the balance among those forces. They thus

---

Great Depression pattern, but also by the cyclical expansion begun in 1904 which would be accounted a short-period phenomenon in the vocabulary used here.

[7] Halevy, op. cit., pp. 270–3 for the combination of long-run and trend forces which affected the budget of 1907; and, more generally, for the basis of working-class discontent in falling real wages, p. 441.

affected the timing and character of political events. The introduction of the Speenhamland System in 1795 was, for example,
connected with the two bad harvests which had immediately
preceded; the appearance of the Luddites in 1811 and again in
1816 was directly connected with the severe unemployment of
those two years. It is significant that the Peterloo massacre occurred in 1819, a year of severe depression; although the pressures which underlay it, as reflected in the banners which were
carried, indicate the influence of long-run and medium-run
forces as well.[8] Similarly, the Reform Bills of 1832 and 1867 both
represented the adjustment of political pressures long in their
generation; but they were passed at or close to cyclical low
points preceded by intervals of working-class unemployment
and unrest.

We have thus distinguished three types of impulse from the
economic system acting on social and political life: a long-run
force which constitutes the framework within which social life
develops and which affects particularly the general balance of
power within the community and the structure of its political
life; a medium-run impulse, associated with economic trends,
which often defines major political issues and generates movements designed to achieve certain concrete political results; and
short-run impulses which in the nineteenth century affect the
timing of political events and their colouring.

This rough and arbitrary formulation, based on the distinction
of the time period over which an economic force operates on
society as a whole, explains in part why the relation of economic
factors to politics is complex. Embedded in any political event
of importance one is likely to find not simply an economic factor,
but a range of economic factors, with different and even conflicting impacts on the minds and public behaviour of men. The

---

[8] The short-run influence was represented at Peterloo by the cry of
cyclical depression, 'A fair-day's wages for a fair-day's work' which Carlyle
made the occasion for extended reflection (*Past and Present,* bk. i, chap.
iii, pp. 23–9). The trend impact of the war-time high food-prices can be
detected in the call for 'No Corn Laws'; and the long-run aspirations of the
working classes in 'Equal Representation or Death' (W. Page, *Commerce
and Industry,* p. 47).

great gathering at St. Peter's Field, Manchester, in August 1819 was not simply a response to a period of cyclical unemployment; nor was it simply a response to several previous decades of painful social adjustment and restricted standards of living; nor was it simply the response of an increasingly large segment of the community to the lack of political representation. It was all of these things.

III

The multiplicity of economic impulses acting on political life is among the lesser complexities which surround the relation between economic factors and politics. More difficult is the mechanics of their operation. Here it is necessary to seek a rough outline of the structure of society which historians and social scientists can take as agreed.

It is a useful convention to regard society as made up of three levels, each with a life and continuity of its own, but related variously to the others. These three levels are normally designated as economic, social, and political. Each is itself capable of elaborate sub-division, and these sub-divisions, too, have their own life and continuity. Within the economy, for example, one can isolate for examination the evolution of its capital market institutions; or the development of iron and steel trades; or the course of wheat prices. Nevertheless the production and distribution of goods and services form a unified and interrelated operation; and the component parts of economic life may be studied in relation to a larger whole (e.g. the national income, or the level of real wages). Similar unity among discrete strands exists in the social and political levels of society although, lacking quantitative measures and refined analytic tools, it is less easy to define and to manipulate.

The economic level of society imparts, as is suggested above, a variety of impulses to social and political life; and these have been distinguished in three arbitrary categories according to the time-period over which they operate. But it also receives back from social and political life other impulses which affect its course. Such interactions are discussed briefly below. For the moment it is sufficient to note that the relations between the economic level of society and its other levels do not run merely in one direction.

The social level of society, as viewed here, is very broad indeed. It includes the way people live, the culture and religion which they generate and regard as acceptable, their scientific pursuits, and above all the general political concepts which serve to rationalize their relationship to the community.[9] In a passage which implies the use of an analytic structure not very different from that developed here, Professor G. M. Trevelyan has written: [10]

> . . . the social scene grows out of economic conditions, to much the same extent that political events in their turn grow out of social conditions. Without social history, economic history is barren and political history unintelligible. But social history does not merely provide the required link between economic and political history. It has also its own positive value and concern.

There are various senses in which this intermediate role for social life may be taken as meaningful. The limited aspect most relevant to present purposes, however, is the manner in which general ideas are formed which serve as the basis for a considerable array of political positions on particular issues.

It appears to be a general characteristic of education, in a broad sense, that the community equips the individual with a set of general ideas which he may modify, reject, or supplant, by which the multiplicity of situations he confronts is reduced to

---

[9] A satisfactory definition of the term 'social' is difficult, although its accepted usage is tolerably clear. A. L. Rowse (The Study of History, p. 69) has defined social history, on a rough-and-ready basis, as how society consumes what it has produced. This is not wholly satisfactory; for the writer, the teacher, the dress designer, are all producing in an economic sense; and it would be an arbitrary distinction that would segregate the work of the scientist in an industrial laboratory from the scientist in a subsidized university laboratory. Social activities appear to arise from human needs or desires over and above the technical minima necessary for food, shelter, clothing, and reproduction. These needs are met by the production of goods and services; and the working force consists of men, not factors of production; therefore, 'social' qualities and objectives suffuse the process of production as well as consumption.

[10] English Social History, p. vii.

order, made explicable, or tolerable. These are the conceptions that relate man to his family, his fellow-men, to his church, and to the state. In terms of nations similar general ideas develop which set, let us say, a Britisher's conception of his relationship to the continent of Europe, or to the African colonies, or to the United States.

These powerful simplifications alter only slowly; but they alter in such a way that they appear adequately to conform to the society's range of interests, and to explain the phenomena which men confront daily in their lives. There is a hard long test of empiricism that societies, as opposed to individuals, apply to the large ideas they accept. Once accepted these ideas have an authority of their own and a great independent reality among the forces which move men to act.

The fact that such general ideas change slowly, and that men's attachment to them is often impervious for considerable periods to evidence of their unreality, irrelevance, or inapplicability, has led to a considerable literature of cynicism in which men's minds are regarded as an anarchic open market for large concepts, unrooted in solid judgement or empirical tests. Pareto's sociology and some of the subsequent literature of fascism enshrined this bias, as did some of the discussion of semantics in the United States during the 1930s.[11] While it is clearly necessary to take

---

[11] J. M. Keynes closed *The General Theory of Employment, Interest, and Money* with a comment on the relative potency of vested interests and ideas in determining the course of history (pp. 383–4): '. . . the ideas of economists and political philosophers, both when they are right and when they are wrong, are more powerful than is generally understood. Indeed the world is ruled by little else. Practical men, who believe themselves to be quite exempt from any intellectual influences, are usually the slaves of some defunct economist. Madmen in authority, who hear voices in the air, are distilling their frenzy from some academic scribbler of a few years back. I am sure that the power of vested interests is vastly exaggerated compared with the gradual encroachment of ideas. Not, indeed, immediately, but after a certain interval; for in the field of economic and political philosophy there are not many who are influenced by new theories after they are twenty-five or thirty years of age, so that the ideas which civil servants and politicians and even agitators apply to current events are not likely to be the newest. But, soon or late, it is ideas, not vested interests, which are dangerous for good or evil.'

Keynes's observation is not at issue with the view developed here. It would be accepted that a given set of special interests confronting a given

into account the very considerable time lags which attend the
rise and fall of ideas, in relation to the situations which they are
designed to explain, and to appreciate the independent power
they exercise over the minds and behaviour of individuals, at
bottom and in the long run, ideas appear to be rooted in real and
substantial changes in the conditions under which men live.

In the period 1790–1914 the eighteenth-century notion of responsible aristocratic government gave way to concepts of representative democracy; notions of *laissez-faire* and self-help
triumphed over older concepts of paternalism and then quite
promptly began to lose ground to a revived conception of state
responsibility for the general welfare. Similarly, the mid-century
hopes of permanent peace and of universal free trade with the
countries of the Empire dropping like ripe fruit from the tree,
hardened into a more exclusive conception of Empire and a
defensive British nationalism *vis-à-vis* Germany. Each of these
massive changes was associated with real events, economic in
character in the first instance. This does not imply that those
who formulated the ideas were personally motivated by economic forces; nor does it imply that individuals accepted the
new ideas by a Machiavellian process of rationalization. It does
imply that the complex of changes in society which in the end
made the new ideas acceptable to the majority of the British
people were, at their basis and in their origin, economic.

While these conceptions may have economic roots, they often
express the widest sensibility and aspiration of which men are
capable; and the shifts in conception which occur affect men's
attitudes towards issues wider than those of politics. In reflecting
genteel doubt concerning the sanctity of mid-Victorian articles

---

situation can find resolution in a variety of ways; that the course followed
in fact may depend on the ideas current, especially in the short run; and that
the long run, in history, is compounded of a series of short-run resolutions
to particular issues and conflicts. The argument here would emphasize,
however, that the ideas available, and their acceptability, depend on
previous or current experience and interests, not excepting the 'General
Theory'. For a comment on the independent power of institutions, apart
from their 'original meaning or purpose', similar in its general implications
to Keynes's observations on the limited rationality of political judgement, see
L. B. Namier, *The Structure of Politics at the Accession of George III,* vol.
i, p. 164.

of faith, Gilbert and Sullivan were no less a product of the Great Depression than Joseph Chamberlain.

As suggested earlier there are many aspects of political life which take their shape from the social level of society; but for these limited purposes the most significant is the generation of wide conceptions in terms of which specific issues are viewed, fought over, and settled. Social life furnishes to politics its vocabulary.

Politics, the third level of society, emerges as the arena in which the various interests and powers of the community negotiate the terms of their common life. In the resolution of any particular issue there is involved not only the network of pressures and formulations arising from the economic and social levels, but also the technique of politics itself: the accepted methods of mobilizing and making effective these pressures according to the rules and procedures which constitute the political system. This is an absorbing human activity demanding special virtuosity. The life of the political system, like that of the economy and the social system, is in a sense autonomous. At any moment of time the terms within which it works are, it is true, given; and the balance of power within the community sets relatively narrow limits to the actions which are permissible to the politician. Nevertheless, within those limits, a complex process of formulation, persuasion, personal initiative, and compromise takes place which, in its detail, bears often relatively little direct relation to the large basic forces outside the level of politics.

In nineteenth-century Britain the types of issue which arose for political settlement can be grouped in three categories:

First, issues of the balance of power in society and of political structure. Of these the Reform Bills are the most obvious example. The great crisis in the early years of this century over the power of the House of Lords would, of course, also fall within this category. The various Acts, legislative and in common law, relating to the status of the trades unions are only a little less important, and might well be grouped with the basic constitutional issues.

Second, issues of the distribution of income in a broad welfare sense. This category would include the Corn Laws and their

repeal; the Factory Acts; education bills; the social legislation of the pre-1914 decade; issues concerning the structure
and incidence of taxation, most notably, perhaps, the question of the income tax. The effects of such legislation over a
period of time may be to alter the balance of power in society, and thus to help induce structural changes at a later
stage. But the issues actually arise and are settled fully
within the existing political structure.

Third, issues concerning the security and relative power of the
community as a whole. Foreign affairs fall within this category, and questions of war and peace; although one might
include, for Britain in the nineteenth century, the problem
of Ireland as well. This general category falls mainly outside
the present discussion, although it is susceptible of analysis
in similar terms.

As between issues of the balance of power and what are here
called issues of income distribution a sharp line is, occasionally,
difficult to draw. The final repeal of the Corn Laws involved pressures almost as various and profound as the passage of the Reform Bill of 1832; although there is a sense in which the Corn
Laws were lost with the passage of the latter act. And a useful
distinction can probably be made between them as distinct
types of political issue. The Reform Bill of 1832 involved specific
consequences which could not be fully foreseen, stretching far
into the future. It was not an issue of measurable gains or losses,
for the segments of the community concerned, like another
penny on the income tax. It shifted political power at its bases
and thus stirred very large hopes and fears. For the landowning
gentry a whole way of life appeared to be at stake; and emotions were brought into play transcending economic factors in
their limited sense. These are the issues in politics which involve the greatest dangers to the process of peaceful adjustment;
and in countries outside Britain in modern times they have often
yielded revolution or civil war.

In terms of the international community, and problems of
diplomacy, many of the issues which have resulted in war have
been of this nature. No significant, peculiarly economic stakes
appear to be involved, but rather the relative power of states

which, it is felt, will determine the decision in a whole range of particular future issues incapable of exact prediction. The role of economic factors in a matter of Corn Laws, taxation, or tariff adjustments between nations is evident and fairly direct. The overtones of high moral or political principle which are occasionally invoked on such occasions are a relatively thin and conventional veneer. In the case of the Reform Bill of 1832, or the German invasion of Belgium in 1914, however, the basic balance of power appears in question for classes within a community and as between different communities. And with the balance of power there enters legitimately the whole way of life to which men are attached and the large ideas to which they owe allegiance.

Much of the dissatisfaction with analyses which place an exclusive emphasis on economic factors in politics arises from the obviously complex nature of the forces and motives which enter into these basic struggles for power, either within states or between them. Men do not usually fight and die for finite economic gains. They are, more generally, moved by a loyalty to ideas. These ideas, in turn, may be largely generated from economic life, and from a social life substantially shaped by the economy. But in war men are often moved by a simple sense of community quite independent of a particular economy or society, except that it is theirs; and in combat soldiers are often dominated by a loyalty that extends not much beyond those who are at their side. In times of peace this primitive loyalty to the community, though muted, can constitute an independent element in politics, acting as a powerful solvent in moments of acute domestic conflict, as the Duke of Wellington showed in 1832 and 1846.[12]

IV

The argument has thus far roughly defined the nature of the impulses generated by the economic system; it has sketched briefly the social and political structure on which they have their impact; and it has indicated some possible routes by which

---

[12] On the eve of the American Civil War the symbols of community were widely invoked, notably in the closing passage of Lincoln's first Inaugural Address; but they failed to produce a resolution.

they may find their way, directly and indirectly, to the arena of politics. As suggested earlier, however, the economic system receives as well as imparts impulses; and these interactions are an additional element of complexity.

One of the more important interactions lies in the field of education. One can trace in nineteenth-century Britain a dynamic reinforcing process: the rise of an industrial and commercial middle class; its insistence on improved facilities for education; and the consequent strengthening of that class in both its economic activities and in politics. In the latter half of the century a similar process affected the economic and political strength of the working classes. Religion, too, and science, and other aspects of social life tended, over the century, to reinforce the economy whose structure and direction of change gave them their special bias. In its broadest sense it is the social level of society which produces or fails to produce men of the type required for the efficient working of the economy.

The influence of politics on the economic system is, of course, very considerable. It sets, in the first place, the framework of law within which goods and services are produced. Among other major issues of the century, British politics was called upon to decide whether the basic framework of the economy was to be one of protection, or of free trade; and whether bargaining in the labour market was, in part, to be collective, or as between individual workingmen and firms.

More than that, the structure of government taxes and disbursements, decreed by politics, constituted an authentic part of the economic process; and the government's intervention was meaningful even when it took the negative form of a Gladstonian obsession with economy. In many of the most important activities of government it is accurate and convenient to regard politics as a way of taking economic decisions alternative to private markets. This is patent in the case of war; notably, in this era, the French wars, when the society, having become engaged in large military enterprise, transferred to the government a significant range of economic decisions (e.g. the scale and terms of foreign loans and subsidies). These decisions, in turn, shaped indirectly many other aspects of economic life. Although the direct role of government in the economy is less marked during times of peace in the nineteenth century, the nature of political intervention, as a minor but real instrument for the taking of economic decisions, is much the same.

Society emerges, then, from this schematic analysis, as a dynamic structure of three levels, each with a quasi-autonomous life of its own, each receiving and imparting impulses from and to the other levels. In the formal sense with which economists are familiar the analysis of society is a dynamic problem: the impulses which are generated within society require time in which to work themselves out.

Movements within the economic system, long-run in character, set the framework within which social life and its concepts evolve, pursuing, on the whole, a sluggish life of their own. The long-run impulses have their main impact on politics, having worked through the social structure, where they have been generalized, associated with non-economic aspirations, and crystallized into ideas and particular, often structural, political objectives. Similarly, the medium-run or trend impulses imparted from the economic system become associated with wider concepts and objectives before they make their full appearance in politics, often in the form of particular non-structural acts of legislation. The short-run economic forces tend to strengthen or weaken the relative forces making for or resisting political change; and they thus affect the timing and character of political events. The political level of society receives from the other levels this complex of impulses and by rules and conventions and ideas which are themselves partially the product of long-run economic and social influences, sorts them out, and seeks to resolve conflicts among them in a manner such as to avoid resort to settlement by trial of brute strength. In performing these functions the political level of society sets the basic terms of both social and economic relationships in society; and, in receiving and disbursing income, it actively engages in current economic activity of significance.

V

It is evident that the unity of the structure of society, and its shape, derive from the character of man: his desires and motives and aspirations. Any complete theory of society would have to begin, formally, with psychological hypotheses. No attempt to supply them will be made in this limited and exploratory discussion. But two observations concerning the position of the individual, in the structure outlined above, appear germane.

It will be noted that, of its nature, this structure is determinist in a loose-jointed way at the most. The economic system imparts certain impulses to the social system; and it constitutes a framework within which social life must develop; but it does not determine the particular manifestations of social life. Romantic poetry may have been connected, by various remote and proximate links, to the coming of the Industrial Revolution; but it was not written by Arkwright or Ironmaster Wilkinson. Similarly, the nature of political problems, and within limits, the nature of their possible resolution is given, at any moment of time, by forces external to political life. The particular solution arrived at, however, may vary substantially; and its particular form may have important consequences for the future. The area for freedom of action afforded to the individual in politics is certainly not infinite; but it is real. Referring to an incident that involved F. E. Smith, Mr. Churchill once wrote: [13] 'This probably turned the scale in favour of Mr. Bonar Law's leadership, and may traceably have altered the course of history. However, it is always being altered by something or other.'

Within economic life, as well, technical conditions and the economic environment are given, but progress is achieved by the efforts of men stretched to the limit of their energy, imagination, and competence, as the history of any great firm will attest. There is, in short, a considerable place for the individual within each level of this structure. On occasion it may be proper to regard the course of history as inevitable, *ex post;* but not *ex ante.*

Secondly, there is the question of motives. Is man in society basically economic man? Here only a very limited observation will be hazarded. It appears necessary to distinguish the behaviour and motives of individuals from those of economic, social, and political groups. In devoting his efforts to the repeal of the Corn Laws John Bright was no doubt helping to effect a shift

---

[13] W. S. Churchill, *Great Contemporaries,* p. 151.

in relative economic advantage among the economic and social classes of Britain. One can scarcely imagine an issue more purely economic in its character or intent; and without its economic substance there would have been no such well-financed agitation. Yet Bright, the Quaker, threw himself into the great crusade out of the broadest of motives, as a whole man; and as his later positions on the Crimean War, the American Civil War, and the Second Reform Bill indicate, he regarded the repeal of the Corn Laws as part of a larger political conception for Britain and the world. There is little doubt that many of his followers shared the Free Trade vision, with its full penumbra of hopes for peace, democracy, and universal prosperity.

More generally, the personal economic motives of a political figure appear often to have little relevance to his position on particular issues. The profession of the politician or statesman, as one who helps press forward or resolve peacefully the pressures thrust from below into the arena of politics, is, in one sense, intrinsically disinterested. The politicians who directly benefit economically from participating in politics are, for Britain in the nineteenth century, rare. And in other countries and in other times, the fact of the connexion rarely appears to be the decisive element in shaping major political events. Men may seek in politics the opportunity to exercise powers of leadership or of oratory; they may enter politics from a sense of service or out of family or social tradition, like Namier's 'Inevitable Parliament Men' of the eighteenth century. The interplay of personal motives and impersonal political forces is, surely, a relevant and interesting aspect of the study of society. It appears necessary, however, to avoid treating them as identical.

At every stage, then, the individual appears to work out his destiny within limits which, while narrow from the perspective of the whole evolution of society, provide, more or less adequately, for the expression of his full energies and aspirations. History seems to be tolerant of the individual if he avoids the larger illusions of grandeur.

[*Victorian Political Thought: Conclusions*]

CRANE BRINTON

It is difficult to make the nineteenth century come out neatly as a period, a decent, well-rounded, historical period. You cannot find any pat phrases for it, like the "Age of Reason" or the "Great Awakening." It did things in its own way, but somehow failed to do them with the final grace of a style. Certain museums, like the Metropolitan Museum of New York, have courageously assembled rooms to illustrate the decorative arts of the nineteenth century, and have placed them, probably without deliberate irony, in their proper time-sequence after the eighteenth century. The result is curious. It is not that a *salon* of the 1840's could possibly be mistaken for anything else. The nineteenth century was avidly antiquarian, but so, too, was the sixteenth. The nineteenth century, like the sixteenth, transmuted what it borrowed, so that Ruskin's Venetian Gothic was as different from that of mediæval Venice as Michelangelo's Renaissance from the Rome of the Cæsars. Whistler might use bamboo and green paint liberally, but his Peacock Room belongs in London, or even in Washington, rather than in Japan. Nineteenth-century decorative art failed to achieve the unity of a style. Its ingredients failed to mingle properly, and remained apart in a kind of hash. The hash indeed is different from any one of its elements and indeed from anything else. It is quite recognizable—as hash.

From Crane Brinton, *English Political Thought in the Nineteenth Century* (London: Ernest Benn Limited, 1933; 2nd ed. London and Cambridge, 1949), pp. 293–304.

This same diversity, this multiplicity of elements unabsorbed into a common thing, is evident in the other aspects of human activity in the nineteenth century. To be sure, there is apparently always a mysterious element in this world making for diversity; or, perhaps, life always escapes the annihilation which the complete success of the thinker or of the artist would bring. At any rate, not even the neatest of centuries, the eighteenth, is comfortable in the strait-jacket of generalizations, whether they be the generalizations of the critic working in the glib medium of words, or the generalizations of the connoisseur seeking a wordless identity of recognition. Right reason did not ride with John Wesley in pursuit of the devil through the slums of England, the tears shed over *George Barnwell* were not rhetorical tears, and Strawberry Hill is at least a symptom of the Gothic revival, if it is not the disease itself. But the nineteenth century is almost perversely resistant to attempts to define it. In literature, "Victorian" has nothing like the precision of "Elizabethan." Not even the simple opposition of romantic and classic, which serves so well in the latter half of the eighteenth century, is of much use in the nineteenth.

So, too, in political thought no great simplifying categories are readily available. The nineteenth century did make certainly underlying assumptions. Victorian Englishmen were as sure of perpetual progress as men of the second century were of the approaching end of the world. But progress hardly adds anything immediately to mere living. Faith in progress is faith in an order constructed out of human desires for quite definite satisfactions, or it is no faith at all. When we come to consider what kind of order nineteenth-century Englishmen embodied in their political faiths, we find their minds as variously furnished as their houses. The nineteenth century is a warring ground of political doctrines. True, so are most other centuries, say notably the seventeenth. But the conflict of men and ideas in seventeenth-century England, or even the more complex conflict of men and ideas in sixteenth-century France, can without too much apparent distortion be dramatized into a kind of unity. Certain doctrines emerge with the imprint, with the style of a given century. Such are the doctrines of the Divine Right of Kings, of the

natural goodness of man, of the separation of powers. Now it is
not impossible so to dramatize the politics of nineteenth-century
England, not impossible to distinguish, in Newman's sense of the
word, certain "notes" of English political thought in the period—
indeed we are about to attempt to do so—but the task seems
harder, and its conclusions more open to exceptions, than for
previous centuries. Perhaps we are too near the nineteenth century to see its true outlines; or perhaps the nineteenth century
really was what it thought itself to be, an exceptional age.

Certainly the nineteenth century agreed with Ranke that its
task was above all one of reconstruction. The revolutions of the
late eighteenth century—the American, the French, and the
industrial revolutions—had struck the Western mind with a
sense of catastrophe which, one is inclined to believe, far ex-
ceeds our present sense of the catastrophic nature of the Russian
Revolution. Men as far apart as St. Simon and Maistre set out
consciously to rebuild an authority and a faith which all men
might accept. Something essential, men felt, had been destroyed,
and there was as yet nothing to put in its place. Quite ordinary
people could agree with Morris that "we not only are, but we feel
also ourselves to be living between the old and the new." The
nineteenth century was consciously an age of transition, an age
of groping. It was sometimes quite romantically proud of the
fact, and invented a phrase, the *mal du siècle,* to consecrate its
uncertainties.

Reconstruction meant that after all, there was something to
build with. The commonplace that the nineteenth century was
a century of history can hardly be questioned. Not that the nineteenth century invented history, or even scientific historical
research, which goes back at least as far as Mabillon. But fashionable eighteenth-century thought had seen in the past little but a
tissue of errors, a hindrance, in so far as it had got itself enshrined in custom, to men who knew so much more than their
fathers had known. If, however, wrote Acton in the true nineteenth-century vein, the past has been a burden, a knowledge of
the past is the surest way of lifting that burden. Liberal and conservative alike sought to reinforce their programmes by explain-
ing that the course of history led surely up to them. Men

appealed to history as their grandfathers had appealed to Nature. When one compares the views of a Brougham and a Disraeli on the history of the Whigs and the Tories, one doubts whether they thereby anchored themselves more firmly in objective fact. Maine spent his life attacking the law of Nature in the name of the law of history, but the historical method led to much the same conclusions on freedom of contract as those the history-scorning Bentham had reached. No doubt the study of history taught the nineteenth century a certain respect for the immobility of social groups, a certain sense of the difficulties confronting the social reformer, without which its vigorous pursuit of social panaceas would have been disastrous. No doubt, too, that its diligent study of the historic and prehistoric past of the race uncovered facts which no political thinker can do without. But it was a little too sure that history, like Nature, explains itself. Here as elsewhere the nineteenth century could not bring itself to a healthy scepticism. M. Paul Valéry has recently revived his countryman's famous *boutade* that history is a "fable convenue"; and M. Croce has long insisted that, if the true historian makes the past live in the present, he thereby identifies the past with his own living will. The nineteenth century, anxious though it was to preserve the sovereignty of the self-conscious individual, insistent though it was on the fact that living things grow and are not made, was unwilling to make full allowance for the subjectivity it postulated. In history it sought for finality, for complete agreement (up to the present at least). In spite of its abandonment of the eighteenth-century world machine, in spite of its acceptance of a universe subject to growth, it would not entertain the possibility that growth is a miracle, and that therefore there is a limit to our ability to predict and control growth. It discovered the dynamic State; but it was a bit aghast at its own discovery.

We are thus brought to a second great commonplace about the nineteenth century. It was the century of progress. Its world was not static, but dynamic. It brought home to ordinary men the notion of evolution. Again, this notion was not wholly new. Histories of the idea of progress commonly go back to Ionian Greece. But the mediæval man was as certain about his earth as he was about his heaven, and he never thought of either as really changing. And, though men like Condorcet are sure of the fact of human improvement, the kernel of eighteenth-century political thought is a conviction that there is a pattern of the State as unchanging, though in motion, as Newton's universe (which of course is also in motion), and that once thought has ascertained that pattern, men have but to conform their actions to it to attain a perfect bliss. The nineteenth century substituted progress for perfectability. The difference may seem purely verbal, but it is real enough at bottom. For the notion of progress leaves the process of growth open at both ends. By implication, it leaves the past as uncertain as the future. It is true enough, as we have pointed out, that the nineteenth century had not the full courage of its belief in progress. Spencer contrived to know as much about the cosmic process as Thomas Aquinas had known. He takes away with the one heavy hand of ethical conviction what the other hand of evolution had offered. So many nineteenth-century evolutionists did this sort of thing, so many identified their private desires with those of the new deity, that it is small wonder that there has been a reaction against the idea of progress. But progress offered us with the winning modesty of a Bagehot or with the generous, if morally indignant, fervour of a Huxley is too attractive a gift to be refused. The doctrine of progress has too often been merely an uncritical extolling of the virtues of the machine age, of Western civilization, of an approaching *pax Anglo-Saxonica*. It has been the peculiar property of a group of sincere but narrow votaries whose world has been formed above all by the Protestant Reformation and the French Revolution, and whose "liberalism" is profoundly distrustful of many of the irrational graces and corporate loyalties of human life. Progress has been wedded to other abstractions like Liberty, Democracy, and Nationality, as if it were not already abstract enough in itself. But for better or for worse, the idea of progress is now an indispensable part of our intellectual equipment. We may not feel for China or Mexico the contempt of the evolutionist who is sure those nations have not properly evolved. But we cannot escape the fact that our lives are different from the lives of the primitive cave-dwellers from whom we almost certainly descend. We rarely limit ourselves to the modest adjective "different," most of us, in our innermost consciousness, commit ourselves to such evaluating terms as "higher" or "fuller." We may not be the masters of the process of evolution, but we are certainly its children.

Nineteenth-century political thought busied itself with the task of reconstructing a social order which had collapsed with the *ancien régime*. It sought that order in the study of history guided by the idea of progress. It formed an amazing number of solutions. Nothing is more striking in nineteenth-century political thought than its variety. Hardly a man of those we have studied in these pages can be said to be anything like in complete agreement with another. What may be called eternal contrasts of temperament, like the contrast between the liberal's optimistic trust in his fellow men, and the conservative's pessimistic distrust of them, run through the century. Maine, like Coleridge, was in this sense a Tory by temperament; yet their programmes differ greatly. English socialists seem to have little but the label in common. Owen, the Ricardian socialists, Morris, Hyndman, and the Fabians are all agreed that poverty must be abolished, but they are far from agreed as to the steps necessary to abolish it. Indeed, one of the obstacles in the way of writing a history of English political thought in the nineteenth century according to the method of ideas rather than that of men is the fact that there seem to be as many ideas as men. Schools of thought indeed there are, like the historical school; and certain common methodological concepts, like that of society as an organism. But to employ such categories is to list together men who have little in common. Spencer, Bagehot, and Kidd all appealed to biology, but with very different results.

A striking thing about these divergent political philosophies is that they led so few men to scepticism. Nineteenth-century Englishmen did indeed come to lose what they called their faith; but they commonly then set about to wail over their loss. To doubt led not to a fertile Pyrrhonism, not to a scientific willingness to rest content with a working hypothesis; it led to the lost-sheep attitude of a Clough. To identify one's scale of values with the order of the universe is perhaps more than a temptation to the thinker; it may well be a necessity of human thought. But it would seem that the nineteenth century committed itself rather unreservedly to this process. It found its own diversity extremely uncomfortable. "We are not made to dwell among ruins," wrote St. Simon after the French Revolution. We must get to work and rebuild—rebuild our society. But there were so many architects, and each was so sure of his own plan! Men built much and variously—Liverpool and Manchester, New Lanark, North Oxford, Regent Street, Letchworth, and Kelmscott. They were all, however, building New Jerusalems. The nineteenth century, we must repeat, was an age of faiths.

If, however, we ask ourselves whether some generalizations can be made to measure the differences between English political thought in 1800 and in 1900, the answer need not be wholly negative. The purely personal elements present at the beginning of the century certainly exist at its end. Making allowance for the differences in their environment, and above all for the discredit which has fallen on the phraseology of the Age of Reason, there is a similarity between the shallow self-confidence and assertiveness of a Brougham and the same qualities in a Winston Churchill. But the balance has altered. In the first place, as the century went on the struggle between *laissez-faire* and State intervention saw the increasing practical triumphs of intervention. At the end of the century, the bland confidence of the Manchester school in self-help for all has given place to the irritated and unheeded protests of Spencer against the Factory Acts. Not even the discovery of the struggle for life could save economic individualism, and we have seen how Kidd found that social legislation was necessary to the "higher" competition. That the nineteenth century solved the antagonism between liberty and authority is obviously not true. But the end of the century saw the problem cleared of a great deal of abstract economic dogmatism with which it had been cluttered at the beginning of the century.

Again, nineteenth-century England, by the very fact that she was forced to experiment with it, did something to make democracy a fact rather than a bugbear. Here, too, we, as heirs of that century, are faced with a problem by no means solved. Democracy is to-day in some circles almost as suspect, its true political implications almost as much in doubt, as in the days of Burke. But after all, the nineteenth century did virtually establish universal suffrage, it did destroy the power of the House of Lords, it did make serious inroads on the sense of caste in Englishmen. We are to-day faced with the problem of leadership—or, if you prefer, that of aristocracy—but we can no longer find a solution in a God-made landed interest. Disraeli's Tory democracy is no longer a living formula. When towards the end of the century Maine attacked democracy in *Popular Government*, he was obviously on the defensive. His irritation at the assumption of the advocates of democracy that that form of government was somehow clothed in inevitability, though it is an irritation with which it is easy to feel an intellectual sympathy, is in itself a tribute to the strength of democracy.

Party alignments throughout the century are with difficulty reconciled with clear-cut distinctions in political thought. Toryism has always had an interventionist tradition, and through the magic of Disraeli took on for a time the guise of democracy. The Tories in 1867 carried through the most radical political reform of the century. Much social, if not socialistic, legislation has had a Tory origin. On the other hand, Liberalism was at first identified with absolute economic freedom, and even radicalism went no farther than the first French Republic. By the end of the century, however, there is discernible a settling-down of party allegiances in conformity with social programmes. Toryism, in accordance with its old habits, has come to rest in the radicalism of a previous generation. The Conservative party is now the party of the victors in the struggle of the industrial revolution. It has indeed its extreme fringe, a group of earnest men who represent the survival of Christian socialism. But on the whole the Conservative party has come to defend the capitalism which has evolved from Manchester. Its very protectionism is no real desertion of Manchester, but a patterning after the successful protectionism of the hitherto most thriving child of the industrial revolution, the United States. It is the Tory to-day who is most likely to regret "Government interference." Liberalism, however, has followed Mill and Green far towards a socialistic organization of society, and in so far as it has any vitality, has merged with Labour to work for a social democracy that aims at the abolition of the kind of inequality the nineteenth century held to be an indispensable foundation for society.

If as regards actual programmes the difference between political thought in 1800 and 1900 is to be summed up as a shift by which radical, democratic, liberal, or popular thought—a precise adjective is hard to find—turned from individualism to collectivism, while conservative, aristocratic, anti-popular thought turned from a collectivism determined by the survival of feudal loyalties to individualism, the difference between the methodological background of political thought in 1800 and in 1900 is by no means so clear. Yet in general it may be said that during the century, conservative and liberal thinkers alike were led to view society less and less as a mechanism, and more and more as an organism. This change is measured by the increased prestige of biology in the minds of political thinkers. We have already emphasized sufficiently the alliance between biology and politics. It was an alliance that hardly taught modesty to political thinkers, and it is not to-day as firm an alliance as it once was. For one thing, we have come to feel that the later nineteenth century, under the influence of biological leads, had altogether too much distrust of the human intellect. Psychology, anthropology, and history combined to teach Bagehot and his contemporaries that civilized man is the creature of centuries of growth, that his vital processes are still the vital processes of the savage, that what we call his reason is the servant, not the master, of his desires, and that therefore reason is still a pretty useless, or even dangerous, tool in politics. Now as a corrective to the eighteenth-century belief in the reasonableness of man, this anti-intellectualism was of great value. But held as an ultimate truth it was almost self-destructive. Reason alone can recognize and remedy unreason, even in politics. Reason may be the youngest child of evolution, but hardly the weakest, and certainly not the most ill-favoured. Kidd's conclusion that reason is impotent, save to destroy, is a caricature on the thought of the century, but a revealing caricature. Even Bagehot praised stupidity with rather less than half-playfulness. The work of the anti-intellectual social psychologists has been of the greatest use. The part of imitation, the *rôle* of the unconscious, the behaviour of mobs, the apparently inevitable sway of symbols and stereotypes, the gap between a man's professions and his practices—a gap which, since he does not perceive it, does not in the least make him a hypocrite—all this is of permanent value for political thought. But the thinkers who analysed all these irrational workings of the political consciousness of the man in the street were at least attempting to free their own minds from the limitations they were studying in others. At the very worst, they might in charity have admitted the possibility of extending their emancipation to others. On the whole they did not, and took refuge in a defensive anti-intellectualism which had its roots in the eighteenth century they disliked. Rousseau's Nature had a strange survival in the work of the evolutionists.

This alliance with biology further strengthened one of the most important currents in nineteenth-century opinion. The eighteenth century had been all but unanimously on the side of nurture; the nineteenth century, if only to show itself a natural and ungrateful child, was to swing violently over to the side of Nature. In the timeless dispute over the question as to whether heredity or environment plays the greater part in human life, the nineteenth century without hesitation took the side of heredity. The French Revolution had made evident the failure of the environmentalists in their attempt to tamper with Nature. Malthus had proved conclusively—at least to his more hasty readers, which is to say the majority—that the more conditions of human existence were bettered, the more misery was stored up for an over-populated and not too distant future. Carlyle and his followers had insisted that schemes for improving men's social environment could not possibly redeem their souls, and that redemption itself was a mystery beyond the search of the environmentalist. Finally, the work of Darwin, especially when capped by that of Weismann, served to make the intellectual temper of the late nineteenth century as fanatically devoted to heredity as that of the late eighteenth had been to environment. Hundreds of ambitious and quite unscientific genealogies showed that virtue and vice bred true, and by the beginning of the present century the Jukeses and the Kallikaks, the Edwardses and the Coleridges had become almost household words.

Now faith in heredity—which must not be confused with the scientific study of genetics—is socially significant as an attempt to stabilize a given society within the limits of existing inequalities of political and economic status. The rich are the able, just as the poor are the incompetent. Both classes breed true. Any attempt to *alter* the distribution of wealth—let alone any attempt to *equalize* its distribution—must be made in defiance of a law of Nature, and is therefore bound to fail. Heredity served the Victorians as original sin had served the Church, to hold together a society unequally privileged. But Victorian society was never really stabilized, never, indeed, achieved more than a fleeting compromise with the forces of social change. Moreover, one of the dangers of an appeal to a scientific principle, even though the appeal is made wholly in the spirit of religion, lies in the undogmatic character of true science. Biologists themselves have gone far beyond Weismann, have ceased, indeed, to put the problem of heredity in the extremely simple terms used during the last century. Social writers are thus obliged either to follow in the steps of the biologists, and abandon their assurance that they have in direct, blending heredity a complete clue to social processes, or else to admit that their "heredity" is merely another god. A considerable body of minority opinion even in Victorian times continued its faith in environment; socialism, indeed, could hardly afford to desert Owen wholly, even in espousing Marxian determinism. Yet such was the prestige of nature as opposed to nurture that many a hopeful soul, meliorist by temperament, was driven to eugenics for a solution of the conflict between his hopes and what his contemporaries assured him were hard facts.

Biology, then, influenced political thought towards an exaggerated distrust of the human intellect and an exaggerated trust in the principle of heredity as understood by Weismann. Yet in spite of, or in part even because of, its alliance with the biological sciences, political thought at the end of the century was richer than at the beginning. It had ramified into a number of special studies which are a bit optimistically called the social sciences. Now these sciences are still in the awkward age. They are noisy, impertinent, and dreadfully sure of themselves. They do not know the virtue of the tentative. They attempt to cover their insufficiencies by an appeal to the methods, or rather to the prestige, of the physical sciences. They confuse their hypotheses with the will of God. They attempt to arrive at a finality beyond judgment and taste, though they can succeed only with the aid of both. But nineteenth-century history, jurisprudence, economics, anthropology, psychology, education, and other social studies did go far towards attaining a discipline of their own. They did an enormous amount of specialized spade-work. Thanks to them, political thought has infinitely more material to work with than it had in the eighteenth century.

How wisely it will use that material it is not for us to hazard a guess. We are perhaps as lost in transition as we can now discern the nineteenth century to have been. But we cannot complain that the last century has left us nothing but ruins. On the contrary, it has left us a vast number of projects of construction in all stages of completion—save the final. It threw itself whole-heartedly into a vast number of social experiments, from infant schools to imperial States. In spite of the World War and the Russian Revolution, the nineteenth century did not end with a cataclysm. It has handed on its experiments pretty well intact. Modern political thought need not profess to repudiate the work of the nineteenth century, as that century professed to repudiate the work of the eighteenth. We may take the lesson of evolution as learned, and be content with the problems we have inherited. We may achieve the contentment the nineteenth century did not achieve, if we will but admit that, since change is inevitable, we do not stop change by calling it progress.

V

The Victorian Years: An Epilogue

G. KITSON CLARK
An Epilogue and a Recapitulation

An Epilogue and a Recapitulation

G. KITSON CLARK

The first thought that comes to mind on looking back at the society that occupied England in the age of Queen Victoria is that one knows very little about it either in detail, or for that matter as a whole, as a subject for generalization. The movement that is going on is so continuous, the variety so great that every historical comment seems fumbling and inaccurate, every generalization inconclusive and incomplete. Even were it possible, as in most contexts it is not possible, to assemble all the necessary facts, or to trace all the relevant actions of all the individuals involved in one movement or transaction, there remains the problem of understanding the motives of a large number of men and women with whom there cannot now be any sort of contact. The situation in any part of England at any moment in the period is, I think, best suggested by those clear photographs of street scenes in various towns, of which a fair number seem to have survived from the second half of the century. They are of things that really happened and of people who really lived and have not been recalled to a reconstructed existence with the help of the historian's ink-bottle; and therefore the result is something we cannot fully understand. The street is filled with people who were once without question there going about their business; but no one can ever recover who they all were, what they were doing before the photograph was taken or what they were going to do afterwards, still less what occupied their minds.

From G. Kitson Clark, *The Making of Victorian England* (Cambridge, Mass.: Harvard University Press, 1962), pp. 275–289.

Nor can anyone recover that sense of common reality, that natural understanding of the world in which they moved as the matter of everyday fact, which they all shared at that moment, and which disappeared for ever as soon as they retreated from life into history.

It is important to remember these things, since men's statements about groups and communities and ways of life which have come to an end tend to seem more precise and inclusive than it is possible for them to be; at best an historical generalization must omit much that is relevant, while even what it does propose as a positive statement is likely to be no more than a tentative hypothesis. Nevertheless, the first general statement which it seems worth while to put forward about the making of Victorian England may seem to be not open to question but rather intolerably trite. It is that the England of Queen Victoria was necessarily a continuation of the periods that immediately preceded it and that in the process of forming it the results of inheritance, in some cases inheritance from very remote periods, played a most important part. It is worth while to emphasize this fact for this reason. The society in which we live is obviously the continuation of Victorian society; there are striking differences between our society and theirs, it is true, but our dress, our political ideals, the mechanized background to our lives and our crowded towns all yield enough resemblance to any society that has existed after the invention of gaslight, railways and the electric telegraph as to lead us to forget that many matters in their society might closely resemble what existed in periods which seem to be absolutely different from our own.

In fact, this error has a more significant cause than a superficial resemblance between ourselves and the Victorians. When an important revolution has taken place it is perhaps always difficult to remember how much of the ordinary world must necessarily survive the revolution and supply part of the background of life after all is over. The nineteenth century was pre-eminently a century of revolutions, and the temptation has been to start history afresh when it begins, assuming that what went on in the centuries of the old régime must by that date have reached its natural end. This is an error that must conceal many of the elements which went to the fashioning of Victorian England. Victorian England was no doubt to a large extent the creation of the political and industrial revolutions of the nineteenth century, but the order of society, which had existed for centuries before those revolutions, lasted robustly into, and in some matters after, the third quarter of the century. Those who were at the head of that order had to make concessions and partially to accept a new system of values, for powerful social forces had come into being which were alien and in some cases hostile to them, while the principle of heredity and prescription upon which their position had been founded was condemned by the political theory that came to be the orthodoxy of the day. Nevertheless, the political power of the old ruling class survived, as did their predominance in society. It is probable that well into the second half of the nineteenth century the landed aristocracy included a large number of the richest men in the country and they certainly remained its social leaders. Till 1867 the grip of their influence on a large section of the electoral system was patent, much of it survived till 1880, some of it probably long afterwards. At least till 1868 the aristocracy normally supplied most of the Cabinet and the Prime Minister, while the paternal sway of nobleman, squire and parson overshadowed much of the countryside.

All this had important results, for it is not only necessary to reckon with this survival in order to understand Victorian England, it is necessary to retain a knowledge of it in order to understand the society that succeeded Victorian England. Not only did some of the native power of the old ruling classes survive into the twentieth century, but as the nineteenth century had gone forward and wealth had accumulated in various hands new social elements had come to amalgamate themselves with the old aristocracy, or to model themselves upon them and to lend to old habits of mind and modes of life a new power of survival, which they would not have otherwise possessed. Therefore, though much that had typified the gentry and the aristocracy had come from the remote pre-revolutionary past, they were enabled to put their trademark on much that went forward with vigour into the future.

Nor was the old order of society all that survived from earlier, and as many hoped irrelevant, centuries. There was also much of the old disorder, and, for many, much traditional degradation. There had been in the eighteenth century, probably there always had been, a cruel primitive background to society, a background of brutality and callousness, of bestiality and heavy drinking and much wretchedness and degradation, inadequately remedied or controlled by any public authority. These things did not vanish when the nineteenth century began, nor had they altogether disappeared by the time it had run half its course. Certainly the law gradually became more effective, and more humane, repressing what was savage and primitive in society, and even eliminating something of what was absurd and brutal in its own operation. Gradually society learnt more of its duty to protect those who were at the mercy of economic and social forces which were too strong for them, to ameliorate their environment and even to educate them. But these processes were often slow, the machinery that had to be used untried and suspect, and many of the lessons to be learnt extremely uncongenial.

Nor did all the forces that were making for change in the nineteenth century inevitably tend to increase the general happiness, or progress, or civilization, of mankind. Two of the most powerful of them were not directed by any conscious human intention to any clearly conceived end; they acted blindly and the evil, or the good, that they achieved were the results of chance. The rapid increase of population in England, Wales and Scotland and, till 1845, in Ireland is on any calculation one of the most important factors in the development of nineteenth-century society, and in many ways its most obvious result was an increase in human misery, particularly in the first half of the century and particularly when the immigrants from Ireland are brought into the picture. In Ireland certainly, and probably in England at least in the early years of the century, it seems to have depressed standards of life by the increase of numbers without a comparable increase in resources. It also probably greatly increased the fluid mass of men, women and children at the bottom of society for whom nothing was provided but casual and unskilled labour and an existence in miserable tenements, hovels and cellars with no necessary provisions for a decent and healthy life, and who received in most cases no intellectual or spiritual training or guidance whatsoever.

Part of this mass provided a social and spiritual problem which Victorian England was unable to solve. Its nature was partly revealed by the activities of various religious missions, by the enquiries of social scientists and by the experience gained by practical philanthropists, though it seems probable that it was only in the last twenty years of the century that men were beginning to learn its full extent and something of the true nature of its challenge. But there were others who might in the middle of the century have been included in the general undifferentiated mass of the poor who were, in due course, rescued, or partially rescued, by another blind force that was at work in nineteenth-century society. In spite of the pretensions, indeed the sincere convictions, of many of those who promoted it, it would be idle to deny that the Industrial Revolution was indeed blind. Those who launched it and furthered it most often had their eyes on the profit immediately to be made or the improvement in machinery or method immediately to be devised, and not normally on the general results their labours might have for mankind. Even when they believed that they knew what they were working for, they were probably liberating forces which in the long run they could not control. Nevertheless, whatever their ideals or their lack of ideals, they produced wealth and gainful employment and an abundance of goods, particularly in the third quarter of the century. As a result Victorian England was not only a much larger, much more dynamic, community than had ever existed before in the island, it was a much richer one, and its wealth percolated down through the various middle classes to a section of the working class who would otherwise have been poor indeed.

Greater wealth brings a man greater self-reliance, and a greater capacity to stand up for his rights, or to join with others for that purpose. The increase in wealth among the working classes led to the development of Trade Unions which were larger than the craft unions which had flourished in the first half of the century and extended to other types of labour than the craft unions had served, while the increase of wealth among the working classes and middle classes led to the developments in politics which began to become noticeable in the general election of 1868. The social, political, industrial revolutions went forward together and the whole movement seems so purposeful that it is difficult to remember how speculative it all was and what a large part chance had had to play in the matter. Even the prosperity which sustained it depended upon payment for exports which the rest of the world might, or might not, continue to take regularly from Great Britain; it depended also upon a system of credit and foreign exchange which was never under secure control. The development of mechanization was morally neutral; it might work good or it might very easily work evil. To some of those who served it it brought wealth and an improved status, to others the destruction of their handicrafts and ruin, and to others exploitation, particularly if they were women and children; while the extension of industrialism was not likely to secure that the towns where its workers lived were places which were fit for human habitation. If poverty and numbers had crowded men and women into slums, the demands of industrialism would make congestion worse and the filth and smoke it produced add to the squalor and misery of the scene.

If standards were to be maintained and improved, if the demands of humanity were to be attended to, it was not going to suffice to rely on the fortuitous development of increasing prosperity, or, for that matter, on voluntary service however devoted, or on private benevolence however munificent. Englishmen of the nineteenth century would have to learn this lesson which many of them were so extremely reluctant to learn. To master the forces which their society had engendered, to do something for the myriads who thronged their streets, to respond at all effectively to the demands of justice and humanity, they had to use increasingly the coercive power of the State and the resources that could only be made available by taxation; only so could conditions in factories be regulated and the more helpless types of labour protected, only so could the towns of England be sewered, scavenged, partially rebuilt and prevented from becoming, or remaining, mere suppurating middens, the breeding-places of misery, degradation and infectious disease, only so could schools be provided for all and all children made to attend school.

It was hard for Englishmen who believed that they had learnt from their history the importance of freedom and the dangers of the power of the State to accept the teaching of these necessities, and perhaps it was fortunate for them that they did not see the full import of what they had to learn. If the power of the community is to intervene effectively in the complicated problems of modern society, it must be guided to its task by experts and applied through regulations which experts have devised. The general public must not only surrender its freedom, but surrender it to the control of servants whose actions it cannot understand. At least from 1833 when the factory inspectors were appointed, or with the appointment of the Poor Law Commissioners, this expert administrative opinion was being developed. It was accumulated through the activities of a number of newly appointed public servants, commissioners and assistant commissioners, inspectors, servants of enlightened local authorities and men in a variety of public offices. They learnt the science of what was to be done and applied their knowledge by influencing legislation or by administrative methods. What was done by such men in the middle of the century with, at best, uncertain support from Parliaments and Ministers, and confronted by a wayward, or recalcitrant, public opinion, is in retrospect very remarkable. It is one of the truly important factors in the making of Victorian England and in this case is an example of the human intelligence definitely directing affairs towards a clearly conceived end. But it is also worth while to recognize this movement for what it was, for it was the beginning of the development of the modern State controlled by civil servants, acting by means of administrative regulations and assuming ever-increasing power. This development started in a liberal society that believed itself to be pledged to the policy of *laissez-faire*, it was largely unwanted, altogether unplanned and in many cases to a curious extent not noticed, but, and this fact seems to be significant, unless that society was to commit moral, or even literal, suicide, it was also inevitable.

Important as the independent actions of public officials were, they could have done nothing unless they had had some support from some form of public opinion, and in fact public opinion did come to their support or the furtherance of the reforms which they were implementing in a variety of ways. There could be a general popular agitation as there was for factory reform, there could be a general wave of opinion, possibly fanned by a momentary newspaper agitation, such as followed Chadwick's revelations about the health of towns, or there could be the pressure of specialized groups such as those which later in the century supported sanitary reform, or there might be the action of dedicated individuals working through local authorities, or through Parliament. The situation was obviously complex, and it is important to realize this. There is sometimes a tendency among historians to impose on the forces supporting or opposing particular social reforms rather too well-defined a pattern, ranging this or that religious group, or this or that class or party, exclusively on one side or other of particularly important issues; but such attempts should be viewed with suspicion, they are very often polemical in origin and they are very often based on impressions which have not been confirmed by what ought to have been rather elaborate and laborious research. Such facts as easily come to hand do indeed suggest that there is a great deal more to be learnt from the analysis of public opinion, particularly of local public opinion in the nineteenth century, and that when the full picture is painted it is not likely to be a simple one.

However, it seems possible now to say this. There was much opposition to proposals for which the moral case must seem to us overwhelming; men were indolent, or obdurate, or stupid, or callous when to us the call to a particular action would have seemed to be urgent and inescapable; they were, as they are now, inclined to be diverted from what was right by a preoccupation with their own interests. But throughout the reign of Queen Victoria there was in most classes in the country a general tendency towards humanitarianism and reform. It acted with dif-

ferent intensity with different people at different times. Where
interest, or ignorance, or prejudice, intervened, it was too often
sluggish, or selective, or non-existent. For some who claimed
allegiance to it it was no doubt the merest lip-service to a rather
loosely conceived ideal. With some it was intermittent, a capacity to be excited by particular revelations or responsive to an
organized agitation but not otherwise continuously active. With
some it meant absorption in some special social need or abuse,
and with some it was a passion for the general welfare of humanity or a clearly conceived social programme. But in whatever
form this tendency existed, it helped to give a shape to English
nineteenth-century history, to secure that on the whole matters
were always moving in a particular direction, if they were not
always moving very fast.

It would be right to keep this general tendency very vague in
conception, if the vague rather meaningless word 'progressive'
is applied to it that is definition enough; indeed probably that is
too precise. But there were two much more definite currents of
opinion which affected men's minds right through the century
and which also played a considerable part in making Victorian
England what it was. One might be called the political revolution, the movement from oligarchy or aristocracy towards democracy, the other was the revival of religion. They are not to be
completely separated from one another, for the revival of religion
helped men who were emerging from obscurity and poverty to
realize themselves, and to define their relations with society and
make their claims upon it, while the political revolution gave
meaning and force to the Dissenters' attack on the privileges of
the Church of England. Each also in particular matters contributed to the general tendency towards humanitarianism. But it
would be wrong to think of either as ancillary to anything else.
Each pursued for its own sake its own well-defined objective
which could occupy the most important place in a man's mind,
possibly to the exclusion of everything else.

The challenge of the political revolution had become an important factor in politics in the eighteenth century. In the agitation for Parliamentary reform that started at the time of the
American Revolution the claim had been made that all English-

men ought to have a share in the government of the country because they were Englishmen or even because they were men; and at the same time men had begun to say that the object of society was the good of every man and to challenge the claims of prescriptive right to be a possible justification for the privileges of particular classes or individuals. The challenge became clearer and more insistent after the French Revolution had broken out, if the resistance to it also became more conscious and more passionate. Thereafter the issue was probably normally present in one form or other in most men's minds all through the century and it continued to affect the general shape and direction of public discussion. The social tensions of the first half of the century gave this challenge urgency and relevance, but when those tensions had relaxed and British politics were stagnant, there was no moment when there were not groups of people working for manhood suffrage, better social equality and the abolition of privilege, and probably very few moments when some people were not acutely apprehensive of the advent of democracy and the excesses associated with it. Naturally, when the pace quickened again in the 'sixties these hopes and fears became more lively and dominant, but the fact that all through the century most men had been conscious of this problem, often enough acutely conscious of this problem, is one of the most important facts about the making of Victorian England. It supplies, so to speak, the plot of the play.

But if the political revolution supplied the natural focusing point of Victorian political discussion, explicit or implicit, the Christian religion coloured what many Victorians, particularly lower- and middle-class Victorians, thought about everything. Mid-nineteenth-century England was very heavily charged with religious feeling, or religiosity. This was not to be wondered at; in the existing state of education Christianity and the Bible supplied the only comprehensive system of thought of which many people were aware. They supplied the only philosophy or ethics easily available, the only cosmology or ancient history. They intruded into all exhortation and instruction and even into what was read or seen for pleasure; the sensational novels revelled in Christian sentiment, or what passed for Christian sentiment, such sentiment was constantly invoked in stirring language on the stage, while the Bible, or Christian symbolism, or mythology, supplied subjects for many of the engravings and oleographs that men and women hung up in their houses.

Christianity was, however, at that moment not only unavoidable and all-intrusive, it was also dynamic. At the stage of cultural and emotional development which many people were passing through in the nineteenth century, the Christian religion in one form or other could present itself in such a way as to present an almost irresistible appeal to the heart. Why this should have been so raises some very difficult problems, but that it was so is clear. Thus was kindled a fire that spread through the whole country. All religious denominations engaged with ever-increasing zeal in the attempt to re-convert England, churches and chapels were built, missions despatched, revivals staged; what was spent on that work in the way of human effort and sacrifice, and for that matter of financial expenditure, is one of the really important facts of English history of the nineteenth century. Indeed, if it were possible to add up the numbers of hours spent by human beings hoping, planning and working for selected objectives in the reign of Queen Victoria, it seems possible that the re-conversion of England and the achievement of democracy and abolition of privilege would come highest on the list.

If, however, this was so, then most of the hopes which were entertained during the century were unfulfilled at the end. In 1900 all England had not been re-converted; there were still large areas of paganism and spiritual dereliction. In 1900 democracy still lagged on the road, manhood suffrage had been achieved, but the House of Lords retained its full powers, in many constituencies the old influences, thinly disguised under democratic forms, were still strong, and social equality was far to seek. This was not, in either case, what many human beings had hoped and had expected to see, but such disappointments are the commonplace of history; the record is studded with incomplete revolutions and unfulfilled missions. Men seem habitually to exaggerate the power of their ideas to control the future, as they habitually underestimate the chance that what opposes them will survive and even increase in strength as time goes on;

or that the whole situation will change and their dearest wishes become irrelevant. These disappointments are therefore not surprising, and since they refer to the twentieth century, they are not really the concern of this book, but as it happens in each case the failure seems to disclose something about the progress of affairs in Victorian England.

Presumably the primary reason for the failure to convert England was the magnitude of the task. The most strenuous endeavours, the utmost devotion, could not keep pace with the increase of population and bring back into the fold, if they had ever been in the fold, the numbers of human beings which the tide of humanity had deposited in miserable physical environments, with no moral traditions and a way of life in which settled habits were difficult and the needs of the moment imperative. But the twentieth century saw something more significant than the mere fact that the Christian mission failed to keep pace with the increase of population; in the twentieth century the absolute number of observing Christians seems to have begun to fall off. Possibly the phenomenon becomes most marked with the empty churches and secularized chapels of the second quarter of that century, but such movements do not start abruptly and it seems likely that the causes of this change stretch back into the nineteenth century.

If so, it would be very interesting to know what these causes were, for they possibly throw some light on the making of Victorian England. Of course, an intellectual case against Christianity had been fairly widely current among well-educated people in the eighteenth century, and had received in the nineteenth century popularization by the positivists and the secularists. Their activities, however, do not seem to have restricted the effectiveness of the Christian mission in the mid-nineteenth century, and it is not easy to learn how many people they reached, particularly how many uneducated people. During the nineteenth century—with the activities of the geologists, or of the people who attacked the morality of such doctrines as that of eternal punishment and finally with the effective emergence between 1860 and 1870 of the doctrine of evolution—the cogency and force of the attack on Christianity as popularly received was very greatly increased, and from the record of a good many personal histories it seems to have been from the late 'sixties onwards increasingly more unlikely that a really highly educated man would be a Christian. But again the difficult question is raised: By what stages and by what dates did these opinions reach very large sections of the public? It is not indeed easy to see what evidence would satisfactorily bear on this problem. It is, of course, possible to find out the circulation of significant books, or to enumerate those who attended secularist meetings, or joined secularist societies, but those numbers seem to cover a relatively small proportion of the population, and possibly a small proportion of those affected by the drift of opinion from Christianity. Indeed, it seems possible that in a good many cases what was most likely to destroy the old beliefs was not so much the acceptance of a theory hostile to Christianity as the development of a doubt, of a general uneasy feeling that Christianity had been disproved by someone, which would combine with the increase in the number of secular interests and amusements to cause a retreat from the old habits and certainties.

All this is unfortunately extremely speculative, and it would be interesting to know more, for perhaps it would be best to take this change, and the changes immediately associated with it, as the significant end of Victorian England. It is also not very easy to trace or to understand some of these associated changes. For instance, there seems to be evidence that in the first half of the twentieth century the power of religious revivalism began to drop off. It still remained a potential weapon, but it seems to have become more difficult to use and less effective and lasting in its results when used. The cause of this might be a growing scepticism about the doctrines commended by revivalists or the importance of the issues they intended to drive home, or it might result from a change of fashion which made a certain type of emotional appeal, which had seemed moving and soul-searching to large sections of one generation, seem silly and slightly disgusting to their successors. Such changes do occur in history and they probably have a very important influence on its course, but they are not easy to isolate. Certainly in the last years of the nineteenth and the early years of the twentieth century a change of fashion was taking place and the satirical attack on the taboos, the sanctities, the sentimentalisms and the rhetoric of the Victorians was beginning, but again the same awkward problem suggests itself: By what stages did an attack which commended itself to the intellectual and fashionable spread to really large sections of the population? Probably it did so in the end with the unfortunate result that for very many people Victorian England became a period to be ridiculed and attacked but never understood, denied both the advantages of contemporary sympathy and objective historical study.

The history of the political revolution offers a contrast to all this. Here there is no reversal of intention. On the contrary, as the century ended the demand for the revolution became more urgent and more comprehensive. It was increasingly realized that political change was useless without important social reforms to accompany it, and one of the strongest counts against Victorian England was the inequalities and injustices which it had permitted to continue. It was an accusation which the facts seemed fully to authenticate. Whatever the causes, and to whatever extent it may be suggested that forces which had developed in the century had mitigated a situation which might have been much worse, the society which the twentieth century inherited was in many ways a cruel and unlovely one. There was much hopeless poverty at the base of society and for many of the working class who were in a slightly more fortunate position there were no extravagant rewards and there was great insecurity. Popular education was only gradually improving. The cities were often both degrading and ugly. There were still considerable slums, and large numbers of dreary streets which were next door to slums. There was a great deal of vulgarity. There may be a difference of opinion about the virtues of good Victorian architecture and design, it is unlikely that there can be any about the mean results of mass production and of a hasty unthinking commercialism. Society could still be very cruel and callous in its treatment of the weak and unfortunate; whether that was the result of inherited callousness, or an inability to civilize a society which had suffered so great an increase in numbers, or to the operations of the capitalist system, may be of great interest to historians but it did not matter so much to the victims.

This all presents a sad contrast to the high hopes for humanity which had so often been entertained in the course of the century. Of course, the answer to this might be that in fact many of the best men had so often hoped for the wrong things, or for the right things to come in the wrong way. Men had hoped for instance that once liberated from the entangling power of the State and the corrupting power of the old aristocracy the forces inherent in society, particularly when reinforced by the new powers of industry and commerce, would liberate mankind from the cruelties and injustices of which it had always been the victim. The experience of the nineteenth century proved that that calculation was mistaken. But the interesting fact is that the philanthropists and the seers had not even secured the reasonably attainable things which they had earnestly desired. They had hoped, for instance, for political democracy and the abolition of hereditary privilege, and by the end of the century these things had not been achieved.

Probably the main reason for these recurrent disappointments was the fact that the political revolution could not outrun the social and economic developments which were required to support it. While the titled and proprietory classes retained their social and economic predominance and before other classes had achieved sufficient wealth and independence to stand clear of them, it was idle to expect them to see their old grip on the country loosened. This was, however, not normally very easy to see at the time. Looking back at the very great power that remained in the hands of the aristocracy and gentry after the repeal of the Corn Laws in 1846, it must seem to us to be extremely unlikely that they would immediately assent to a reform of Parliament which would mean the surrender of that power; but that fact was not obvious to John Bright. The situation in 1885 must have seemed even more promising. Electoral reform was reasonably complete, the old aristocratic power seemed to be breaking up and the end of the battle probably in sight. That it was not so was probably due in part to the remaining strength of the old classes, which was always greater than their opponents credited and to the explosive impact of the Irish question which they could not have foreseen. But it may also have been due to a possibility which the promoters of a political revolution were not able to realize and accept. The process of social and economic development may increase the power of those elements in society which demand change, but it may also increase the power of forces to whom changes, at least those changes which are most insistently demanded, are increasingly repugnant.

If this diagnosis is true, it seems to agree with a general view of the process by which Victorian England can be said to have been made, upon which my book is in some sort based. The forces which control history are partly intellectual and conscious, and partly unconscious and blind. What happened in England in the nineteenth century was partly controlled by conscious human reason, as in this matter of the challenge of the political and social revolution which ran through the whole century and gave logic and direction to its history. But it was also powerfully affected by such blind forces as the increase of population and the progress of the Industrial Revolution and the increase of wealth, and not by these only but by other factors less easy to trace, by fashion, by the flux and reflux of opinions which might seem to be tangential to the main argument of history, by the kind of emotional appeal which affects particular people at a particular moment, by snobbery—one of the most elusive but not the least powerful of the factors that influence human affairs —and probably by other things not identified. Historical analysis may find it necessary to treat these forces separately, but it must be remembered that they are all, conscious or blind, the power of fashion or the deposit of wealth, working on the same people at the same time in the same community. Like the different currents in a fast-moving river, they rush forward together in the same bed, through a period like the reign of Queen Victoria, past the observer of a later date and into the future to make and remake that in its turn.

VI

A Victorian Chronology, 1830-1901

A VICTORIAN CHRONOLOGY, 1830–1901

Events	Births, Deaths	Publications in England	Publications outside England
1830 William IV ascends throne Whig Ministry (Nov.) Grey, PM	d. Hazlitt (b.1778) b. C. Rossetti (d.1894)	Lyell, *Principles of Geology* Tennyson, *Poems, Chiefly Lyrical*	Comte, *The Positive Philosophy* Holmes, "Old Ironsides" Hugo, *Hernani* Stendhal, *The Red and the Black*
1831 Defeat of Reform Bill		Elliot, *Corn-Law Rhymes* Peacock, *Crotchet Castle*	Hugo, *Notre Dame de Paris* Poe, *Poems* Whittier, *Legends of New England*
1832 First Reform Bill	d. Bentham (b.1748) d. Scott (b.1771) b. L. Carroll (C. L. Dodgson((d.1898)	Bulwer-Lytton, *Eugene Aram* Darwin, *Narrative of the Surveying Voyage of H.M.S. Adventure and Beagle* (conc. 1836) H. Martineau, *Illustrations of Political Economy* (conc. 1834) F. Trollope, *Domestic Manners of the Americans*	Bryant, *Poems* Goethe, *Faust, II* Irving, *The Alhambra*

Events	Births, Deaths	Publications in England	Publications outside England
1833 Keble's Sermon, "National Apostasy," Start of the Oxford Movement Abolition of slavery in colonies Factory Act Irish Church Temporalities Bill	d. A. H. Hallam (b.1811)	E. B. Barrett, *Prometheus Bound* Browning, *Pauline* Carlyle, *Sartor Resartus* (in *Fraser's Magazine* from November, 1833 to August, 1834; separately: Boston, 1835; London, 1838) Newman, et al., *Tracts for the Times* (90 numbers, 1833–41) Surtees, *Jorrock's Jaunts and Jollities* Tennyson, *Poems*	Balzac, *Eugénie Grandet* Longfellow, *Outre-Mer* Poe, "A MS Found in a Bottle" G. Sand, *Lélia*
1834 Whig Ministry (July) Melbourne, PM Conservative Ministry (Dec.) Peel, PM New Poor Law Slavery Act Establishment of London University	d. Coleridge (b.1772) d. Lamb (b.1775) d. Malthus (b.1766) b. Acton (d.1902) b. Du Maurier (d.1896) b. Morris (d.1896) b. Whistler (d.1903)	Bulwer-Lytton, *The Last Days of Pompeii*	Balzac, *Père Goriot* Bancroft, *History of United States*, I Pushkin, *Queen of Spades*

Events	Births, Deaths	Publications in England	Publications outside England
1835 Whig Ministry (April) Melbourne, PM Municipal Corporations Act	*d.* Cobbett (*b.*1762) *b.* A. Austen (*d.*1913) *b.* Butler (*d.*1902)	Browning, *Paracelsus* Dickens, *Sketches by Boz*	Tocqueville, *Democracy in America* Strauss, *Das Leben Jesu* Vigny, *Chatterton*
1836 Marriage Act Tithe Commutation Act	*d.* Godwin (*b.*1756) *d.* J. Mill (*b.*1773) *b.* Gilbert (*d.*1911)	Dickens, *Pickwick Papers* (monthly from April, 1836 to November, 1837; separately, 1837) Lockhart, *Life of Sir Walter Scott* Pugin, *Contrasts*	Emerson, *Nature* Gogol, *The Inspector General* Holmes, *Poems* McGuffey, *Eclectic Readers*
1837 Victoria ascends throne	*d.* William IV (*b.*1765) *b.* Swinburne (*d.*1909)	Browning, *Strafford* Carlyle, *The French Revolution* Dickens, *Oliver Twist* (in Bentley's Miscellany, 1837–38; separately, 1838) Thackeray, *Yellowplush Papers* (in *Fraser's Magazine*, 1837–38)	Emerson, *The American Scholar* Gogol, *Dead Souls* Hawthorne, *Twice Told Tales* Hugo, *Poems* Whittier, *Poems*

Events	Births, Deaths	Publications in England	Publications outside England
1838 People's Charter published Chartist Movement begins First railroad train enters London Irish Poor Law	b. Lecky (d.1903)	Dickens, *Nicholas Nickleby* (monthly from April, 1838 to October, 1839; separately, 1839) Lyell, *Elements of Geology*	Cooper, *American Democrat* Emerson, "Divinity School Address" Hugo, *Ruy Blas* Lamartine, *La Chute d'un Ange* Whittier, *Ballads and Anti-Slavery Poems*
1839 Bedchamber Plot First Factory Inspectors' Report Opium War Royal Commission on Police	b. Ouida (d.1908) b. Pater (d.1894)	Ainsworth, *Jack Sheppard* Baily, *Festus* Carlyle, *Chartism* Darwin, *Voyage of the Beagle* Thackeray, *Catherine* (in *Fraser's Magazine*, 1839–40)	Longfellow, *Hyperion; Voices of the Night* Poe, *Tales of the Grotesque and Arabesque* Stendhal, *The Charterhouse of Parma*
1840 Annexation of New Zealand Health of Towns Committee Marriage of Victoria Penny Postage Act Parliamentary Charity Commissions	b. Hardy (d.1928) b. Symonds (d.1893)	Browning, *Sordello* Bulwer-Lytton, *Money* Dickens, *Master Humphrey's Clock, The Old Curiosity Shop, Barnaby Rudge* (weekly from April, 1840 to November, 1841; separately, 1840–41)	Cooper, *The Pathfinder* Dana, *Two Years Before the Mast* Lermontov, *Hero of Our Time*

Events	Births, Deaths	Publications in England	Publications outside England
1841 Conservative Ministry (Sep.) Peel, PM Factory Commission Handloom Weavers Commission *Punch* founded		Browning, *Pippa Passes* Carlyle, *Heroes, Hero-Worship, and the Heroic in History* Newman, *Tract XC* Thackeray, *The History of Samuel Titmarsh and the Great Hoggarty Diamond* (in *Fraser's Magazine*; separately, 1849)	Dumas, *The Count of Monte Cristo* Emerson, *Essays* Feuerbach, *Essence of Christianity* Lowell, *A Year's Life*
1842 Ashley's Factory Act Chartist riots Income tax Webster-Ashburton Treaty *Illustrated London News* founded	*d.* T. Arnold (*b.*1795)	Browning, *Dramatic Lyrics* Dickens, *American Notes* Macaulay, *Lays of Ancient Rome* Newman, *Essay on Miracles* Tennyson, *Poems*	Griswold, *Poets and Poetry of America* Longfellow, *Ballads and Other Poems*
1843 Free Church of Scotland founded Wordsworth Poet Laureate	*d.* Southey (*b.*1774)	Browning, *Blot in the 'Scutcheon* Carlyle, *Past and Present* Dickens, *A Christmas Carol*; *Martin Chuzzlewit* (monthly from January, 1843 to July, 1844; separately, 1844)	Prescott, *The Conquest of Mexico*

Events	Births, Deaths	Publications in England	Publications outside England
		Hood, *Song of the Shirt* Macaulay, *Critical and Historical Essays* J. S. Mill, *System of Logic* Ruskin, *Modern Painters*, I (II, 1846; III–IV, 1856; V, 1860)	
1844 Bank Charter Act Children's Factory Act Railway Act Rochdale Pioneers Royal Commission on Health of Towns	b. R. Bridges (*d*.1930) b. Hopkins (*d*.1889)	E. B. Barrett, *Poems* Chambers, *Vestiges of Creation* Disraeli, *Coningsby* Patmore, *Poems* Thackeray, *The Luck of Barry Lyndon* (in *Fraser's Magazine*, reprinted in *Miscellanies* in 1855, and as *The Memoirs of Barry Lyndon* in 1856)	Dumas, *The Three Musketeers* Emerson, *Essays*, II Heine, *New Poems* Whittier, *Voices of Freedom*
1845 Newman enters Roman Catholic Church	*d*. Grey (*b*.1764) *d*. Hood (*b*.1799) *d*. S. Smith (*b*.1771)	Browning, *Dramatic Romances and Lyrics* Carlyle, *Cromwell* Dickens, *The Cricket on the Hearth* Disraeli, *Sybil* Newman, *Essay on Development of Christian Doctrine*	Poe, *The Raven and Other Poems*

Events	Births, Deaths	Publications in England	Publications outside England
1846 Whig Ministry (July) Russell, PM Establishment of free trade Irish potato famine Repeal of Corn Laws		Brontës, *Poems by Currer, Ellis, and Acton Bell* Dickens, *Dombey and Son* (monthly from October, 1846 to April, 1848; separately, 1848) Eliot (trans.), *Life of Jesus* Lear, *A Book of Nonsense*	Hawthorne, *Mosses from an Old Manse* Holmes, *Poems* Melville, *Typee* Poe, "The Philosophy of Composition"
1847 British Museum opened Hampden Controversy Ten Hour Act	d. O'Connell (*b.*1775)	A. Brontë, *Agnes Grey* C. Brontë, *Jane Eyre* E. Brontë, *Wuthering Heights* Disraeli, *Tancred* Landor, *Hellenics* Tennyson, *The Princess* Thackeray, *Vanity Fair* (serially from January, 1847 to July, 1848; separately, 1848)	Emerson, *Poems* Griswold, *Prose Writers of America* Longfellow, *Evangeline* Melville, *Omoo* Prescott, *The Conquest of Peru*
1848 Chartism fails Pre-Raphaelite Brotherhood founded Public Health Act Queen's College for Women established	d. E. Brontë (*b.*1818) d. Marryat (*b.*1792) d. Melbourne (*b.*1779)	A. Brontë, *Tenant of Wildfell Hall* Bulwer-Lytton, *Harold* Clough, *Bothie of Toper-na-Fuosich* Gaskell, *Mary Barton*	Lowell, *Biglow Papers; A Fable for Critics; Vision of Sir Launfal* Marx, *Communist Manifesto* Poe, *Eureka*

Events	Births, Deaths	Publications in England	Publications outside England
		Kingsley, *Yeast* (in abridged form in *Fraser's Magazine*; separately and in complete form, 1851) J. S. Mill, *Principles of Political Economy* Newman, *Loss and Gain* Thackeray, *The History of Pendennis* (serially from November, 1848 to December, 1850; separately, 1849–50)	
1849 Free Libraries Committee Navigation Acts repealed *Household Words* founded	*d.* A. Brontë (*b.*1820) *d.* M. Edgeworth (*b.*1767) *b.* Henley (*d.*1903)	Arnold, *The Strayed Reveller and Other Poems* E. Brontë, *Shirley* Dickens, *David Copperfield* (monthly from May, 1849 to November, 1850; separately, 1850) Macaulay, *History of England*, I–II (III–IV, 1855) Ruskin, *The Seven Lamps of Architecture*	Melville, *Mardi; Redburn* Parkman, *The Oregon Trail* Thoreau, *A Week on the Concord and Merrimack Rivers;* "Civil Disobedience"
1850 Clayton-Bulwer Treaty	*d.* Peel (*b.*1790)	Beddoes, *Death's Jest Book* E. B. Browning, *Sonnets from*	Emerson, *Representative Men* Hawthorne, *The Scarlet Letter*

Events	Births, Deaths	Publications in England	Publications outside England
Factory Act Ministry of Education Reestablishment of Catholic hierarchy in England Tennyson Poet Laureate *The Germ* founded	*d.* Wordsworth (*b.*1770) *b.* R. L. Stevenson (*d.*1894)	the Portuguese Browning, *Christmas Eve and Easter Day* Carlyle, *Latter-Day Pamphlets* Kingsley, *Alton Locke, Tailor and Poet* Tennyson, *In Memoriam* Wordsworth, *Prelude*	Melville, *White Jacket* Whittier, *Songs of Labor*
1851 Ecclesiastical Titles Act Great Exhibition Window Tax repealed	*d.* M. Shelley (*b.*1797)	Borrow, *Lavengro* E. B. Browning, *Casa Guidi Windows* Carlyle, *Life of John Sterling* Gaskell, *Cranford* (in *Household Words* from December, 1851 to May, 1853; separately, 1853) Meredith, *Poems* Newman, *The Present Position of Catholics in England* Ruskin, *Pre-Raphaelitism; The Stones of Venice*, I (II-III, 1853) Spencer, *Social Statics*	Hawthorne, *The House of the Seven Gables* Heine, *Romanzero* Longfellow, *The Golden Legend* Melville, *Moby Dick* Parkman, *The Conspiracy of Pontiac*

Events	Births, Deaths	Publications in England	Publications outside England
1852 Conservative Ministry (Feb.) Derby, PM Coalition Ministry (Dec.) Aberdeen, PM Annexation of Burma Oxford and Cambridge Magazine founded	d. Pugin (b.1812) d. Wellington (b.1769) b. Asquith (d.1928) b. G. Moore (d.1933)	Arnold, Empedocles on Etna, and Other Poems Dickens, Bleak House (monthly from March, 1852 to September, 1853; separately, 1853) Newman, The Idea of a University Thackeray, The History of Henry Esmond	Gautier, Poems Hawthorne, The Blithedale Romance Melville, Pierre Stowe, Uncle Tom's Cabin Turgenev, Sketches of a Sportsman
1853 Charity Commission		Arnold, Poems C. Brontë, Villette Kingsley, Hypatia Thackeray, English Humorists of the 18th Century; The Newcomes (serially from October, 1853 to August, 1855; separately, 1854–55) Yonge, The Heir of Redclyffe	Hawthorne, Tanglewood Tales
1854 Crimean War (to 1856) Working Men's College founded		Dickens, Hard Times (weekly in Household Words and separately) Gaskell, North and South (in	Thoreau, Walden; or, Life in the Woods

Events	Births, Deaths	Publications in England	Publications outside England
		Household Words from September, 1854 to January, 1855; separately, 1855; Patmore, Angel in the House, Part I (II, 1856; III, 1860; IV, 1862); Ruskin, Lectures on Architecture and Painting	
1855 Whig Ministry (Feb.), Palmerston, PM; Adulteration of Food Commission; Fall of Sebastopol; Limited Liability Act; Daily Telegraph founded; Saturday Review founded	d. C. Brontë (b.1816)	Arnold, Poems, II; Browning, Men and Women; Dickens, Little Dorrit (monthly from December, 1855 to June, 1857; separately, 1857); Kingsley, Westward Ho!; Meredith, The Shaving of Shagpat; Spencer, The Principles of Psychology; Tennyson, Maud and Other Poems; Thackeray, The Rose and the Ring; Trollope, The Warden	Bulfinch, Age of Fable; Irving, The Life of George Washington (conc. 1859); Melville, Benito Cereno; Whitman, Leaves of Grass
1856 Limited Liability Act	b. Shaw (d.1950)	E. B. Browning, Aurora Leigh	Emerson, English Traits

Events	Births, Deaths	Publications in England	Publications outside England
Treaty of Paris	b. Wilde (d.1900)	Froude, History of England, I–II (III–IV, 1858; V–VI, 1860; VII–VIII, 1863; IX–X, 1866; XI–XII, 1870) Newman, Callista F. W. Robertson, Sermons	
1857 Bank Crisis Divorce Act Indian Mutiny	b. Conrad (d.1924) b. Gissing (d.1903)	Borrow, The Romany Rye Buckle, The History of Civilization in England, I (II, 1861) Eliot, Scenes of Clerical Life Gaskell, The Life of Charlotte Brontë Hughes, Tom Brown's School Days Kingsley, Two Years Ago Ruskin, Political Economy of Art Thackeray, The Virginians (monthly, from November, 1857 to October, 1859; separately, 1858–59) Trollope, Barchester Towers	Baudelaire, Fleurs du Mal Flaubert, Madame Bovary
1858 Conservative Ministry (Feb.)	d. R. Owen (b.1771)	Arnold, Merope Carlyle, Frederick the Great I–II (III, 1862; IV, 1864;	Holmes, The Autocrat of the Breakfast Table

Events	Births, Deaths	Publications in England	Publications outside England
Derby, PM India Act Jews admitted to Parliament Removal of property qualification for House of Commons		V–VI, 1865) Clough, Amours de Voyage Kingsley, Andromeda, and Other Poems Morris, The Defence of Guenevere, and Other Poems Trollope, Doctor Thorne	Longfellow, The Courtship of Miles Standish
1859 Whig-Liberal Ministry (June) Palmerston, PM All the Year Round founded	d. J. Austen (b.1790) d. DeQuincy (b.1785) d. H. Hallam (b.1777) d. L. Hunt (b.1784) d. Macaulay (b.1800) b. A. C. Doyle (d.1930) b. H. Ellis (d.1939) b. Housman (d.1936) b. F. Thompson (d.1907)	Darwin, The Origin of Species Dickens, A Tale of Two Cities (serially from April to November in All the Year Round, and separately) Eliot, Adam Bede Fitzgerald, The Rubáiyát of Omar Khayyám Meredith, The Ordeal of Richard Feverel J. S. Mill, On Liberty Smiles, Self-Help Tennyson, Idylls of the King	Hugo, La Légende des Siècles
1860 Formation of London Trades Council Cornhill Magazine founded	b. Barrie (d.1937)	Collins, The Woman in White Dickens, Great Expectations (in All the Year Round, 1860–61; separately, 1861)	Emerson, The Conduct of Life Hawthorne, The Marble Faun Whittier, Home Ballads

Events	Births, Deaths	Publications in England	Publications outside England
		Eliot, *The Mill on the Floss*	
		Essays and Reviews	
		Meredith, *Evan Harrington* (in *Once a Week*; separately, 1861)	
		Ruskin, *Unto This Last*	
		Swinburne, *The Queen Mother; Rosamond*	
		Thackeray, *The Four Georges* (in *Cornhill Magazine*; separately, 1861)	
1861	*d.* Prince Albert (*b.*1819)	Arnold, *On Translating Homer*	Holmes, *Elsie Venner*
Newcastle Commission (elementary education)	*d.* E. B. Browning (*b.*1806)	Eliot, *Silas Marner*	Turgenev, *Fathers and Sons*
Repeal of paper tax	*d.* Clough (*b.*1819)	J. S. Mill, *Representative Government; Utilitarianism* (in *Fraser's Magazine*; separately, 1863)	
Morris and Company founded		Palgrave, *Golden Treasury*	
		Reade, *The Cloister and the Hearth*	
		D. G. Rossetti, *Early Italian Poets*	
		Spencer, *Education: Intellectual, Moral, and Physical*	
		Thackeray, *Adventures of Philip* (in *Cornhill Magazine*, 1861–	

Events	Births, Deaths	Publications in England	Publications outside England
1862 Colenso Controversy Lancashire cotton famine	d. Buckle (b.1821)	62; separately, 1862) Trollope, *Framley Parsonage*	Hugo, *Les Misérables*
1863	d. Thackeray (b.1811)	Eliot, *Romola* (in *Cornhill Magazine* from July, 1862 to August, 1863; separately, 1863) Meredith, *Modern Love* C. Rossetti, *Goblin Market and Other Poems* Spencer, *A System of Synthetic Philosophy: First Principles* Trollope, *Orley Farm*	Bryant, *Thirty Poems* Hawthorne, *Our Old Home* Longfellow, *Tales of a Wayside Inn* Renan, *Vie de Jésus* Thoreau, *Excursions*
		Huxley, *Man's Place in Nature* Kingsley, *Water Babies* Lyell, *Antiquity of Man* Reade, *Hard Cash* Thackeray, *Roundabout Papers*	
1864 Public Schools Commission	d. Landor (b.1775)	Browning, *Dramatis Personae* Dickens, *Our Mutual Friend* (monthly from May, 1864 to November, 1865; separately, 1865)	Taine, *History of English Literature*

Events	Births, Deaths	Publications in England	Publications outside England
		Gaskell, *Wives and Daughters* (in *Cornhill Magazine*, 1864–66; separately, 1866; completed by F. Greenwood) Newman, *Apologia Pro Vita Sua* (republished in 1865 as *History of My Religious Opinions*; original title in subsequent editions) Spencer, *Principles of Biology*, I (II, 1867) Tennyson, *Enoch Arden and Other Poems* Thackeray, *Denis Duval* (in *Cornhill Magazine*, separately, 1867) Trollope, *The Small House at Allington*	
1865 Whig-Liberal Ministry (Oct.) Russell, PM Fenian Conspiracy	*d.* Cobden (*b.*1804) *d.* Gaskell (*b.*1810) *d.* Palmerston (*b.*1784) *b.* Kipling (*d.*1936)	Arnold, *Essays in Criticism*, I L. Carroll, *Alice's Adventures in Wonderland* Lecky, *History of Rationalism* Kingsley, *Hereward the Wake* (in *Good Words*, January to December, 1865; separately, 1866)	Lowell, *Commemoration Ode* Thoreau, *Cape Cod* Tolstoy, *War and Peace* Whitman, *Drum Taps*

Events	Births, Deaths	Publications in England	Publications outside England
Insurrection in Jamaica *Fortnightly Review* founded *Pall Mall Gazette* founded	b. Yeats (*d.*1939)	Newman, *Dream of Gerontius* (in *The Month*; separately, 1866) Robertson, *Caste* Ruskin, *Sesame and Lilies* Swinburne, *Atalanta in Calydon*	
1866 Conservative Ministry (June) Derby, PM Atlantic cable opened Hyde Park riots Suspension of Habeas Corpus Act in Ireland *Contemporary Review* founded	*d.* Keble (*b.*1792) *b.* Wells (*d.*1946)	Eliot, *Felix Holt* Ruskin, *Crown of Wild Olive* Swinburne, *Poems and Ballads,* I Trollope, *The Last Chronicle of Barset* (in parts; separately, 1867)	Dostoyevsky, *Crime and Punishment* Howells, *Venetian Life* Ibsen, *Brand* Verlaine, *Poems* Whittier, *Snow-Bound*
1867 Second Reform Bill Dominion status for Canada Royal Commission on Trade Unions	*b.* Bennett (*d.*1931) *b.* Galsworthy (*d.*1933)	Arnold, *New Poems* Bagehot, *English Constitution* Carlyle, *Shooting Niagara* Morris, *Life and Death of Jason* Ruskin, *Time and Tide*	Emerson, *May-Day and Other Poems* Ibsen, *Peer Gynt* Longfellow (trans.), *Divine Comedy* Marx, *Das Kapital,* I Turgenev, *Smoke*

Events	Births, Deaths	Publications in England	Publications outside England
1868 Conservative Ministry (Feb.) Disraeli, PM Liberal Ministry (Dec.) Gladstone, PM Prosecution of Eyre fails		Browning, The Ring and the Book Collins, The Moonstone Eliot, The Spanish Gypsy Morris, The Earthly Paradise, I (II, 1869; III, 1870) Newman, Verses on Various Occasions	L. Alcott, Little Women Hawthorne, Passages from the American Note-Books
1869 Disestablishment Law Imprisonment for debt abolished Suez Canal opened	d. Derby (b.1799)	Arnold, Culture and Anarchy Blackmore, Lorna Doone Clough, Poems and Prose Remains Lecky, History of European Morals J. S. Mill, On the Subjection of Women Ruskin, Queen of the Air Tennyson, Holy Grail and Other Poems Trollope, Phineas Finn	Flaubert, L'Education Sentimentale Twain, Innocents Abroad Verlaine, Poems
1870 Civil Service Reform Act	d. Dickens (b.1812)	Arnold, St. Paul and Protestantism	Emerson, Society and Solitude Hawthorne, Passages from the

Events	Births, Deaths	Publications in England	Publications outside England
Elementary Education Act Irish Land Act		Dickens, *The Mystery of Edwin Drood* (monthly from April to September; unfinished) Huxley, *Lay Sermons, Addresses, and Reviews* Morris, *Volsunga Saga* Newman, *Grammar of Assent* D. G. Rossetti, *Poems* Ruskin, *Lectures on Art* Spencer, *Principles of Psychology* (conc. 1872)	English Note-Books
1871 Abolition of purchase of army commissions Abolition of religious test at universities	b. J. M. Synge (*d.*1909)	Arnold, *Friendship's Garland* L. Carroll, *Through the Looking-Glass* Darwin, *The Descent of Man* Eliot, *Middlemarch* (in parts, 1871–72) Hardy, *Desperate Remedies* Ruskin, *Fors Clavigera* (conc. 1887) Swinburne, *Songs Before Sunrise*	Lowell, *My Study Windows* Rimbaud, *Bâteau ivre* Whitman, *Democratic Vistas*
1872 Australian Ballot Act	d. Maurice (*b.*1805)	Bagehot, *Physics and Politics* Butler, *Erewhon*	Holmes, *Poet at the Breakfast Table*

Events	Births, Deaths	Publications in England	Publications outside England
		Hardy, *Under the Greenwood Tree* Ruskin, *Munera Pulveris* Swinburne, *Under the Microscope*	Nietzsche, *Birth of Tragedy* Twain, *Roughing It*
1873 Judicial Reform Act	*d.* Bulwer-Lytton (*b.*1803) *d.* J. S. Mill (*b.*1806)	Arnold, *Literature and Dogma* Bridges, *Poems* Huxley, *Critiques and Addresses* J. S. Mill, *Autobiography* Pater, *Studies in the History of the Renaissance* Trollope, *The Eustace Diamonds*	Howells, *A Chance Acquaintance* Rimbaud, *Une Saison en Enfer* Tolstoy, *Anna Karenina* Twain, *The Gilded Age*
1874 Conservative Ministry (Feb.) Disraeli, PM		Hardy, *Far from the Madding Crowd* (in *Cornhill Magazine*, January to December, and separately) J. S. Mill, *Three Essays on Religion* Morley, *On Compromise* Stephen, *Hours in a Library*, Series I (II, 1876; III, 1878; collected, 1907) Swinburne, *Bothwell, a Tragedy* Thomson, *City of Dreadful Night* (in *National Reformer*, March–May; separately, with other poems, 1880) Trollope, *Phineas Redux*	Flaubert, *La Tentation de Saint-Antoine* Verlaine, *Romances sans Paroles*

Events	Births, Deaths	Publications in England	Publications outside England
1875 British control of Suez Canal Employees' and Workmen's Act Public Health Act Trade Union Act	d. Kingsley (b.1819) d. Lyell (b.1797)	Arnold, *God and the Bible* Gilbert and Sullivan, *Trial by Jury* Symonds, *Renaissance in Italy* (conc. 1886) Tennyson, *Queen Mary* Trollope, *The Way We Live Now*	Howells, *A Foregone Conclusion*
1876	d. H. Martineau (b.1802)	Bradley, *Ethical Studies* Eliot, *Daniel Deronda* Meredith, *Beauchamp's Career* Morris, *Sigurd the Volsung* Spencer, *Principles of Sociology*, I (II, 1882; III, 1896) Swinburne, *Erechtheus, a Tragedy* Tennyson, *Harold* Trevelyan, *Life of Macaulay* Trollope, *The Prime Minister*	H. James, *Roderick Hudson* Mallarmé, *L'Après-Midi d'un Faune* Twain, *The Adventures of Tom Sawyer*
1877 Transvaal annexed Victoria Empress of India	d. Bagehot (b.1826)	Arnold, *Last Essays on Church and Religion* Huxley, *American Addresses* Mallock, *New Republic*	Ibsen, *Pillars of Society* H. James, *The American*

Events	Births, Deaths	Publications in England	Publications outside England
		Meredith, *An Essay on Comedy, and the Uses of the Comic Spirit* (in *New Quarterly Magazine*; separately, 1897) Patmore, *The Unknown Eros and Other Poems*	Lanier, *Poems* Zola, *L'Assommoir*
1878 Congress of Berlin Economic depression Factory and Workshops Act		Bagehot, *Literary Studies* Browning, *La Saisiaz* Gilbert and Sullivan, *H.M.S. Pinafore* Hardy, *The Return of the Native* (in *Belgravia*, January to December, and separately) Swinburne, *Poems and Ballads*, II	H. James, *Daisy Miller*
1879 Irish famine		Browning, *Dramatic Idyls*, I Meredith, *The Egoist* Spencer, *Principles of Ethics* (conc. 1893) Trollope, *Thackeray*	Cable, *Old Creole Days* Ibsen, *A Doll's House* H. James, *The Europeans*
1880 Liberal Ministry (April)	d. G. Eliot (*b*.1819)	Browning, *Dramatic Idyls*, II Disraeli, *Endymion*	Adams, *Democracy* Dostoyevsky, *Brothers Karamazov*

Events	Births, Deaths	Publications in England	Publications outside England
Gladstone, PM Compulsory education Employers' Liability Act		Gissing, *Workers in the Dawn* Tennyson, *Ballads and Other Poems* Trollope, *The Duke's Children*	Maupassant, *Tales* Twain, *A Tramp Abroad* Wallace, *Ben Hur* Zola, *Nana*
1881 Irish Land Act Married Women's Property Act Parnell imprisoned Browning Society founded *Evening News* founded	d. Carlyle (b.1795) d. Disraeli (b.1804)	Carlyle, *Reminiscences* Gilbert and Sullivan, *Patience* Huxley, *Science and Culture* D. G. Rossetti, *Ballads and Sonnets* Swinburne, *Mary Stuart, a Tragedy* Wilde, *Poems*	France, *Le Crime de Sylvestre Bonnard* Harris, *Uncle Remus* Ibsen, *Ghosts* H. James, *Portrait of a Lady; Washington Square*
1882	d. Darwin (b.1809) d. D. G. Rossetti (b.1828) d. Trollope (b.1815) b. Joyce (d.1941)	Arnold, *Irish Essays and Others* Froude, *Life of Carlyle* (conc. 1884) Morris, *Hopes and Fears for Arts* Shaw, *Cashel Byron's Profession* Swinburne, *Tristram of Lyonesse, and Other Poems*	Howells, *A Modern Instance* Maupassant, *Une Vie* Twain, *The Prince and the Pauper* Wagner, *Parsifal* Whitman, *Specimen Days in America*
1883 Corrupt Practices Act Fabian Society founded	d. Fitzgerald (b.1809)	Huxley, *Man's Place in Nature* Meredith, *Poems and Lyrics of the Joy of Earth*	Nietzsche, *Thus Spoke Zarathustra* Twain, *Life on the Mississippi*

Events	Births, Deaths	Publications in England	Publications outside England
1884 Third Reform Bill	d. Reade (b.1814)	Gissing, The Unclassed Meredith, Diana of the Crossways (in the Fortnightly Review, 1884-85; separately, 1885) Moore, A Mummer's Wife Tennyson, Becket Toynbee, The Industrial Revolution	Moore, A Modern Lover Shaw, An Unsocial Socialist Stevenson, Treasure Island Trollope, Autobiography Daudet, Sapho Huysmans, A Rebours Ibsen, The Wild Duck Jewett, A Country Doctor Lowell, "On Democracy" Parkman, Montcalm and Wolfe Twain, The Adventures of Huckleberry Finn
1885 Conservative Ministry (June) Salisbury, PM Fall of Khartoum Housing the Poor Act Commonweal founded	b. D. H. Lawrence (d.1930)	Arnold, Discourses in America Burton, The Arabian Nights (conc. 1888) Dicey, The Law of the Constitution Dictionary of National Biography, I Gilbert and Sullivan, The Mikado Pater, Marius the Epicurean	Howells, The Rise of Silas Lapham Royce, The Religious Aspect of Philosophy Zola, Germinal

Events	Births, Deaths	Publications in England	Publications outside England
		Ruskin, *Praeterita* (conc. 1889) Stevenson, *A Child's Garden of Verses* Swinburne, *Marino Faliero, a Tragedy* Tennyson, *Tiresias and Other Poems* Whistler, *The Ten O'Clock Lecture*	
1886 Liberal Ministry (Feb.) Gladstone, PM Conservative Ministry (Aug.) Salisbury, PM Irish Home Rule Bill defeated		Froude, *Oceana* Gissing, *Demos* Hardy, *The Mayor of Casterbridge* (in the *Graphic*, January to May, and separately) Kipling, *Departmental Ditties* Moore, *A Drama in Muslin* Stevenson, *Dr. Jekyll and Mr. Hyde; Kidnapped* Tennyson, *Locksley Hall, Sixty Years After*	Chekhov, *Ivanov* Howells, *Indian Summer* Ibsen, *Rosmersholm* H. James, *The Bostonians; Princess Casamassima* Rimbaud, *Les Illuminations*
1887 First Colonial Congress Irish Crimes Act Trafalgar Square riots		Browning, *Parleyings with Certain People* Doyle, *A Study in Scarlet* Gissing, *Thyrza*	Dewey, *Psychology* Strindberg, *The Fathers*

Events	Births, Deaths	Publications in England	Publications outside England
Victoria's Golden Jubilee		Meredith, *Ballads and Poems of Tragic Life* Pater, *Imaginary Portraits* Stevenson, *Underwoods*	
1888 Local Government Act	*d.* Arnold (*b.*1822) *b.* T. S. Eliot (*d.*1965)	Arnold, *Essays in Criticism, II* Doughty, *Travels in Arabia Deserta* Gissing, *A Life's Morning* Hardy, *Wessex Tales* Henley, *A Book of Verses* Kipling, *Soldiers Three* Meredith, *A Reading of Earth* Moore, *Confessions of a Young Man* Morris, *Dream of John Ball* Ward, *Robert Elsmere* Wilde, *The Happy Prince and Other Tales*	Bellamy, *Looking Backward* H. James, *Aspern Papers* Lowell, *Political Essays* Strindberg, *Miss Julie* Whitman, *November Boughs*
1889 London dock strike Parnell Commission	*d.* Browning (*b.*1812) *d.* Collins (*b.*1824) *d.* Hopkins (*b.*1844)	Browning, *Asolando* Morris, *House of the Wolfings* Pater, *Appreciations* Shaw, ed., *Fabian Essays, I* Stevenson, *Master of Ballantrae*	Adams, *History of the United States of America* Tolstoy, *Kreutzer Sonata* Twain, *A Connecticut Yankee in King Arthur's Court*

Events	Births, Deaths	Publications in England	Publications outside England
		Swinburne, *Poems and Ballads, III* Tennyson, *Demeter and Other Poems* Yeats, *The Wanderings of Oisin*	
1890 Housing of the Work- ing Class Act Parnell divorce Kelmscott Press founded	d. Burton (*b.*1821) d. Newman (*b.*1801)	Bridges, *Shorter Poems* Frazer, *The Golden Bough*, I (conc. 1915) Morris, *News from Nowhere* (in the *Commonweal*; separately, 1891) Whistler, *The Gentle Art of Making Enemies*	Dickinson, *Poems* Howells, *Hazard of New Fortunes* Ibsen, *Hedda Gabler* H. James, *The Tragic Muse* W. James, *Principles of Psychology*
1891 Factory Act Free Education, Act		Barrie, *The Little Minister* Doyle, *Adventures of Sherlock Holmes* Gissing, *New Grub Street* Hardy, *Tess of the D'Urbervilles* (in the *Graphic*, July to December, and separately) Kipling, *The Light that Failed* Morris, *Poems by the Way* Shaw, *Quintessence of Ibsenism* Wilde, *Picture of Dorian Gray; Intentions*	Dickinson, *Poems*, II Garland, *Main-Travelled Roads* Hofmannsthal, *Poems and Lyrical Dramas* Howells, *Criticism and Fiction*

Events	Births, Deaths	Publications in England	Publications outside England
1892 Liberal Ministry (Aug.) Gladstone, PM Small Holdings Act	d. Tennyson (b.1809)	Du Maurier, Peter Ibbetson Gissing, Born in Exile Henley, Song of the Sword Huxley, Essays upon Some Controverted Questions Kipling, Barrack-Room Ballads Meredith, Poems Shaw, Widowers' Houses Tennyson, Death of Oenone, and Other Poems Wilde, Lady Windermere's Fan	Hauptmann, The Weavers Ibsen, The Master Builder Zola, La Débâcle
1893 Independent Labour Party organized Local Government Act	d. Symonds (b.1840)	Bradley, Appearance and Reality Gissing, The Odd Women Huxley, Collected Essays (conc. 1894) Meynell, Poems Pater, Plato and Platonism Pinero, The Second Mrs. Tanqueray C. Rossetti, Verses Shaw, Mrs. Warren's Profession F. Thompson, Poems Yeats, Celtic Twilight	Crane, Maggie: A Girl of the Streets: A Tale of New York (privately printed; first published edition, 1896)

Events	Births, Deaths	Publications in England	Publications outside England
1894 Liberal Ministry (March) Roseberry, PM	d. Froude (b.1818) d. Pater (b.1839) d. C. Rossetti (b.1830) d. Stevenson (b.1850)	Du Maurier, *Trilby* Grossmith(s), *The Diary of a Nobody* Hardy, *Jude the Obscure* (in *Harper's New Monthly Magazine*, December 1894 to November, 1895; separately, 1896) Kipling, *Jungle Book* Moore, *Esther Waters* Pater, "The Child in the House" Shaw, *Arms and the Man* Swinburne, *Astrophel and other Poems* Webb(s), *History of Trade Unionism* Yeats, *Land of Heart's Desire*	D'Annunzio, *Triumph of Death* Santayana, *Sonnets* Twain, *The Tragedy of Pudd'n-head Wilson*
1895 Conservative Ministry (June) Salisbury, PM Wilde scandal	d. Huxley (b.1825)	Acton, *A Lecture on the Study of History* Conrad, *Almayer's Folly* Pater, *Greek Studies* Wells, *The Time Machine* Wilde, *The Importance of Being Earnest* Yeats, *Poems*	Crane, *The Red Badge of Courage*

Events	Births, Deaths	Publications in England	Publications outside England
1896 Conciliation Act Austen Poet Laureate *Daily Mail* founded	*d.* Du Maurier (*b.*1834) *d.* Morris (*b.*1834) *d.* Patmore (*b.*1828)	Barrie, *Sentimental Tommy* Dowson, *Verses* Housman, *A Shropshire Lad* Kipling, *The Seven Seas* C. Rossetti, *Poems, Unpublished or Uncollected* Swinburne, *Tale of Balen*	Dickinson, *Poems, III* Frederic, *The Damnation of Theron Ware* Hauptmann, *Sunken Bell* Jewett, *Country of the Pointed Firs* Santayana, *Sense of Beauty*
1897 Victoria's Diamond Jubilee Workmen's Compensation Act		Conrad, *The Nigger of the Narcissus* Kipling, *Captains Courageous* Maugham, *Liza of Lambeth* F. Thompson, *New Poems* Wells, *Invisible Man*	H. James, *What Maisie Knew;* *The Spoils of Poynton* W. James, *The Will to Believe* Robinson, *Children of the Night* Rostand, *Cyrano de Bergerac*
1898	*d.* Beardsley (*b.*1874) *d.* L. Carroll (*b.*1838) *d.* Gladstone (*b.*1809)	Hardy, *Wessex Poems* Moore, *Evelyn Innes* Shaw, *Plays Pleasant and Unpleasant* Wells, *The War of the Worlds* Wilde, *Ballad of Reading Gaol*	Crane, *The Open Boat* H. James, *Turn of the Screw* Zola, *J'Accuse!*

Events	Births, Deaths	Publications in England	Publications outside England
1899 Boer War (to 1902) Federation of Trades Unions London Government Act		H. Ellis, *Psychology of Sex* Gissing, *The Crown of Life* Mackail, *Life of William Morris* Maugham, *Orientations* Yeats, *The Wind Among the Reeds*	Chekhov, *Uncle Vanya* H. James, *The Awkward Age* Norris, *McTeague* Tarkington, *Gentleman from Indiana* Veblen, *Theory of the Leisure Class*
1900 British Labour Party founded Labor Representative Committee	*d.* Blackmore (*b.*1825) *d.* Ruskin (*b.*1819) *d.* Wilde (*b.*1856)	Conrad, *Lord Jim* Saintsbury, *A History of Criticism*, I (conc. 1904) Stephen, *English Utilitarians* Symons, *The Symbolist Movement in Literature* Yeats, *Shadowy Waters*	Dreiser, *Sister Carrie* Freud, *Interpretation of Dreams* Howells, *Literary Friends and Acquaintances* London, *Son of the Wolf* Tolstoy, *Resurrection*
1901 Accession of Edward VII	*d.* Victoria (*b.*1819)	Barrie, *Quality Street* Butler, *Erewhon Revisited* Kipling, *Kim* Meredith, *A Reading of Life* Shaw, *Three Plays for Puritans*	Chekhov, *Three Sisters* H. James, *The Sacred Fount* Mann, *Buddenbrooks* Norris, *Octopus*

VII

A Selected Bibliography

I
The Historical Background

II
The Victorian Environment

III
The Literary Background

IV
A Bibliographical Note

A Selected Bibliography

I. The Historical Background

Briggs, Asa. *The Age of Improvement 1783–1867*. London, 1959.

Bryant, Arthur. *The Pageant of England, 1840–1940*. New York, 1941.

Burn, W. L. *The Age of Equipoise: A Study of the Mid-Victorian Generation*. London, 1964.

Butler, J. R. M. *The Passing of the Great Reform Bill*. London, 1914.

Clark, G. Kitson. *The Making of Victorian England*. Cambridge, 1962.

Court, W. H. B. *A Concise Economic History of Britain from 1750*. Cambridge, England, 1954.

Ensor, R. C. K. *England, 1870–1914*. Oxford, 1949.

Gregg, Pauline. *A Social and Economic History of Britain 1760–1950*. London, 1950.

Halévy, Elie. *A History of the English People in the Nineteenth Century*, trans. E. I. Watkin and D. A. Barker. 2nd ed., 6 vols., London, 1949–52.

Smellie, K. B. *A Hundred Years of English Government*. Rev. ed., London, 1951.

Temperley, H. W. V., and L. M. Penson. *Foundations of British Foreign Policy*. Cambridge, England, 1938.

Trevelyan, G. M. *British History in the Nineteenth Century, 1782–1919*. 2nd ed., London, 1937.

Trevelyan, G. M. *Illustrated English Social History: The Nineteenth Century*. London, 1952.

Woodward, E. L. *The Age of Reform 1815–1870*. 2nd ed., Oxford, 1962.

Young, G. M., ed. *Early Victorian England, 1830–1865*. 2 vols., London, 1934.

Young, G. M. *Victorian England: Portrait of an Age*. 2nd ed., London, 1957.

Young, G. M., and W. D. Handcock, eds. *English Historical Documents, 1833–1874*. London, 1956.

II. The Victorian Environment

Aiken, Henry D., ed. *The Age of Ideology: The Nineteenth Century Philosophers*. New York, 1956.

Appleman, Philip, William A. Madden, and Michael Wolff, eds. *1859: Entering An Age of Crisis*. Bloomington, 1959.

Aspinall, Arthur. *Politics and the Press. c.1750–1850*. London, 1949.

Barnard, Howard Clive. *A Short History of English Education*. Rev. ed., London, 1952.

Beer, Max. *A History of British Socialism*. 2 vols., London, 1920.

Bernal, John D. *Science and Industry in the Nineteenth Century*. London, 1953.

Blaug, Mark. *Ricardian Economics*. New Haven, 1958.

Boas, Louise S. *Women's Education Begins: The Rise of the Women's Colleges*. London, 1938.

Boner, Harold A. *Hungry Generations: The Nineteenth Century Case Against Malthusianism*. New York, 1955.

Bradbury, Ronald. *The Romantic Theories of Architecture in the Nineteenth Century in Germany, England, and France*. New York, 1934.

Brand, Carl F. *The British Labour Party: A Short History*. Stanford, 1964.

Briggs, Asa. *Victorian Cities*. New York, 1965.

Briggs, Asa. *Victorian People: A Reassessment of Persons and Themes, 1851–67*. London, 1954.

Brinton, Crane. *English Political Thought in the Nineteenth Century*. 2nd ed., Cambridge, 1949.

British Broadcasting Corporation. *Ideas and Beliefs of the Victorians*. London, 1949.

Brooke, Iris, and James Laver. *English Costume in the Nineteenth Century*. London, 1947.

Bury, J. B. *The Idea of Progress*. New York, 1932.

Cassirer, Ernst. *The Myth of the State*. New Haven, 1946.

Casson, Hugh. *An Introduction to Victorian Architecture*. London, 1948.

Christensen, Torben. *Origin and History of Christian Socialism*. Copenhagen, 1962.

Clapham, J. H. *An Economic History of Modern Britain*. 2nd ed., 3 vols., Cambridge, England, 1930–38.

Clark, Kenneth. *The Gothic Revival: A Study in the History of Taste*. 3rd ed., London, 1962.

Clarke, Basil F. L. *Church Builders of the Nineteenth Century*. London, 1938.

Cockshut, A. O. J. *Anglican Attitudes: A Study of Victorian Religious Controversies*. London, 1959.

Cole, G. D. H. *A Short History of the British Working Class Movement, 1789–1947*. London, 1948.

Crowther, James G. *British Scientists of the Nineteenth Century*. London, 1935.

Curtis, S. J., and M. E. A. Boultwood. *An Introductory History of English Education Since 1800*. 2nd ed., London, 1962.

Davies, Horton. *Worship and Theology in England: From Watts and Wesley to Maurice, 1690–1850*. Princeton, 1961.

Davies, Horton. *Worship and Theology in England: From Newman to Martineau, 1850–1900*. Princeton, 1962.

Dawson, Christopher. *The Spirit of the Oxford Movement*. London, 1933.

Dicey, A. V. *Lectures on the Relation between Law and Public Opinion in England during the Nineteenth Century*. 2nd ed., London, 1914.

Dingle, Herbert, ed. *A Century of Science, 1851–1951*. London, 1951.

Dodds, John W. *The Age of Paradox: A Biography of England, 1841–1851*. New York, 1952.

Eiseley, Loren. *Darwin's Century. Evolution and the Men Who Discovered It*. New York, 1961.

Elliott-Binns, Leonard E. *Religion in the Victorian Era*. London, 1936.

Faber, Geoffrey. *The Oxford Apostles*. London, 1936.

Fay, Charles Ryle. *Life and Labour in the Nineteenth Century*. Cambridge, England, 1920.

Ferriday, Peter, ed. *Victorian Architecture*. London, 1963.

Frazer, William M. *A History of English Public Health 1834–1939*. London, 1950.

Fryer, Peter. *Mrs. Grundy: Studies in English Prudery*. London, 1963.

Gash, Norman. *Politics in the Age of Peel*. London, 1953.

Gillispie, Charles C. *Genesis and Geology*. Cambridge, 1951.

Gloag, John. *Victorian Taste*. London, 1962.

Gooch, G. P. *History and Historians in the Nineteenth Century*. 2nd ed., rev., London, 1958.

Grampp, William D. *The Manchester School of Economics*. Stanford, 1960.

Halévy, Elie. *The Growth of Philosophic Radicalism*, trans. Mary Morris. London, 1949.

Hammond, J. L. and Barbara. *The Age of the Chartists*. London, 1930.

Harrison, J. F. C. *Learning and Living, 1790–1960: A Study in the History of the English Adult Education Movement*. London, 1961.

Harrison, Royden. *Before the Socialists: Studies in Labour and Politics, 1861–1881*. Toronto, 1965.

Heilbroner, Robert L. *The Worldly Philosophers: The Lives, Times, and Ideas of the Great Economic Thinkers*. New York, 1953.

Himmelfarb, Gertrude. *Darwin and the Darwinian Revolution*. London, 1959.

Hinde, R. S. E. *The British Penal System 1773–1950*. London, 1951.

Hitchcock, Henry Russell. *Early Victorian Architecture in Britain*. 2 vols., London, 1954.

Hobhouse, Christopher. *1851 and the Crystal Palace*. London, 1937.

Houghton, Walter E. *The Victorian Frame of Mind, 1830–1870*. New Haven, 1957.

Howarth, O. J. R. *The British Association for the Advancement of Science: A Retrospect 1831–1921*. London, 1922.

Hubbard, H. *A Hundred Years of British Painting 1851–1951*. London, 1951.

Inglis, K. S. *Churches and the Working Classes in Victorian England*. London, 1963.

Ironside, Robin. *Pre-Raphaelite Painters*. London, 1948.

Irvine, William. *Apes, Angels, and Victorians: A Study of Darwin, Huxley, and Evolution*. New York, 1955.

Kellett, Ernest E. *Religion and Life in the Early Victorian Age*. London, 1938.

Klingender, Francis D. *Art and the Industrial Revolution*. London, 1947.

Knickerbocker, Frances W. *Free Minds: John Morley and His Friends*. Cambridge, 1943.

Lewis, Roy, and Angus Maude. *The English Middle Classes*. London, 1949.

Lippincott, Benjamin E. *Victorian Critics of Democracy*. Minneapolis, 1938.

Lynd, Helen M. *England in the Eighteen Eighties*. New York, 1945.

McCord, Norman. *The Anti-Corn Law League, 1838–1846*. London, 1958.

McDowell, R. B. *British Conservatism, 1832–1914*. London, 1959.

McDowell, R. B. *The Irish Administration, 1801–1914*. London, 1964.

McLean, Ruari. *Victorian Book Design and Colour Printing*. London, 1963.

Maccoby, Simon. *English Radicalism 1832–1914*. 3 vols., London, 1935–53.

Mack, Edward C. *Public Schools and British Opinion Since 1860.* New York, 1941.

Madsen, Stephen T. *Sources of Art Nouveau.* New York, 1957.

Marchand, Leslie A. *The Athenaeum: A Mirror of Victorian Culture.* Chapel Hill, 1941.

Marcus, Steven. *The Other Victorians. A Study of Sexuality and Pornography in Mid-Nineteenth Century England.* New York, 1966.

Mead, George H. *Movements of Thought in the Nineteenth Century,* ed. M. H. Moore. Chicago, 1936.

Meeks, Carroll L. V. *The Railway Station: An Architectural History.* London, 1957.

Métraux, Guy S., and François Crouzet, eds. *The Nineteenth Century World.* New York, 1963.

Metz, Rudolf. *A Hundred Years Of British Philosophy.* London, 1938.

Morison, Stanley. *The English Newspaper.* Cambridge, England, 1932.

Newman, Charles. *The Evolution of Medical Education in the Nineteenth Century.* New York, 1957.

Owen, David. *English Philanthropy, 1660–1960.* Cambridge, 1964.

Pease, Edward R. *The History of the Fabian Society.* New York, 1916.

Peterson, A. D. C. *A Hundred Years of Education.* London, 1952.

Pevsner, Nikolaus. *High Victorian Design: A Study of the Exhibits of 1851.* London, 1951.

Plamenatz, John. *Utilitarianism, with a Study of the English Utilitarians.* Oxford, 1949.

Price, R. G. G. *A History of Punch.* London, 1957.

Randall, John H. *The Making of the Modern Mind.* Rev. ed., New York, 1940.

Raven, C. R. *Christian Socialism.* London, 1920.

Roberts, David. *Victorian Origins of the British Welfare State.* New Haven, 1960.

Roe, F. Gordon. *Victorian Furniture. London,* 1952.

Rostow, W. W. *British Economy of the Nineteenth Century.* Oxford, 1948.

Routh, H. V. *Towards the Twentieth Century: Essays in the Spiritual History of the Nineteenth.* New York, 1937.

Russell, G. W. E. *A Short History of the Evangelical Movement.* London, 1915.

Sandall, Robert. *The History of the Salvation Army.* 3 vols., London, 1947, 1950, 1955. Vol. IV by Arch R. Wiggins, London, 1964.

Schuyler, Robert L., and Corrine C. Weston. *British Constitutional History Since 1832*. Princeton, 1957.

Singer, Charles J. *A Short History of Science in the Nineteenth Century*. London, 1941.

Singer, Charles J., *et al.*, eds. *A History of Technology*. Vol. IV: *The Industrial Revolution c1750 to c1850*. Vol. V: *The Late Nineteenth Century c1850 to c1900*. Oxford, 1958.

Smith, Kenneth. *The Malthusian Controversy*. London, 1951.

Somervell, D. C. *English Thought in the Nineteenth Century*. London, 1929.

Spring, David. *The English Landed Estate in the Nineteenth Century: Its Administration*. Baltimore, 1963.

Stephen, Leslie. *The English Utilitarians*. 3 vols., London, 1900.

Storr, Vernon F. *Freedom and Tradition: A Study of Liberal Evangelicalism*. London, 1940.

Tawney, R. H. *Religion and the Rise of Capitalism*. London, 1926.

Thompson, E. P. *The Making of the English Working Class*. London, 1963.

Thompson, F. M. L. *English Landed Society in the Nineteenth Century*. London, 1963.

Turnor, Reginald. *Nineteenth Century Architecture in Britain*. London, 1951.

Ward, John Trevor. *The Factory Movement, 1830–1855*. London, 1962.

Wearmouth, Robert F. *Some Working Class Movements of the Nineteenth Century*. London, 1948.

Webb, Sidney and Beatrice. *History of Trade Unionism*. New ed., London, 1950.

Wilenski, R. H. *English Painting*. Rev. ed., London, 1954.

Williams, Raymond. *Culture and Society, 1780–1950*. New York, 1958.

Woodroofe, Kathleen. *From Charity to Social Work in England and the United States*. London, 1962.

Young, G. M. *Victorian Essays,* chosen and introduced by W. D. Handcock. Oxford, 1962.

III. The Literary Background

Allott, Miriam, *Novelists on the Novel*. New York, 1959.

Altick, Richard D. *The English Common Reader: A Social History of the Mass Reading Public, 1800–1900*. Chicago, 1957.

Baker, Joseph E. *The Novel and the Oxford Movement*. Princeton, 1932.

Baker, Joseph E., ed. *The Reinterpretation of Victorian Literature*. Princeton, 1950.

Batho, E. C., and Bonamy Dobrée. *The Victorians and After, 1830–1914*. Rev. ed., London, 1950.

Beach, Joseph Warren. *The Concept of Nature in Nineteenth Century Poetry*. New York, 1936.

Beebe, Maurice. *Ivory Towers and Sacred Founts: The Artist as Hero in Fiction from Goethe to Joyce*. New York, 1964.

Benziger, James. *Images of Eternity: Studies in the Poetry of Religious Vision from Wordsworth to T. S. Eliot*. Carbondale, 1962.

Buckley, Jerome Hamilton. *The Victorian Temper: A Study in Literary Culture*. Cambridge, 1951.

Bush, Douglas. *Mythology and the Romantic Tradition in English Poetry*. Cambridge, 1937.

Bush, Douglas. *Science and English Poetry*. New York, 1950.

Cazamian, Louis. *Le Roman Social en Angleterre, 1830–1850*. Paris, 1904.

Cecil, David. *Early Victorian Novelists: Essays in Revaluation*. London, 1934.

Chesterton, G. K. *The Victorian Age in Literature*. London, 1913.

Cruse, Amy. *The Victorians and Their Books*. London, 1935. (American title: *The Victorians and Their Reading*.)

Dalziel, Margaret. *Popular Fiction 100 Years Ago: An Unexplored Tract of Literary History*. London, 1957.

The Eighteen Sixties: Essays by Fellows of the Royal Society of Literature, ed. John Drinkwater. New York, 1932.

The Eighteen Seventies: Essays by Fellows of the Royal Society of Literature, ed. Harley Granville–Barker. New York, 1929.

The Eighteen Eighties: Essays by Fellows of the Royal Society of Literature, ed. Walter de La Mare. Cambridge, England, 1930.

Elton, Oliver. *A Survey of English Literature, 1780–1880*. 4 vols., New York, 1920. (See vols. 3 and 4.)

Evans, B. Ifor. *English Poetry in the Later Nineteenth Century*. London, 1933.

Fairchild, Hoxie N. *Religious Trends in English Poetry*. Vol. IV: *1830–1880*. New York, 1957. Vol. V: *1880–1920*. New York, 1962.

Ford, Boris, ed. *From Dickens to Hardy*, Vol. 6 of the *Pelican Guide to English Literature*. Baltimore, 1958.

Ford, George H. *Dickens and His Readers. Aspects of Novel-Criticism Since 1836*. Princeton, 1955.

Ford, George H. *Keats and the Victorians: A Study of His Influence and Rise to Fame, 1821–1895*. New Haven, 1944.

Fredeman, William E. *Pre-Raphaelitism: A Bibliocritical Study*. Cambridge, 1965.

Gaunt, William. *The Aesthetic Adventure*. London, 1945.

Gaunt, William. *The Pre-Raphaelite Tragedy*. London, 1942. (Retitled in 1943: *The Pre-Raphaelite Dream*.)

Hanley, E. A. *Stoicism in Major English Poets of the Nineteenth Century*. New York, 1948.

Holloway, John. *The Victorian Sage: Studies in Argument*. London, 1953.

Hough, Graham. *The Last Romantics*. London, 1949.

Hyman, Stanley Edgar. *The Tangled Bank: Darwin, Marx, Frazer, and Freud as Imaginative Writers*. New York, 1962.

Jackson, Holbrook. *The Eighteen Nineties: A Review of Art and Ideas at the Close of the Nineteenth Century*. London, 1913.

James, Philip. *English Book Illustration, 1800–1900*. London, 1947.

Johnson, E. D. H. *The Alien Vision of Victorian Poetry*. Princeton, 1952.

Kermode, Frank. *Romantic Image*. London, 1957.

Knoepflmacher, U. C. *Religious Humanism and the Victorian Novel: George Eliot, Walter Pater, and Samuel Butler*. Princeton, 1965.

Langbaum, Robert W. *The Poetry of Experience: The Dramatic Monologue in Modern Literary Tradition*. New York, 1957.

Leavis, F. R. *The Great Tradition*. London, 1948.

Leavis, Q. D. *Fiction and the Reading Public*. London, 1932.

Lukacs, Georg. *The Historical Novel*, trans. Hannah and Stanley Mitchell. London, 1962.

Maison, Margaret Mary. *The Victorian Vision: Studies in the Religious Novel*. New York, 1962. (Published in London in 1961 as *Search Your Soul, Eustace: A Survey of the Religious Novel in the Victorian Age*.)

Miller, J. Hillis. *The Disappearance of God*. Cambridge, 1963.

Neff, Emery. *The Poetry of History: The Contribution of Literature and Literary Scholarship to the Writing of History since Voltaire*. New York, 1947.

Pascal, Roy. *Design and Truth in Autobiography*. Cambridge, 1960.

Peckham, Morse. *Beyond the Tragic Vision. The Quest for Identity in the Nineteenth Century*. New York, 1962.

Phelps, Gilbert. *The Russian Novel in English Fiction*. London, 1956.

Praz, Mario. *The Hero in Eclipse in Victorian Fiction*, trans. Angus Davidson. London, 1956.

Praz, Mario. *The Romantic Agony*, trans. Angus Davidson. 2nd ed., London, 1951.

Rowell, George. *The Victorian Theatre*. London, 1956.

Schilling, Bernard N. *Human Dignity and the Great Victorians*. New York, 1946.

Stang, Richard. *The Theory of the Novel in England, 1850–1870*. New York, 1959.

Stevenson, Lionel. *Darwin Among the Poets*. Chicago, 1932.

Tillotson, Geoffrey. *Criticism and the Nineteenth Century*. London, 1951.

Tillotson, Kathleen. *Novels of the Eighteen-Forties*. Oxford, 1954.

Tindall, William York. *Forces in Modern British Literature, 1885–1946*. New York, 1947.

Tinker, Chauncey B. *Painter and Poet. Studies in the Literary Relations of English Painting*. Cambridge, 1938.

Walker, Hugh. *The Literature of the Victorian Era*. Cambridge, England, 1910.

Warren, Alba H. *English Poetic Theory, 1825–1865*. Princeton, 1950.

Welland, D. S. R. *The Pre-Raphaelites in Literature and Art*. London, 1953.

Wellek, René. *A History of Modern Criticism, 1750–1950*. Vol. IV: *The Later Nineteenth Century*. New Haven, 1965.

Willey, Basil. *Nineteenth Century Studies: Coleridge to Matthew Arnold*. New York, 1949.

Willey, Basil. *More Nineteenth Century Studies: A Group of Honest Doubters*. New York, 1956.

Wright, Austen, ed. *Victorian Literature: Modern Essays in Criticism*. New York, 1961.

IV. A Bibliographical Note

In addition to standard bibliographical works (Vol. III of *The Cambridge Bibliography of English Literature*, for example), the following are the most helpful guides to Victorian studies:

Annual Victorian Bibliography
— first published in 1933 (covering work done in 1932) in *Modern Philology;* continued in each May issue through 1957.
— since 1958 in each June issue of *Victorian Studies*.
Bibliographies of Studies in Victorian Literature, 1932–1944, ed. William D. Templeman. Urbana, 1945.

Bibliographies of Studies in Victorian Literature, 1945–1954, ed. Austin Wright. Urbana, 1956.

Guide to Doctoral Dissertations in Victorian Literature, 1886–1958, ed. Richard D. Altick and William R. Matthews. Urbana, 1960.

Victorian Fiction: A Guide to Research, ed. Lionel Stevenson. Cambridge, 1964.

The Victorian Poets: A Guide to Research, ed. Frederic Faverty. Cambridge, 1956.